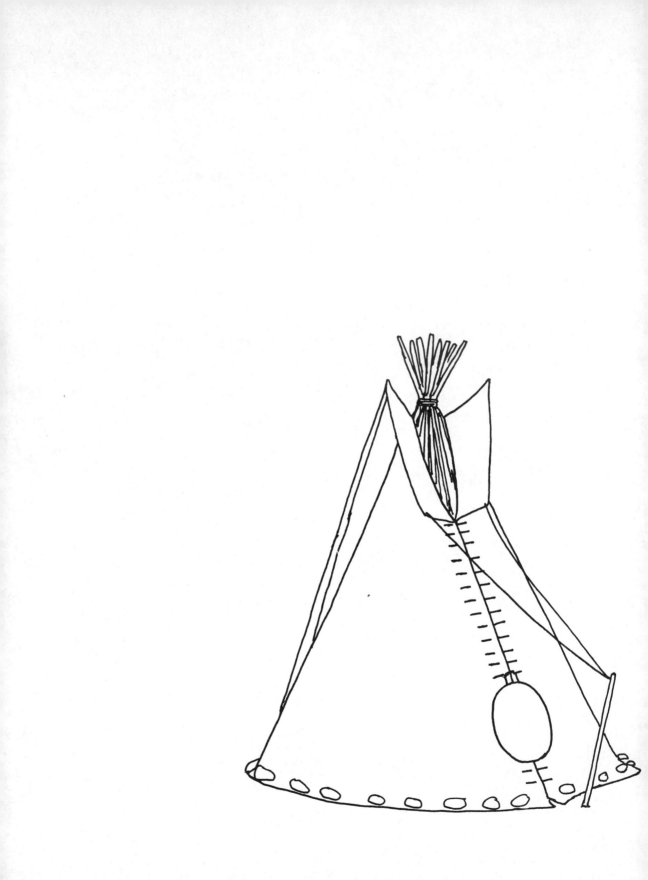

Peter Goodchild

Survival Skills of the North American Indians

Chicago Review Press

For my parents

Library of Congress Cataloging in Publication Data

Goodchild, Peter.
  Survival skills of the North American Indians.

  Bibliography: p.
  1. Indians of North America—Industries. 2. Indians
of North America—Economic conditions. 3. Handicraft—
North America. 4. Survival skills. I. Title.
E98.I5G66 1984   609'.7   84–23255
ISBN 0–914091–64–6
ISBN 0–914091–69–7–pa

Jacket and text design by Arlene Sheer

Contents

Introduction

How did the North American Indians manage to stay alive? In most parts of the continent they had no metal tools, grew no crops, and had no domesticated animals. Large parts of North America consist of rather inhospitable terrain, yet the Indians managed to solve the problems of daily living for thousands of years before the arrival of white people.

Before attempting to answer the above question, it would be worth keeping in mind that North American Indian culture was not homogeneous. The continent can be divided into a number of somewhat arbitrary "culture areas." On the technological level, as we shall see, many traits of Indian life were universal or at least widespread, but there were also regional variations.

Arctic

The first people to enter the New World came through the western Arctic from Siberia, yet the Canadian Arctic remained largely uninhabited long after most of North America had been populated, until the Eskimos developed a rather unique technology and began to spread eastward from Alaska. Eskimo life depended on the hunting of seals, caribou, and, to a varying extent, walruses and whales, while fish were important to the Alaskan Eskimos. The kayak and umiak made the sea's resources accessible. Well tailored caribou-skin clothing made the cold winters endurable. The igloo was the principal winter house in the central Arctic, while in other areas the winter house was most often made of stone, logs, turf, or whalebone. The summer dwelling was often a hide-covered tent.

Subarctic

The Subarctic forest, predominantly spruce but including other evergreens and occasional hardwoods such as birch, poplar, and willow, is a vast area stretching from Alaska southeast to Lake Superior and eastward to Newfoundland. Spruce forest gives the illusion of lush vegetation, yet little else grows in such areas. The soil is thin and acidic, and the trees block out the sunlight. The lack of other vegetation means that animal life may also be scarce. It was largely the thousands of lakes and rivers that made both human and animal life possible in the Subarctic. These waterways were the main routes of travel in the summertime, and fish provided food. But moose and caribou both live in the Subarctic forest, and these animals were the most important sources of food. Snowshoe hares, beaver, and bear were also part of the Subarctic diet. The Indians of this region lived in small nomadic bands. They wore clothing that covered the entire body, somewhat like the tailored clothing of the Eskimos. The principal type of house was a conical lodge of hides or birch bark. The two principal means of transportation, snowshoes and birch-bark canoes, were invented in Siberia, but they were perfected by, respectively, the Athapaskans and the Algonquians, the two major language groups of the Subarctic.

Northwest Coast

The culture area of the Northwest Coast stretches from the Alaskan Panhandle to northern California. The abundant rain and long growing season fostered the growth of enormous trees. The thick forests and mountainous coasts made inland travel difficult except along large rivers and a few well established trails, but the Indians of this area had little need to leave the coast. Like the giant trees, the enormous schools of salmon are a thing of the past, but in aboriginal times it was the annual spawning runs of salmon that made permanent villages possible. Several other kinds of fish were also caught, and the oil from eulachon (candlefish) substituted for the lack of carbohydrate foods in the diet. Woodworking was highly developed on the Northwest Coast. Soft, straight-grained cedar was split into planks for large houses or carved into large ocean-going canoes. Carved house-posts and totem poles (more heraldic than totemistic) are typical of Northwest Coast art.

Plateau

The Plateau is the region drained by the Columbia River system, including parts of British Columbia, Washington,

Oregon, and Idaho. The culture of the Plateau was largely a composite of all the surrounding cultures, though a fairly unique type of house was built, consisting of a large circular pit and a low conical log roof covered with dirt. Fishing and hunting were of roughly equal importance. In addition to the usual berries, several root plants, including camas bulbs, bitter root, biscuit root, and tobacco root, were important constituents of the diet.

Plains

The Plains dominate the center of the continent and consist of the true short-grass, treeless Plains of the west, as well as the long-grass, partly wooded Prairies of the east. Five hundred years ago the true Plains were sparsely inhabited, but the introduction of horses by the Spanish resulted in the culture we most often think of as typically "Indian." Horses made travelling and hunting much easier. Buffalo supplied food, clothing, tools, and weapons, and well designed buffalo-hide tipis were the main type of dwelling, though on the Prairies large permanent earth lodges and several other types of dwellings were built.

Eastern Woodlands

The Eastern Woodlands is a region of hardwood forest, mixed with pines and other conifers, with pines predominating in much of the south. Most of this region, stretching from the St. Lawrence River to the Gulf of Mexico, was densely inhabited by sedentary people with strong political organization. Deer and fish supplied food, but cultivated maize, beans, and squash formed a large part of the diet. Houses were large, well built, and permanent. Among the most familiar tribes are the Iroquois to the north, who lived in large elm-bark longhouses. Further south, in prehistoric times, lived various people commonly known as the "Mound Builders," whose cultures may have arisen as a result of Mexican influence. As long ago as the eighteenth century, Eastern Woodland culture had been so affected by European immigration that it bore little resemblance to its original form. Though we have a general idea of the aboriginal culture from the notes of early explorers, our knowledge is often lacking in detail.

California

Most of California consists of forests of oak and pine, with juniper, redwood, and other conifers dominant in a few areas. But down the middle of the State are the grass-lands and marshes of the Sacramento and San Joaquin River valleys, while the southeastern part of the State is dominated by the Mohave Desert. Most of California once had a dense native population. The people of the coast caught salmon and other fish, like the inhabitants of the Northwest Coast. Acorns were a major source of food in most areas, and pine nuts were also a common food. Most tribes lived in domed houses thatched with various plant materials, though some lived in crude conical lodges of bark or thatch. Basketry was highly developed, especially among the Pomo of the northern coast.

Great Basin

Utah and Nevada form the center of the Great Basin, but this sparsely inhabited region stretches into most of the surrounding States. Most of the rivers drain into lakes rather than into the sea, and the Basin is the driest part of the continent. The Indians of the Great Basin lived in small subconical lodges with a willow frame and a covering of grass, cattails, or bark, though a very crude brush shelter was used for travelling. The main plant food was pine nuts, and animal food consisted of rodents, insects, fish, and wildfowl.

Southwest

The multi-storied pueblos are the most familiar image of the Southwest, which consists of most of Arizona, New Mexico, and western Texas. Many Indians of this area lived in these permanent villages, and maize often supplied the largest portion of the diet, supplemented by beans, squash, and sunflowers. The climate is dry, but the soil is good, and with various techniques it was possible to grow these crops. There was even a considerable amount of grassland in aboriginal times, before overgrazing began to have its effect. Rabbits were the principal game animal. Basketry and pottery were highly developed, and cotton was spun and woven for clothing. The Pueblo culture was descended from that of the Anasazi or "Old People," whose impressive buildings and roads are still visible. In the eleventh century, northern Athapaskan tribes such as the Navaho and Apache also entered this land.

Mexico and Central America

The most technologically advanced North American cultures all belong to Mexico and Central America. The Mayas of Central America built great stone temples, and their knowledge of astronomy and mathematics surpassed that of the Romans. Mayan picture-writing was a complex written language. The Aztecs dominated southern Mexico for several centuries before the arrival of the Spanish. Tools and ornaments were made from smelted gold, silver, and copper, though obsidian was widely available and often used. Many plants were cultivated, with maize again as the principal food. Since this book is concerned with primitive technology, the advanced cultures of Mexico and Central America will only be mentioned in passing.

Each culture was a response to its environment—its fauna, flora, climate, and even its geology. Tradition also played a part, of course; when a tribe moved into a new area, it brought its own language, religion, political organization, and technology. But eventually the environment would have its effect.

Along with the variety in material culture I have just described, there was also a considerable amount of unity. Many tools, weapons, traps, and nets were similar everywhere. The bow, which arrived rather late on the American scene (about A.D. 500), was used by all tribes. Conical or domed lodges of bark or hide were the principal type of house in most of North America. Pottery was absent only in the north. Woven baskets or bags were made to some extent by nearly all tribes, though replaced in the eastern Subarctic by birch-bark vessels. Maize, beans, and squash were cultivated over a large area from South America to eastern Canada.

This unity extends even further. The skills described in this book are those of the North American Indians, but in fact they are merely the North American version of a universal "Stone Age" technology, traces of which can still be seen on other continents. A fishing net, a basket, or an herbal potion made in a small European village, for example, might closely resemble a North American product.

Only in a few parts of North America are the old skills somewhat in use, though modern tools have everywhere replaced those of stone and bone. But the old techniques and devices were described by white explorers and scholars, and it is their records that I have used as my principal source of information. I have also spent a fair amount of time experimenting with Indian techniques in order to corroborate or expand on the records.

Many of the techniques described in this book are now subject to legal restrictions, for a very good reason: they are quite effective. Human overpopulation, pollution, and over-exploitation are now destroying the native flora and fauna of North America, so even simple hunting and gathering practices must be curtailed. Endangered plants and animals should only be utilized in emergency situations.

Ironically, it is the present condition of our environment that makes an understanding of primitive technology essential. Most of us have forgotten the basic skills required to support human life and have become dependent on high technology. There is a psychological loss in not understanding our relationship to the natural world. But our dependence also means that we are in danger if our technology should ever fail. War, plague, and famine still exist, and our own society is only one more in a long list of cultural experiments.

1

Plant food

The North American Indians used about fifteen hundred species of plants as food, though relatively few were regarded as important.

In the Arctic, plants were rarely eaten, since the vegetation there is neither abundant nor palatable. The only plant food commonly eaten in most of the Arctic was reindeer moss taken from the first stomach of the caribou after its slaughter and eaten raw. With the exception of certain berries, plants also contributed little to subsistence in the Subarctic. In the Eastern woodlands, maize, beans, and squash, all cultivated foods, were of great importance, though wild plants contributed considerably to the diet. The Plains Indians depended mainly on the buffalo, but chokecherries, juneberries, and bread root (*Psoralea* spp.) supplemented the diet. In the Southwest, maize, beans and squash were vital. In other parts of the Southwest, as well as on the Northwest Coast, the Plateau, the Great Basin, and in California, many different species of wild plants formed a large part of the diet.

Many alien plants (i.e. foreign plants, in most cases brought by white settlers), such as dandelions and certain mustards, were also quickly adopted into the Indian diet.

This chapter discusses some of the more important food plants; the Appendix gives a more complete listing.

Cultivated plants

The gap between cultivated and wild plants was not always great. What is sometimes called "semi-agriculture" was fairly common. Especially in the Southwest, patches of ground were roughly cleared to allow certain wild plants to grow, and edible "weeds" were left to grow among the cultivated plants. In many areas, patches of ground were burned over to prevent the encroachment of trees and bushes that might impede the growth of more desirable plants. In the Subarctic and the Eastern Woodlands, blueberry bogs were periodically burned to produce heavier crops. Deer were frequently hunted by encircling them with fire, and this burning of the undergrowth opened up the forest; the result was an increase in the growth of plants eaten by both humans and deer, and this in turn led to an increase in the deer population. On the Northwest Coast, raspberry bushes were sometimes pruned to remove the dead growth that might restrict the growth of new shoots. In the east, much of the wild rice was allowed to fall into the water to produce a new crop, and similar conservation methods throughout North America can be regarded as incipient agriculture.

Beans (*Phaseolus* spp.) were cultivated, but several species exist as both wild and cultivated plants. Squash (*Cucurbita* spp.) was cultivated, but the seeds and unripe fruit of closely related wild species were also eaten. Maize, (*Zea mays*) on the other hand, does not grow wild.

Long before maize, beans and squash were cultivated, quite a number of other plants were both gathered from the wild and grown as crops. We may never know exactly how many species were used in this manner, but chenopodium, amaranth, and sunflowers are a few of the plants that were grown in very early times. Some of these early cultivated plants supported large human populations.

Maize, beans, and squash, known to the Iroquois as "the three sisters," eventually became the principal crops of North America. Maize was first developed in Mexico or Central America about 4000 B.C., but over the centuries many races and varieties were developed in various parts of North and South America. Maize was eventually grown in an area that extended from southern Quebec to nearly the tip of South America. Maize, beans, and squash were usually grown together. Maize removes nitrogen from the soil, while beans, like other legumes, draw nitrogen from the atmosphere and put it back into the soil. Maize and beans also complement each other in human diet, providing a better form of protein than when eaten separately. Some kinds of beans form vines and grow up the maize stalks, allowing a more intensive use of the land.

Sunflowers (*Helianthus* spp.) were prized for their oily seeds, but one type of sunflower, the so-called Jerusalem artichoke (*H. annuus*), was grown for its edible tubers. Cotton, gourds, and tobacco were the principal non-food crops. In Mexico, a great number of other plants were also grown, including many tropical fruits that will not grow further north.

Fertilizers seem to have been unknown in aboriginal

times—it was probably the Europeans who taught the Indians to bury fish and ground shells in the maize fields. But the eastern practice of burning the undergrowth added ashes to the soil, making it easier to work and also more fertile.

Agriculture in the Southwest

Water was always the critical factor in Southwestern agriculture. The soil was rich because there was little rain to leach out the minerals, but the low precipitation caused its own problems. Long periods of drought might make agriculture impossible; on the other hand, a sudden flood could just as easily destroy a crop.

Several techniques were developed to solve the water problem. The simplest technique was to plant crops in the flood plains and wait for the annual (sometimes biannual) floods to water the young crops. A less dangerous technique was to build dikes or dams to control the flooding. These dikes both protected the plants against excessive flooding and prevented the water from escaping too quickly once it had arrived. The Hopi designed their fields in a checkerboard pattern, with each "square" enclosing only one or two stalks of maize, while other Indians built a series of vein-like dams to control the flood. A third technique was to dig irrigation ditches to bring water from the rivers. Water was sometimes carried to the fields in jars, particularly if the season was dry. Some crops were planted where they could be watered directly by the runoff from cliff walls. Any rain that might fall, of course, was highly appreciated.

Quite often the Southwestern Indians planted their crops in more than one place, hoping that if one crop failed, the other would survive. However, since the soil was rich and not easily exhausted, the same patch of ground could be cultivated year after year, whereas in the Eastern Woodlands it was necessary to abandon a plot of ground after a few years. Often two crops were planted each year.

It was a common Southwestern practice to grow enough food so that some could be dried and stored for emergencies. If emergency supplies also ran low, the Indians turned to the local wild plants. If these also failed, the Indians moved up into the mountains to gather the wild plants that might have survived in the cooler atmosphere.

The Pueblo Indians had an official Sun Watcher, who called the people to work on a day when the sun rose at a particular point on the horizon. The ground was then broken up with a digging stick. The digging stick was also used to make holes several feet apart and a foot or more deep, and about twenty kernels of maize were dropped into each hole—enough to ensure the survival of some plants, regardless of drought and hungry birds and rodents. The plants that emerged grew in clumps and were by no means as tall as the maize that is grown by modern agricultural methods.

A paddle-shaped hoe was used to cut down the weeds. A greater problem was the birds and rodents that arrived to eat the new shoots. To scare the birds, the Pueblo Indians tied rags to string stretched across the fields, and they also built some fairly elaborate scarecrows. The children and old people of the village were recruited to scare the birds and rodents away. Traps were placed in the fields: multiple snares of horse or human hair for birds, rock-and-stick deadfalls for rodents.

After the maize was harvested, the best ears were saved for seed, and the rest was either eaten or stored. There were dozens of ways of preparing maize. "Green" maize (i.e. soft maize, like our modern "corn on the cob"), usually from an early crop, was left in the husk and roasted in a fire, a pit, or an oven. Most maize was sun-dried and stripped from the cobs. Dried maize and beans were boiled together, sometimes with meat, to provide a dish known today by one of its eastern names, succotash. An ancient method of preparing certain kinds of maize was to pop it in a pottery jar over a fire. Roasted dry maize was also ground to a powder to be mixed with cold water and drunk as pinole, a popular food for travellers.

Maize was most often prepared by grinding, which involved the use of a small cylindrical stone, known today by the Spanish name of "mano," and a larger slightly hollowed flat stone, the "metate." Pueblo women used three or four sets of these stones to grind the maize increasingly finer, requiring hours of daily labor. The meal became slightly moist during the grinding and needed to be toasted occasionally in a pot. Gruel, a breakfast drink, was a small amount of ground maize added to boiling water. Meal was also mixed with a small amount of water (sometimes ash water), rolled into balls, and dropped into boiling water to make dumplings. Bread of various kinds, sometimes wrapped in maize husks, was baked in the ashes of a fire.

Hominy was prepared from maize kernels soaked for a few days in water with ashes. The ashes were made by burning juniper wood, maize cobs, saltbush (atriplex), or bean vines. The amount of ash used was between one-tenth and one-half as much as the amount of maize. The soaking separated the hulls from the starch. The hulls and water were then discarded, and the grains were washed. Ash water—lye—was also prepared separately and strained through a grass or sage stirring brush to separate the ashes from the water before the maize was added. Ash water might also be prepared by boiling.

Lye increased the nutritional value of maize, reducing some amino acids but greatly increasing the content of lysine and niacin.

Tortillas were made by grinding the hominy, shaping it into balls, and then patting it flat between the hands and baking it on an ungreased griddle.

A Pueblo girl considered herself a good cook when she had learned to make piki bread. Blue maize meal was mixed with boiling water, and strained ash water and plain cold water were added to make a thin batter. A griddle was used, consisting of a rectangular flat stone set on four corner-stones, with a fire underneath. The griddle was lightly greased with crushed toasted seeds of various sorts. Using her fingers, the cook spread a very thin layer of batter over the griddle. The bread was cooked for only a few seconds before it was rolled up and served.

There were several recipes for maize "beer." Sometimes the kernels were soaked until they sprouted, then crushed, boiled, and mixed with mesquite flour or saguaro syrup. The mixture was left to ferment in a jar. The jar was never washed, so some of the wild yeast would remain for the next batch of beer.

Several species of beans were grown, notably kidney beans (*Phaseolus vulgaris*) and the highly variable teparies (*P. acutifolius*). Both beans and squash were usually planted between the maize plants, again in deep holes with several seeds to a hole.

Beans were allowed to dry on the vines and then were shelled and further dried in the sun. They were usually roasted or boiled and eaten whole, though sometimes boiled beans were mashed and mixed with cornmeal for bread. Dried raw beans were ground into flour and made into cakes, and the young whole pods were also eaten.

Squash was peeled, cut in half, and allowed to partly sun-dry. Each half was then cut in a spiral and further sun-dried. The squash seeds were also saved; they were roasted and eaten whole, or crushed to grease the stone griddles. The flowers, which fall off as the fruit begins to form, were sometimes cooked.

Agriculture in the north and east

Iroquois production of maize more closely resembled modern methods. Like the Indians of the Southwest, the Iroquois had many varieties of maize and many ways of preparing it.

To prepare a new field, the underbrush was burned, and the loam was scraped into piles and burned. The trees were girdled (the bark removed in a ring around the tree) and left to die, then burned down a year later. If an old field was being replanted, the stubs of the previous year's maize were dug up and burned in piles, though the ashes were not scattered on the fields as fertilizer. The fields gradually became exhausted and were abandoned after about five or ten years.

Before planting, the maize kernels were soaked until they began to sprout slightly. Hellebore juice (a poisonous member of the lily family) and other toxins were added to the water to discourage vermin. A few days before planting, the soil was dug up with a right-angled hoe of wood, bone, or antler. Holes were dug about four inches deep and about a yard apart, and four or five grains were placed in each hole.

Soil was placed around each plant from time to time to prevent the shallow-rooted plants from being blown over by the wind. The fields were hoed when the maize was about a foot high and again when it was knee-high. The maize eventually grew to five or six feet in height.

Only one crop was grown each year, but some parts of the fields were planted later than others, to produce a staggered harvest.

To dry the maize, the husk was pulled back, and the husks of several ears were braided together and hung up to dry. The kernels were then stripped from the cob and stored in elm-bark barrels or in underground pits lined with elm bark.

The mano and metate were sometimes used for grinding, but the wooden mortar and pestle were more common. A log about twenty inches wide and equally long was stood on end, and a fire was built on top to hollow it out. Sometimes clay was put on the rim to protect it. The hollow was burned and chopped to a depth of about a foot. The pestle was a maple pole, about five inches wide and two feet long, narrowed in the center to form a handle.

The maize was cooked and served in many ways: boiled, baked, roasted, made into soup, pudding, or bread. The dried kernels were also soaked in lye, then put into loosely woven baskets which were immersed in fresh water and soused up and down until the hulls floated loose.

Like the Indians of the Southwest, the Iroquois planted beans and squash among the maize plants. Squash was sun-dried after cutting it into spirals or slices, and beans were also sun-dried.

Agriculture in the southeastern United States differed only slightly from that of the Iroquois. The southeastern Indians did not grow as much maize as the Iroquois, and they only used the fertile lowlands along the rivers, where occasional flooding brought fresh topsoil to increase fertility. The trees were girdled and either burned later or left to rot. With a longer growing season, the southeastern Indians, like the Indians of the Southwest, frequently grew two crops of maize each year. After a few years, the fields were abandoned and new ones were started. Beans and squash were also grown, as in other areas. Because of the greater precipitation, nearly all foods in the Southeast were dried on racks over a fire.

The Indians of the Prairies also grew their crops in forest soils rather than on grassland. It was far too difficult to remove the prairie sod with the available tools, and the forest soil was more fertile. The Prairie Indians often piled brush on the fields and burned it to add ashes to the soil, making it easier to work.

Fruits and berries

Over the greater part of North America, blueberries (*Vaccinium* spp.) were an important part of the diet, and in the Subarctic they were the most important of all plant foods. Of nearly equal importance were the various types of raspberries (*Rubus* spp.), including salmonberries, thimbleberries, cloudberries, and all the other localized varieties.

Wild blueberries and raspberries are also eaten by white people nowadays, while many other types of berries gathered by the Indians are ignored, including many that have an excellent flavor.

Juneberries (*Amelanchier* spp.) go by several other names—service-berry, Saskatoon, shadbush, etc. Somewhat related to apples, and with a slightly apple-like taste, they were often added to pemmican by the Plains Indians, but, like blueberries and raspberries, they grow in most parts of North America and were enjoyed by many Indian groups. There are many species, and some taste better than others. Wild cherries and plums (*Prunus* spp.) were known to most Indians. The stones contain somewhat toxic amounts of prussic acid, but choke cherries (*P. virginiana*) were crushed with their stones as an ingredient of pemmican. Grapes (*Vitis* spp.) were popular in most of the United States. Strawberries (*Fragaria* spp.) were popular almost everywhere. Other widespread types of fruit are currants and gooseberries (*Ribes* spp.), rose hips (*Rosa* spp.), mulberries (*Morus* spp.), hackberries (*Celtis* spp.), and ground cherries (*Physalis* spp.). Clusters of sumac berries (*Rhus* spp.) were added to hot or cold water for a beverage.

Other kinds of fruit and berries are limited to the northern United States and Canada. Cranberries (*Vaccinium* spp.) belong to the same genus as blueberies. Crowberries (*Empetrum nigrum*), small black berries growing on low shrubs with needle-like leaves, were important in some parts of Alaska. Bearberries (*Arctostaphylos uva-ursi*) were eaten in many parts of Canada, though it was the leaves that were more important, as an additive to smoking tobacco. High-bush cranberries (*Viburnum trilobum*) were popular in the northern United States and southern Canada, and related types of *Viburnum* were also eaten, though some are quite bitter.

The Southwest has some characteristic types of fruit. The fruit of several kinds of cactus was a major element in the diet of the Indians living in the desert. Wolfberries (*Lycium* spp.) were popular. Squawberries (*Rhus trilobata*), a type of sumac, were used as a beverage or ground into bread. Manzanita berries (*Arctostaphylos manzanita*) belong to the same genus as the more northern bearberries.

Other types of fruits and berries were also harvested in more limited areas. Papaws (*Asimina triloba*), persimmons (*Diospyros virginiana*), sour-gum berries (*Nyssa sylvatica*), and palmetto berries (*Serenoa repens*) are typical of the southeastern United States. Huckleberries (*Gaylussacia* spp.) were harvested in the eastern United States. A few berries that might not appeal to the contemporary palate were once regarded as luxuries: silverberries (*Eleagnus commutatus*) were eaten by the Plains Indians, and the related but very bitter buffalo-berries or soap-berries (*Shepherdia* spp.) were mixed with water and beaten into a frothy "Indian ice cream" on the Northwest Coast. Salal berries (*Gaultheria shallon*) and Oregon grapes (*Berberis aquifolium* and *B. nervosa*) are also found on the Northwest Coast. Crab-apples (*Pyrus* spp.) were eaten in some parts of the northern and eastern United States and in

British Columbia. May-apples (*Podophyllum peltatum*) were eaten mainly in the northeastern United States.

Some types of fruit, though perhaps widely available, remained minor items in the diet. Hawthorn fruit (*Crataegus* spp.) was eaten sparingly in many areas, though it is a rather dry and insipid type of food. Juniper berries (*Juniperus* spp.) were usually eaten in small amounts. Elderberries (*Sambucus* spp.), also very widespread, were a minor item in the diet of several Indian cultures. Honeysuckle berries (*Lonicera* spp.) were eaten by some Indians and ignored by others. Mountain-ash berries (*Pyrus* spp.) were also of minor importance. Bunchberries (*Cornus canadensis*) are pleasant tasting but not usually abundant; more bitter-tasting members of the same genus were also eaten. Most types of barberry (*Berberis* spp.) were also not sufficiently abundant to be worth much attention.

Some kinds of fruit were regarded as more palatable after the first frost had softened and sweetened them. This was the case with, among others, choke cherries, crab-apples, rose hips, mountain-ash berries, and high-bush cranberries.

The Indians were more serious than we are about harvesting berries. Instead of picking the berries one by one, they often raked the berries with their fingers, picking out the leaves and twigs later, or they beat the bushes with a stick and let the berries fall onto a blanket.

Probably every kind of fruit that was gathered in large enough quantities was also dried to preserve it for winter. By far the most common method of drying was to place the berries on mats or trays in the sun, making sure that no rain fell on them. In the Southeast, berries and other foods were dried over a fire. In a few areas, fruit was boiled to a pulp, which was then spread out to dry; this method (accidentally or otherwise) destroyed the eggs of harmful insects.

Roots, bulbs, and corms

Ferns. Ferns were eaten by Indians on both sides of the continent. The edible parts are the rhizomes (rootstocks) and the young fronds, the "fiddleheads." Ferns were used most often by the Indians of British Columbia, who inhabited wet forests rich in ferns, mosses, and other primitive plants. The most important fern, and one of the most common, was bracken (*Pteridium aquilinum*), identified by its unique three-part branching, which can also be seen in the fiddlehead. These fiddleheads were usually boiled. The rhizomes were dug up at various times of the year and hung up to dry. They were roasted over an open fire until the bark could be peeled off. The rootstock was then ready to be eaten, though the hard core was discarded. Other tribes preferred to steam the rootstocks in pits.

Cattail (*Typha* spp.)   Cattail is one of the most useful of all plants. Its leaves provided mats, baskets, capes, hats, cradles, and rope, its fluff provided "diapers," absorbent dressings for wounds and menstrual pads, and one or more parts of the plant provided food at any time of year. Cattail is found in nearly all temperate regions of the world, but in North America it was mainly used by the tribes of the Great Basin, California, and the Southwest.

In the spring the foot-high shoots were gathered by snapping them off where they join the rootstock. The outermost layer was discarded, and the remaining white portion was eaten raw or cooked. A few weeks later the cigar-shaped flowering head develops, which was boiled while still in the green stage. This flowering head later turns brown, and for about one week out of the year it produces a brilliant yellow pollen that was used for bread or mush in the lower Southwest.

The thick rootstocks were pit-roasted, pit-steamed, or simply roasted over an open fire. These cooked rootstocks have a lot of internal fibers and an exterior "bark," and the usual method seems to have been to chew the entire rootstock and spit out the inedible parts. (Several methods have been developed by white people to separate the starch from the fibers. Most of the methods I have tried seem both time-consuming and wasteful; the Indian approach was probably best.)

The Paiutes of the Great Basin even managed to separate the minute seeds from the mature stalk. They stripped the dried heads from the stalk, sprinkled the cottony mass with a little water to hold it together, held it between two sticks over a fire, and then winnowed the seeds from the ashes.

Arrowhead (*Sagittaria* spp.).   Arrowhead tubers were eaten in many parts of the United States, and in some parts of the Eastern Woodlands they were a major food. The plant grows along the edges of lakes, usually in several inches of water, and the egg-shaped tubers grow just under the mud, at the ends of the thin fragile roots. They were gathered in the fall by wading in the mud, feeling for them with the toes. Beavers and muskrats also collected the tubers, and Indians sometimes stole these caches.The tubers were usually prepared by boiling them. The Ojibwa also preserved them for winter by boiling and slicing them, and then stringing them on basswood-bark fiber to dry.

Jack-in-the-pulpit   (*Arisaema triphyllum*); *elephant's ear (Colocasia esculenta)*, also known as taro and dasheen; golden club (*Orontium aquaticum*); and arrow-arum (*Peltandra* spp.). The starchy corms (bulb-like underground parts) of these various members of the arum family were the "breadroot" of the Eastern Woodlands. All these plants are poisonous when raw, since they contain a great deal of calcium oxalate, and even a small bite of the raw corm leaves a painful burning sensation in the mouth. The corms were made edible by drying, cooking, or a combination of the two. They were preserved for winter by slicing, threading them on strings, and drying.

Lilies.   Several different genera of the lily family were sometimes abundant enough to rate as important foods.The bulbs of many kinds of Mariposa lily (*Calochortus* spp.) were popular in the western United States. The bulbs were dug in the spring, usually before the plant was in bloom, and eaten raw, boiled, or roasted, pounded into flour for gruel, or dried for winter use. The bulbs of trout lily (*Erythronium* spp.—there are several common names) were gathered in spring and eaten raw or cooked, though the raw bulbs of some species may be toxic. Fritillary or chocolate lily (*Fritallaria* spp.), also known as rice root because its bulblets look like a handful of steamed white rice, was also dug in the spring and eaten raw or cooked, or dried for later use. The bulbs of the true lilies (*Lilium* spp.) were eaten on both sides of the continent. The bulbs were dug in either spring or fall; some species are bitter and need to be boiled in several changes of water. The large tender rootstocks of false Solomon's seal (*Smilacena stellata* and *S. racemosa*), found across North America, were eaten raw or cooked, and the berries were eaten raw in small quantities.

Overgrazing is now endangering many species of the lily family.

Camas (*Camassia quamash* and *C. leichtlinii*).   A member of the lily family, camas was the most important plant food of the Plateau and the western Plains. The bulbs were harvested while the plant was in bloom. They were pit-steamed or pit-roasted for about three days, until they had turned black. The Blackfeet also boiled the bulbs in soup. The cooked or (less often) raw bulbs were also sun-dried for later use. Edible camas can be confused with death camas (*Zygadenus* spp.).

Greenbrier (*Smilax* spp.).   The roots of the various greenbrier vines were the most important wild plant of the Southeast. They were dug in fall, winter, or spring, and chopped up for bread or soup. The shoots and fruit were also eaten.

Onions (*Allium* spp.).   The wild species of onion generally resemble the cultivated "green onion" or scallion. Onions can be mistaken for the young growth of certain poisonous plants, but the distinguishing characteristic of onions is their unmistakeable odor. The various species were eaten raw or cooked in nearly every part of North America.

Brodiaea, fool's onion (*Brodiaea* spp.).   The bulbs of brodiaea were harvested in the spring, preferably before the leaves appeared, and eaten raw, boiled, roasted, or dried. They were eaten in several parts of western North America, and in California they formed a major part of the diet.

Spring-beauty (*Claytonia lanceolata* and other species).   Spring-beauty is a small plant with white or pink five-petalled blossoms. The plants are sometimes quite abundant in the west, especially on moist soil or mountain slopes. The corms were dug in the spring or fall and eaten raw, boiled, or roasted. They were also dried raw, or boiled, mashed, and formed into cakes before being dried.

Bitter-root (*Lewisia* spp.).   The roots of these species, especially *L. rediviva*, were an important food in much of western North America, but especially on the Plateau. In the spring, before the plants were in full bloom, the roots were dug up and peeled, and the small red "heart" of the next year's growth was removed. The roots were then steamed, boiled, or pit-roasted. The cleaned roots were also strung up or spread on mats to dry. Bitter-root is now becoming rare.

Waterlilies.   In the northern and eastern United States, the American lotus (*Nelumbo lutea*) was an important carbohydrate food. The tubers at the end of the rootstocks, collected in the spring and the fall, were roasted and then boiled. They were also sliced raw and strung up to dry. The seeds and young leaves were also eaten.

Yellow pond-lily or spatterdock (*Nuphar advena*) was eaten in the northern and eastern United States. The rootstocks were collected in the fall or spring before the plant was in bloom, and eaten raw, boiled, or roasted. The seeds were sometimes ground into meal for soup.

The related wokas (*Nuphar polysepalum*) supplied edible tubers and seeds in the central and western United States.

Hog peanut (*Amphicarpa bracteata* and *A. pitcheri*). The roots and the beans of hog peanut were collected and cooked in the central and eastern United States. They were harvested in fall, winter, and spring.

Groundnut, potato bean (*Apios americana*).   Groundnut tubers were gathered at any time of the year and eaten raw, boiled, or roasted in the central and eastern United States. They were also boiled, sliced, and dried for winter.

Prairie turnip, bread-root (*Psoralea esculenta* and other species).   The roots of several species of prairie turnip were peeled and eaten raw, boiled, roasted, or ground into flour for soup or bread, throughout the United States. They were peeled, dried, and powdered for later use, or simply dried whole and unpeeled. Bread-root was the most important carbohydrate food of most of the Plains Indians, especially on the central Plains where the other major root-plants did not grow.

Yampa (*Perideria gairderi* and other species).   The roots of yampa, a genus of the celery family, were dug in the spring and eaten raw, boiled, or steam-cooked in many areas west of the Rocky Mountains. The roots were also preserved for later use by cooking, drying, and powdering them, or by simply sealing the roots in pits.

Biscuit-root, cous (*Lomatium* spp.).   The roots of the many species of biscuit-root, also of the celery family, were dug up in the spring and eaten raw, boiled, steamed, or roasted in many parts of the western United States. The roots were also dried and ground into flour, which was often formed into cakes. The flowers, stems, seeds, and leaves were also eaten. Chocolate tips (*L. dissectum*) was used as a fish poison and considered inedible by some, though others ate the roots and shoots.

Tobacco-root, edible valerian (*Valeriana edulis*). Tobacco-root was an important food in the Plateau region. The roots were cooked for one or two days in pits, until they lost their rank smell, and used for bread or soup. The roots were also stored in undried form underground. They are said to be poisonous when raw.

Balsam-root (*Balsamorhiza sagittata*). Balsam-root was used as food in the Plateau region. The roots (peeled), the young leaves, and the young stems were gathered in the spring and eaten raw or cooked. The seeds were roasted and eaten either whole or ground into flour.

Jerusalem artichoke (*Helianthus tuberosus*). Jerusalem artichoke is actually a type of sunflower. The tubers were eaten raw or boiled in the northern and central United States.

Seeds and nuts

Grasses. Over fifty different species of grass were eaten in North America. Probably all grass seeds are edible, at least if they have not been infected by ergot or other fungi. Maize, of course, was the most important cultivated grass. In the Great Lakes region, wild rice was the most important plant food. In the Great Basin, the Southwest, and California, many different kinds of grass seed were included in the diet.

Grass seeds were usually harvested by beating them into a basket with a woven spoon-like beater, a smaller basket, a stick, or sometimes the bare hands. As the basket became full, it was emptied into a large conical burden basket which the harvester carried on her back with a tumpline across the forehead.

In California the conical burden basket was held in the left hand, dispensing with the intermediate basket.

The next step was threshing (loosening the chaff), which was usually done by pounding a basketful of seeds with a stick. To winnow the seeds (separate the seeds from the chaff), a basketful of seed was tossed up and down in the wind, or the seeds were poured from one basket to another, letting the wind blow away the chaff. Another common method was to simply allow the chaff to accumulate at the top of the basket as the seeds were being threshed, moisten it slightly, and then burn it away with a firebrand.

The winnowed seeds were then put into a shallow basket, a few live coals were added, and the mass was dextrously shaken and tossed until the coals had roasted the seeds.

Among the more important western grasses are rice grass (*Oryzopsis hymenoides*) and dropseed (*Sporobolus* spp.). The Paiutes cut the stalks of rice grass, moistened the heads slightly, and tossed them onto a fire, allowing the roasted seeds to fall into the ashes. The seeds and ashes were separated with a winnowing basket, and the cleaned seeds were husked by crushing between stones. Dropseed has the unique advantage, as its name suggests, that no threshing is required: the ripe seeds fall from the heads, leaving the chaff behind.

Other important western grasses include brome, wild-rye (not a true rye), wild barley, and panic grass.

Wild rice (*Zizania aquatica*). Wild rice—which is not closely related to true rice, though both are grasses—grows in much of the eastern United States, but it was especially important to the Ojibwa and other tribes around the western Great Lakes.

Among the Ojibwa, each plot was owned by a particular family. In order to waste less grain, the stalks were sometimes tied in bundles before ripening. When the grain was ripe, each family went out into the marshes in a canoe pushed by a forked pole. The heads were pulled toward the canoe with a "rice hoop," a long stick held in a crescent shape by a string. Another stick beat the grain from the stalks. Some grain was allowed to fall into the water for the next year's crop.

When the canoe was loaded, it was poled back to the shore. The rice was first trampled to remove the spiny awns. Then it was spread on birch bark and stirred occasionally to dry in the sun for about a day.

The next stage was parching. The rice was put on raised trays which had been coated with clay, while a slow fire burned under each tray. To thresh the grain, it was put into a buckskin-lined pit and trampled.

A later method was to roast the grain in a kettle, stirring occasionally with a paddle; this method threshed the grain at the same time.

The rice was then winnowed by tossing it up and down in a birch-bark tray. The wind blew the chaff away. If it was not a windy day, the chaff could be removed anyway, since it tended to accumulate above the grain. Sometimes the chaff was saved and cooked separately.

The rice was finally washed to reduce the smoky flavor, dried, and stored in bags.

Nuts. Hickory and pecan nuts (*Carya* spp.) were eaten in the eastern and central United States. Walnuts and butternuts (*Juglans* spp.) were eaten fresh, cooked in soup, or stored for winter in most of the United States. Hazelnuts (*Corylus* spp.) were likewise treated in most of the United States and southern Canada. Hazelnuts were often collected and roasted while still green. Chestnuts (*Castanea* spp.) were eaten in the eastern United States. Large chestnut trees are now rare in North America because of an Asian blight that attacks the trees once they have reached a certain stage of growth. Chinquapins (*Chrysolepsis* spp.) were eaten in California and Oregon.

Oil was extracted from most types of nuts. They were crushed without being shelled, and both meat and shell were dropped into boiling water, so that the oil rose to the top and could be scooped off. Vegetable oils were important in Indian diet, especially whenever a lack of animal food meant a deficiency of fat in the diet.

Acorns (*Quercus* spp.). Acorns were eaten in both the east and west of the continent. In California, they were the principal plant food. Some kinds of acorns were simply roasted, but most acorns are bitter and slightly toxic because they contain tannic acid, and a number of methods were used to get rid of the tannin. As a general rule, acorns of the white-oak group (with rounded lobes to the leaves) contain less tannin than those of the black-oak group (with pointed lobes) and require little or no treatment.

In California, acorns were shelled by tapping them with a stone, then crushed with a stone pestle in a bottomless basket placed on a flat stone. The meal was put in a deep hole in wet sand. Water was poured onto the meal and left for a few hours until the tannin had leached out; more water might be added from time to time. Usually some sand remained in the finished product. Other California tribes simply left the whole acorns in swampy ground for six to twelve months.

In the Eastern Woodlands acorns were placed in a bag and immersed in hot water to which wood ashes had been added ("just enough to bite the tongue"), and then soaked in several changes of fresh water to remove the lye.

Acorns were eaten roasted, boiled, or crushed into flour to make bread, and oil was extracted from the acorns of live oak (*Q. virginiana*), a southeastern species.

Green vegetables

Mountain sorrel (*Oxyria digyna*). Common in the northern and mountainous parts of western North America, mountain sorrel leaves were frequently eaten raw or boiled in the spring.

Bistort, knotweed, wild rhubarb (*Polygonum* spp.). The shoots, seeds, and rhizomes of several species of bistort were eaten raw or roasted, from Alaska to California. The rhizomes and leaves of *P. bistorta* were also an important food in Europe not long ago.

Dock and canaigre (*Rumex* spp.). The seeds, young leaves, and roots of dock were eaten in many parts of western North America, from Alaska to Mexico. Many of the species are alien but were soon adopted into Indian diet. The most important native species is canaigre, *Rumex hymenosepalus*; the young leaves and stems were boiled or roasted in the Southwest.

Sea blite, seep weed (*Dondia* spp.). The leaves and seeds of sea blite were cooked in Arizona, Utah, Nevada, and California. The plant is common on alkali (salt) flats.

Amaranth, pigweed (*Amaranthus* spp.). The leaves and seeds of amaranth were cooked in many parts of the United States and Mexico, and several species were cultivated.

Miner's lettuce (*Montia* spp.). The entire plant of miner's lettuce, including the roots, was eaten raw or cooked in many parts of western North America.

Mustards (*Brassica, Barbarea, Rorippa, Sisymbrium, and Nasturtium* spp.). Many different members of the mustard family were important wild vegetables, including several alien species. The "true" mustards, such as *Bras-*

sica campestris and *B. nigra*, both alien, were soon adopted into the Indian diet. Various kinds of peppergrass, cress, watercress, and hedge mustard, most of which are alien, were also gathered and eaten raw or cooked in the spring. Three major native western plants are squaw cabbage (desert candle, *Caulanthus inflatus*), tansy mustard (*Descurainia* spp.), and Indian cabbage (princes plume, *Stanleya* spp.). The edible parts of all three are the young leaves and seeds, though Indian cabbage sometimes draws toxic levels of selenium from the soil.

Saltbush (*Atriplex* spp.).   The boiled young leaves and the ground seeds of many species of saltbush supplied food in the western United States and Mexico. Like sea blite, this is a typical plant of alkali flats.

Chenopodium (*Chenopodium* spp.).   The leaves and seeds of various species of chenopodium were eaten, primarily in the west. Some species, particularly the common lamb's quarters (*C. album*), are alien. Mexican tea (*C. ambrosioides*) was used more often as a medicine to dispel worms than as food, though the somewhat toxic seeds were sometimes used as an ingredient in bread. *C. nuttalliae* was both a wild and a cultivated food in Mexico and the southeastern United States.

Beeweed (*Cleome serrulata*).   The leaves and flowers of beeweed were boiled in New Mexico. This plant was the most important wild green vegetable of the Hopi, though cooking it produced a black dye that was used to decorate pottery.

Clover (*Trifolium* spp.).   The entire clover plant was gathered in the spring and eaten raw or cooked in British Columbia, Arizona, and California, and the seeds were added to pinole in California.

Monkeyflower (*Mimulus* spp.).   The shoots and leaves of monkeyflower were often eaten raw or cooked in the southwestern United States.

Dandelion (*Taraxacum offinale*).   The young leaves of this now-widespread alien plant were gathered and cooked in the spring before the plant was in bloom, in many parts of the United States. The roots were also sometimes eaten. (I might add that the crowns, cut off at the root and trimmed about an inch higher, make an excellent boiled vegetable.)

Desert plants

Agave, mescal, century plant (*Agave palmerii, A. parryi,* and other species).   Agave was a major food of the southwestern United States. In the spring, the plants were cut down with a chisel-shaped stick. The tops of the leaves were cut away, and the remaining crown was pit-roasted for one or two days. The burnt portions were removed, and the pulp was scraped from the fiber and eaten, or the cooked plants were spread in the sun to dry for later use. The young stalks were sometimes cooked in pits or over coals. The flowers and seeds were also sometimes cooked, and the juice from the roasted crowns was allowed to ferment for a few days for an alcoholic drink.

The raw plant causes a serious irritation of human tissue, especially in the mouth. *A. palmerii* and *A. parryi* are probably the least toxic, while *A. lecheguilla* is especially dangerous.

Yucca, datil, palmilla, spanish bayonet (*Yucca* spp.). Yucca was a major food plant of the southwestern United States, as well as a source of soap from the roots and fiber from the leaves. The ripe fruit of datil, *Yucca baccata* and *Y. arizonica*, was eaten raw or cooked, and the unripe fruit was roasted. The pulp of the roasted fruit was sometimes spread out to dry for later use, and the seeds were ground into meal. The flowers and peeled stems of palmilla, *Y. elata*, were gathered and cooked in the spring.

Mesquite and screwbean (*Prosopis* spp.).   The ripe beans of mesquite were ground into meal, which was mixed with water to form cakes. The cakes were dried and eaten raw or cooked. Sometimes the beans were parched before being ground, and sometimes the entire pod was ground for food. Ripe beans were also sun-dried for later use. The Pima ate the catkins. Mesquite meal was mixed with water and left to ferment into an alcoholic drink. These plants were the most important food of northwestern Mexico and the adjacent United States.

Cacti.   Many cacti supplied food in the desert. The saguaro (*Cereus gigantea*) provided a fruit which was eaten, rind, seeds, and all; the juice was often allowed to ferment.

The fruit and stems of the hedgehog cactus (*Echinocereus* spp.) were eaten. The fruit of the barrel cactus (*Ferocactus* spp.) was also eaten, though this genus is best known as a thirst-quencher; the top of the plant can be cut off and the pulp of the stem crushed to supply a refreshing drink. The oxalic acid in the juice, however, can cause nausea if consumed in too great a quantity. The seeds of one barrel cactus, *F. wislizeni*, were also eaten, and the Pima cut the stems into strips and ate them after boiling them for a day. The fruit and seeds of the organpipe cactus (*Lemaireocereus thurberi*) and the fruit of the ball cacti (*Mamillaria* spp.) were also enjoyed. A very widespread genus is *Opuntia*, which varies from the tiny prickly pears to the tree-like chollas. The fruit was eaten raw or cooked, and the stems, flowers, and seeds were eaten cooked.

Other food from trees

Many trees supplied familiar nuts and berries, but trees also supplied other kinds of food.

An important general source of plant food was the cambium layer of several species of trees, particularly when other food sources failed. These trees included various species of pine (most frequently), fir, hemlock, larch, birch, and poplar, plus eastern white cedar, western red cedar, Sitka spruce, Douglas-fir, sugar maple, silver maple, red alder, basswood, slippery elm, red ash, and undoubtedly others.

It is often said that the Indians ate the "inner bark" of trees, but the term is ambiguous. Around the wood of a tree are three layers vaguely referred to as "bark": the cambium, the cortex, and the cork. The thin cambium, the innermost layer, produces both new wood and new bark. In the spring it is tender and mucilaginous and can be easily scraped from the wood or (later) the bark. The next layer, the cortex, is generally fibrous and in many cases was used for cordage. From my own experience, I would say that cortex is no more edible than cork. Whether or not "inner bark," in the sense of "cortex," was eaten very often or at all remains a bit of a mystery.

Maple, willow, and poplar supplied edible buds. All conifer needles, except those of yew, made a hot beverage, rich in Vitamin C. The Ojibwa added the young staminate catkins of white pine to soup, and the Pima ate the catkins of cottonwood.

In many parts of western North America, the seeds of pine trees were eaten. The most important were several large-seeded pines, loosely known as "pinyon pines," of the southwestern United States.

The Paiutes of the Great Basin gathered pine seeds by beating the trees with a pole, or by pulling the cones off with a long hooked stick. The nuts were cleaned of pitch and debris, then tossed in a basket with hot coals. The roasted nuts were put on a grinding stone and rubbed with another stone to crack the shells. The nuts were winnowed by being tossed in a tray so that the wind blew away the shells. The nuts were roasted again and given a final winnowing. A ball of pine-nut paste was rolled over the nuts to remove the last of the debris. The nuts were then crushed to flour, mixed with water, and boiled as gruel.

Unripe cones were kept to ripen in pits. Unripe cones were also roasted in pits to cook the nuts.

Another important food from trees is maple sugar. There is some question of the extent to which the sap was collected in earlier times, before there were metal buckets to make the processing easier, but in historical times the people of the Great Lakes prepared large quantities of maple sugar. In the early spring (when the first crows returned, according to the Menominee), a transverse cut was made in the tree, a foot or two above the ground. A stake was driven into this cut to direct the flow of sap into a birch-bark vessel on the ground. The full vessels were emptied into a kettle, and the sap was boiled and stirred until it began to granulate, then poured into wooden troughs and stirred until it solidified.

Sometimes maple sap was drunk directly as it came from the tree. It was also allowed to partly freeze; the sugarless ice at the top was discarded, and after the process had been repeated a few times, the remaining sap had a higher concentration of sugar.

2

Animal food

There are few members of the animal kingdom that are not potential sources of food, as the Indians fully realized. The Eskimos hunted seals, walruses, polar bears, and whales. Caribou were hunted in the spring and fall, and were especially important to the Eskimos living in the area west of Hudson Bay. Fish (to be discussed in chapter 6) were a major source of food to the Alaskan Eskimos and their Athapaskan neighbors. Fish, particularly salmon, were also the center of Northwest Coast economy. Some of the Subarctic people also depended largely on fish, while others spent more time hunting woodland caribou and moose. In the Eastern Woodlands, the white-tailed deer was the principal source of meat, supplementing a largely vegetarian diet. Buffalo, of course, was the mainstay of Plains economy. Deer, elk, and antelope contributed to the diet of the western Indians, but most Indians of the Southwest, the Great Basin, and California relied on a largely vegetarian diet.

There were only a few restrictions in the use of animals as food. Some insects are bitter, and West Coast shellfish sometimes become toxic (this is discussed below). A steady diet of rabbit or freshwater fish can lead to a deficiency of fat in the diet. The livers of polar bears and ringed and bearded seals can have excessively high levels of vitamin A.

Shellfish

The abundant shell heaps along the Atlantic and Pacific coasts, and along certain river banks, attest to the great importance of shellfish in Indian diet. The Archaic Sioux lived largely on freshwater mussels, and California Indians ate a few land snails, but it was saltwater shellfish that were most often eaten. The great advantage of shellfish is that harvesting it required no elaborate methods and no particular tools or other devices, except perhaps a digging stick.

All North American shellfish are basically edible. However, the bivalves (two-shelled creatures, such as clams and oysters) of the West Coast often become poisonous during the summer because they ingest dinoflagellates (one-celled organisms regarded as either animals or plants) of the genus *Gonyaulax*, which may give a murky color to the water.

Mussels are especially prone to ingest these organisms, clams slightly less so, and oysters are the least susceptible. The risk of poisoning can be reduced somewhat by removing the gills, siphon, and stomach of clams, then boiling the remainder and discarding the water, but some risk remains. It was a Northwest Coast habit to cut off the tip of the clam's siphon, where the toxin is especially prone to concentrate.

Certain univalves (snail-like shellfish), such as whelks and moon snails, which eat other shellfish, can ingest this poison indirectly. Limpets and barnacles, seaweed-eaters, are not affected. Shrimps and crabs are also said to be free from the toxin. However, the Northwest Coast Indians avoided all marine invertebrates when the sea appeared murky or when poisoning had been reported.

Similar toxic organisms also occur on the East Coast, but only rarely.

Most shellfish spawn during the summer, and so at this time they may be rather lean and poor-tasting; this is the source of the belief that "one should only eat oysters in months containing an 'r'."

Different kinds of shellfish prefer different habitats, as noted below. Also, the various species are found at different levels of the beach, from the very-high-tide level to well offshore. Each day there are two high tides and two low tides. The tides are determined by the position of the moon, and to a lesser extent the sun, but in any region with an irregular coastline the various bays and islands will cause so many cross-currents that the correlation of moon and tide becomes very difficult to predict. Unusually low tides occur about two days after the full moon and the new moon. The level of the tides is also related to the time of year.

East coast shellfish. Periwinkles and other univalves were usually just picked up whenever available. (The Common Periwinkle, *Littorina littorea*, was introduced from Europe in the nineteenth century, but other species are native.) Moon snails were "hunted" by following their mole-like burrowings across the sand, then digging down where the trail ended.

Mussels, oysters, and some types of clams could simply be picked up, cooked, and eaten. Other bivalves were harvested by looking for their holes and "squirts" along sandy or muddy beaches, then digging them out with a pointed digging stick. In general, the larger clams are found further below the surface of the sand; clams also burrow deeper in cold weather.

Littlenecks or quahogs (*Venus mercenaria*) are generally found on somewhat muddy beaches along inlets. They were harvested at low tide by walking along the water's edge and feeling for them with the bare feet.

The surf clam (*Spisula solidissima*) is found on sandy exposed beaches. Surf clams could be collected with the bare hands, since they lie just beneath the sand.

The soft-shell clam or steamer (*Mya arenaria*) is found anywhere between the high-tide and the low-tide marks, several inches below the surface of fairly muddy sand, often in areas of low salinity, such as river mouths. They are very sandy and need to be left for two or three days in fresh or salt water (not necessarily running water). Soft-shell clams have been introduced to the West Coast.

The East Coast Indians caught fiddler crabs on the mud flats by surrounding them and walking towards them, forcing them into a mass.

Eelgrass was tied to poles to catch shrimp; the shrimp clung to the eelgrass as the poles were removed from the water the next day.

Lobsters were once extremely common on the East Coast and grew to six feet in length. They were simply picked up from along the shore.

West coast shellfish. Univalves, including limpets and abalones as well as the more "snail-like" types, were removed from the rocks and cracked open, and the meat was often eaten raw.

Mussels were lightly cooked by roasting, steaming, or boiling; they were rarely if ever eaten raw.

The native littleneck clam (*Protothaca staminea*) was dug from just below the surface of gravelly beaches and eaten raw or cooked. The Japanese littleneck (*Venerupis japonica*) is alien.

The Olympia oyster (*Ostrea lurida*) was dug from gravel beaches at low tide; this small shellfish is now becoming rare. The larger Pacific oyster (*Crassostrea gigas*) is alien.

Basket cockles (*Clinocardium nuttalli*) were dug from just below the sand at low tide. The bent-nose clam (*Macoma nasuta*) was dug from several inches below the surface of mud flats. Butter clams (*Saxidomus giganteus* and *S. nuttalli*) were found at low tide on sandy beaches; they were harvested by digging a fairly deep hole, then digging outwards towards the clams to expose them. Clams were eaten raw, or lightly roasted, steamed, or boiled.

Several other types of marine invertebrates were also eaten on the West Coast. The large West Coast barnacles were struck from the rocks with a digging stick and steamed. Goose barnacles were also eaten, though the skin of the "neck" was peeled off and discarded after cooking. Sea urchins were picked up from seaweed beds, caught between the three long wooden prongs of a spear designed for the purpose, or gathered with a dip net. The mouth parts were cracked open, and the star-shaped white or orange gonads were eaten raw. Crabs were usually caught with a pronged spear, though the Alaskan Eskimos used baited nets fastened to a circular frame; the net was left on the sea bed for a few hours, then slowly raised. Octopus was speared repeatedly until it was weakened enough to be picked up. Chitons were roasted, steamed, or boiled. The shell was pounded and peeled off after cooking, and the viscera were discarded, though the orange gonads and the flesh were saved. Chitons were also cleaned and eaten raw.

Shellfish were preserved by removing the meat from the shells, threading it on skewers or string (or laying it on racks), and drying it in the sun or over a fire. The meat was often cooked before being dried.

Insects

All insects—as eggs, larvae, pupae, or adults—are edible if they are not bitter. Most adult beetles are bitter, however, and so are many butterflies, moths, and caterpillars. Indians of the Subarctic commonly ate live warble-fly larvae (*Hypoderma lineata*) taken from the skin of the caribou. Lice from human hair and clothing were usually eaten as soon as they were removed. The larvae of bees and wasps were eaten in many areas. Quite a number of (largely unidentified) species of caterpillars and flies were eaten in the southwestern United States. California Indians caught ants by leaving a piece of damp skin or fresh bark on the ground; the ants were shaken into a bag, left to die, and then sun-dried. Cicadas (*Tibecen* spp.) were eaten on both sides of the continent.

Grasshoppers were the most important of insect foods. In California, patches of woods were burned, and the grasshoppers were picked up already roasted. They were also caught in nets, or driven into pits; they were then roasted and reduced to powder. The Plains Indians caught grasshoppers by burning patches of prairie grass.

It was the people of the Great Basin who used grasshoppers most extensively. A hole was dug, about ten feet wide and about four feet deep. The hunting band spread out in a four-or five-acre circle and walked towards the pit, driving the grasshoppers forward by beating the ground with branches of sagebrush.

The grasshoppers were boiled, strung on rods and roasted, or crushed and dried in the sun or in front of a fire. The northern Shoshone roasted grasshoppers, crickets, and ants by tossing them in a woven tray to which live coals had been added.

Reptiles and amphibians

Reptiles and amphibians were generally ignored except in the lower Great Basin and parts of California. There do not seem to have been many specialized techniques for taking these creatures; probably spears and clubs were most often used. Turtles were sometimes caught by fastening a piece of meat to a line, which in turn was fastened to a pole stuck in a river bank. The turtle swallowed the meat, which acted as a gorge to keep the animal captive.

Birds

Small birds. A common technique for harvesting small birds for food was "bushing": when a flock of birds was roosting in bushes at night, hunters went out with torches, carrying sticks or forked branches to club the sleeping birds.

Small birds were also caught in multiple set snares made of a fine material such as horse hair or human hair. The snares were attached to a rope or pole, which was usually fastened on the ground, and baited with seed, though the snares did not need to be baited if they were placed in maize fields.

A simple device used in the Subarctic consisted of a snowshoe supported at one edge by a vertical stick to which a long string was tied. Grain or other bait was scattered under the snowshoe. When a bird approached, the string was pulled to release the prop.

Ptarmigan. Most Eskimos shot ptarmigans with bows and arrows, though the chances of getting much food in this way were not very great.

The Alaskan Eskimos used a salmon net fifty to a hundred feet long to catch ptarmigan. The net was stretched flat over open ground when the ptarmigan were migrating. One person stood at each end of the net, and another at the middle. As the birds flew past, close to the ground, the net was quickly raised and thrown over the birds.

During the mating season, the Alaskan Eskimos stuffed the skin of a ptarmigan, mounted it on a stick to hold the head upright, and placed this decoy on a knoll or snowdrift. A net, about sixteen feet long and one foot high, made of sinew cord, was placed on stakes around the decoy. The hunter imitated the challenge note of the ptarmigan, and the birds flew towards the decoy and became entangled.

A simpler method was to make a decoy out of snow, place some moss around the neck to imitate the ptarmigan's changing plumage, call the birds, and then shoot them as they arrived to chase off the "intruder."

Sea birds. The Alaskan Eskimos let a man down a cliff where murres were breeding. The birds were easily caught with a scoop net as they sat on their eggs. Auklets were caught in the same manner.

Auklets were also caught by stuffing the skin of one as a decoy. The decoy was placed on a rocky ledge, and fine nets or snares were placed around it. Since auklets have the habit of alighting near each other, they approached the nets or snares and became entangled.

Ducks and geese. The Eskimos caught ducks and gulls with a straight gorge, a piece of bone or antler pointed at both ends. A sinew or rawhide cord was tied to a groove around the middle of the gorge, and the other end of the cord was fastened to any sort of anchor. Sometimes two cords were fastened to the gorge, and the other ends were attached to floats. The gorge was placed inside a fish used as bait.

The Alaskan Eskimos used a chute to catch ducks and

geese in August. At this time of year, the older birds are molting and unable to fly, and the young have still not begun to fly. Salmon nets were stretched on stakes across the marshes, in the form of a V, and the birds were driven to the apex of this chute, then killed with sticks.

Another Eskimo device for waterfowl was the bola, consisting of from four to eight wooden, bone, or ivory weights, usually in the form of an oval ball. Cords about two or three feet long, made of rawhide or braided sinew, were attached to these weights. The other ends were gathered together and bound with grass or wood shavings into a handle. The bola was used in places where birds were accustomed to fly past. It was held by the handle and swung once or twice around the head, and then released into the passing flock.

The Yurok suspended a net horizontally a few inches below the surface of a lake, then sprinkled huckleberries or salal berries on the bottom of the water. The ducks dived for the berries, became entangled in the net, and drowned.

Other California tribes stretched nets above the water and set wooden decoy ducks near them. When the real ducks appeared, the hunters scared them into the nets.

The Maidu suspended the nets on two parallel horizontal poles, allowing the net to sag a little. Birds flying by became caught in the meshes and dropped down onto the rest of the net.

The Miwok used a net stretched between two poles lightly planted in the mud. A long string was attached to the center of the net. Acorns were scattered under the net as bait, and the net was pulled over when the birds approached.

The Shoshone went out into the marshes in tule boats to shoot ducks and mud-hens, but they also used nets stretched between poles, and decoys made of a duck skin stretched over a body made of tules.

The Paiutes caught waterfowl by supporting a net at an angle in the mud with forked sticks. When the birds swam near the net, the hunter jumped up and frightened them so that they became entangled in the net, which was then pulled down on top of them.

The Plains Cree also took waterfowl during the molting season, but their technique was simply to wade towards the shore and kill the birds with digging sticks, while the women waited on the shore to kill any birds that left the water.

The Montagnais of Quebec caught grouse, ducks, and

loons with fishing nets stretched out horizontally above the ground. Two nets, each between sixty and a hundred feet long, were fastened together longitudinally to form the necessary width. They were supported on poles about five feet long. Notches were cut in the bark of these poles to hold the net, and small weights were suspended from the net at points where the net was attached to the poles. Long strings were attached to the net, and the hunter spread sand below it. The birds ate the sand, which they used for digestion. When enough birds had gathered, the hunter pulled on the strings, and the net came down.

A similar type of net was used in snow, except that the net was firmly fastened to the poles, and the poles fell with the net when the strings were pulled.

Turkeys. The Southeastern Indians simply followed and shot turkeys, which apparently made only feeble attempts to escape. In deep snow, turkeys were run down. In the Southeast, artificial calling devices were used, though they have not been described in detail.

Turkeys were domesticated in the Southwest and in Mexico.

Mammals

Many techniques were used for taking mammals: stalking, chasing, ambushing at the den or burrow, driving, and encircling. Game animals were also killed, of course, when accidentally encountered. Traps (discussed in Chapter 5), nets and pits were often used. Lone hunters in particular often wore disguises.

Each technique had several variations or merged with others, and often several techniques were used in combination. The specific method used at any time was dependent on the behavior of the species, the environment, the time of year, and many other factors.

Nevertheless, a few general principles can be stated. Stalking and ambushes of one type or another were widely used for most larger mammals. Driving and encircling were mainly used for animals that live in flocks or herds. Driving and encircling imply community hunts; a solitary hunter might still employ stalking or ambushing for any of these gregarious animals.

Driving, especially for the large herbivores, was often used in combination with several other techniques. Quite common was the use of a *chute*, a pair of fences or lines of logs, poles, brush, or stones set in the shape of a V. At the apex of the chute there might be a cliff, a pit, a corral, or snares, or there might simply be other hunters awaiting the herd. Sometimes the animals were brought to this fence, not by a drive, but by a hunter in disguise, though disguises were more commonly used in stalking.

A narrow valley or cul-de-sac often served as a natural alternative to the chute.

Deadfalls were used primarily in the north for beaver, the weasel family, and bear. In the southwestern regions, small deadfalls were mainly used to kill rodents, either because they endangered the crops or, in the Great Basin, because they were a source of food. Snares were used (though not on the Plains) for most mammals, though usually not for rodents (including beaver), which tend to slip out of such devices. Pitfalls were less common, though they were used in many regions for various large animals. Nets, primarily associated with fishing, were also often used for birds, seals, and beaver.

Stalking was a highly refined art. The hunter had to be able to identify the species of animal that had made the tracks, of course, but sometimes he also had to be able to recognize very indistinct tracks. The sandy deserts of the Southwest made tracking easy at most times of the year. In wooded regions, tracking was more difficult in the summertime; snowfall made the tracker's job easier.

The age of the tracks was important. New tracks might have sharp edges, and water might be seeping into them. Older tracks might be partly obscured by dust, rain, or drifting snow, but changes in the weather had to be considered: a recent period of rain, wind, or thaw might make new tracks look old. Tracks more than a day old, no matter how abundant, might not be worth following, since the animal that had made them was likely to be far away.

If the tracks were widely spaced and continued in a straight line, the hunter might conclude that the animal was travelling at great speed and was not worth pursuing; more tightly-grouped wandering tracks implied that the animal was feeding and perhaps not suspicious of hunters or predators.

Whenever possible, the hunter travelled upwind, since most animals rely more on scent than on sight.

Tracks were not all that the hunter paid attention to. If feces along the trail were moist and warm, they were probably recent. A large animal might reveal its presence by trampled undergrowth; the undergrowth would also be affected if the animal had been feeding. The hunter would look for the low neatly clipped vegetation eaten by rabbits, the coarsely ripped vegetation eaten by members of the deer family, or a berry patch recently devastated by a bear.

Sounds were important. A large animal might reveal its presence by the noise it made walking through the undergrowth. The hunter also had to consider the sounds he was making himself. Wind and rain were a mixed blessing, tending to obscure the sounds of both hunter and prey. But if the hunter was travelling upwind, he knew that any animal ahead of him was not likely to hear him.

The hunter had an advantage in his sense of sight. The large herbivores have poor vision. They detect movement fairly well, but they are colorblind and seem unable to recognize details. In autumn and winter, when the leaves had fallen from the trees, the hunter was especially able to take advantage of his better sense of vision.

Time was an important factor in all methods of hunting and trapping. Most game animals feed during the early morning and evening, and at these times they come down to the water to drink. During the rest of the day they might stay well hidden. These same animals might feed more at night when the moon was bright, and go into cover by dawn.

The seasons also have their effects on animal behavior. Caribou, like most birds, gather in large groups to head south along fairly predictable routes in the autumn, though some animals would be available all winter. In the spring, they return north to give birth. The males of all members of the deer family become belligerent and less cautious of hunters during the autumn mating season. Midwinter was often a time of hardship for the Indians of the Subarctic forest. Snowshoes made it possible to travel on the snow, but in extremely cold weather the animals might stay in seclusion for days.

Arrows do not have the same power as bullets, and game was sometimes only wounded instead of killed right away—a reason why spears and harpoons were sometimes preferred, though they are short-range weapons. If a wounded animal escaped, it was often considered wiser not to follow it right away, since the frightened animal might lead the hunter on a long chase. Instead, if the animal was left alone, it might soon lie down and die from loss of blood, and the hunter could return the next day to find it.

Rats and mice.   Deadfalls made of flat stones were used in the Southwest to rid the fields of rats and mice. On the

Great Basin, they were trapped in the same way as a source of food.

Tree squirrels.   Tree squirrels were usually considered prey for young boys learning to hunt. They were shot with a bow and arrows, though in the Southeast cane blowguns were also used. Dogs were sometimes used to locate squirrels.

Ground squirrels.   Stone deadfalls were commonly used in the Southwest and the Great Basin to catch ground squirrels. The Paiutes sometimes ran the animals down when they became fat in early summer. They also hunted ground squirrels by chasing them into their burrows, closing all the entrances but one, and then shooting the animals as they emerged from the remaining hole.

Porcupines.   In most of North America, porcupines were regarded as a good source of meat when other sources failed. They were usually clubbed when encountered on the ground or in trees. Porcupines were sometimes cooked by singeing the quills off in a fire, after which the animals were baked in the ashes or boiled. Others considered the quills valuable as a decoration for leatherwork, especially before trade beads were introduced by white people.

Prairie dogs.   In aboriginal times, prairie dog "towns" containing millions of animals were common in the western United States, and they formed an important source of food. They were shot with bow and arrow at most times of the year, or dug out of their burrows. Sometimes they were frightened so that, in their haste, several animals ran down one burrow, from which they were then dug out.

When the summer floods arrived in the Southwest, ditches were dug to divert the water into the burrows, and the animals were either shot or grabbed by the neck as they emerged.

Sometimes a hole was plugged with grass and manure, and an earth wall was built around the hole. Water was poured from jars into the basin thus created. The plug was then suddenly pulled out, flooding the burrow.

A Navaho trick was to put a sheet of mica on a cleft stick planted in front of the burrow. The device was set so that it reflected sunlight into the burrow. The prairie dog was blinded as it emerged and could be more easily shot.

Stone-slab deadfalls were commonly used, and tether snares of horse hair were placed at the burrow entrances.

Beavers.   Beavers were an important source of food long before they became the principal item in the fur trade. They were frequently shot with bow and arrow, especially at night during the full moon when beavers, like other animals, are more active. But the most common technique for killing beavers was to destroy their dams and kill the animals as they emerged from the lodges or their holes in the river bank.

The Labrador Eskimos caught beaver by planting a stake in front of the entrance to the lodge, preventing the animal's escape, and then breaking into the lodge from above. The animal had to be seized quickly by the hind legs or it would inflict a serious bite.

In the Arctic and the Subarctic, a common technique was to plant a net across the entrance to the lodge. The Alaskan Eskimos used a square net about four or five feet wide with a mesh large enough for the beaver's head to enter. The Labrador Eskimos used a purse-like net of caribou hide, with an opening about two feet wide; when the beaver left the lodge, it swam into the net, causing it to close.

In winter, Subarctic Indians planted a row of stakes through the ice and down into the mud, across a fairly shallow creek containing beaver lodges. A parallel row of stakes was usually planted on the other side of the lodges, though if the ice was too deep for the beaver to swim on this side, the second row might be omitted. A gap was left in the center of one of the rows, and a purse-like net with a six-foot-wide opening was attached lightly to two poles by means of short strings set into slits in the bark. The poles and net were set into the gap in the fence. The beaver lodges were broken into, and the animals that were not immediately killed swam towards the fence and finally into the net, which was quickly hauled up before the animals managed to gnaw their way free.

Rabbits and hares.   In the southwestern United States, the hunting of rabbits was usually a community affair. The simplest type of community hunt was a drive with men forming a straight line, walking towards the animals and throwing sticks at them as they tried to escape.

The Pueblo and Navaho Indians more often hunted rabbits, not in a straight line, but by forming two large semicircles of people who gradually closed in on the animals.

The Hopi used a curved flattened stick, somewhat like the non-returning type of Australian boomerang. If the stick failed to strike a rabbit before it hit the ground, it might hit one or more animals on the rebound. Other Indians in the west and east used clubs narrowed at one end to form a handle, or merely sections cut from a sapling.

The tribes of the Great Basin drove rabbits into nets, where they could more easily be killed with clubs. Sometimes the nets were at the apex of a chute of sagebrush. The nets of the individual owners were joined end to end and set up in a semicircle or three-sided rectangle, sometimes well over a hundred yards in length. Paiute nets were made of spun Indian hemp (*Apocynum cannabinum*), had a two-inch mesh, and were about two feet high. They were supported on bushes or forked sticks. As the rabbits ran into the nets, they were seized, clubbed, or shot with arrows.

In historical times, the Indians of the Southeast hunted rabbits by driving them with dogs, but this seems to be a modern practice.

Several other techniques were used in the Southwest. A simple deadfall was built, consisting of a stone slab and a stick with a maize kernel under it. Snares were sometimes hung from trees, and the rabbits were driven into them. The Pueblo Indians sometimes herded rabbits into a chute and corral of brush, or into a natural cul-de-sac. Rabbits and hares were also run down on foot, though this was considered more of a sport than a serious method of hunting. In deep snow, however, this was a fairly practical method.

If a rabbit ran into a burrow, it might be pulled out with a crook-shaped stick, or a barbed stick might be twisted into the rabbit's fur to pull it out. The same sort of stick was also used for rodents.

A southeastern technique was for one hunter to attract the attention of a rabbit while another hunter crept up behind it with a club.

Throughout the Subarctic, snowshoe hares were generally trapped in winter, when their trails were visible. Toss-pole snares were most common in northern Canada, but spring-pole snares were used in the Subarctic and in the northern parts of the Eastern Woodlands, though many Indians felt that spring-pole snares lost their flexibility in cold weather.

Sometimes willow and other types of vegetation were cut down and placed in piles to attract the hares; the hunter returned later to shoot them. In order to make a running hare stop, the hunter gave a series of short whistles—a trick used further south for other small animals.

Seals.   The Eastern Cree simply shot or clubbed seals in the summertime as they came ashore. Indians of the Northwest Coast used dugouts to reach islands where seals basked on the shore, then paddled swiftly towards them and harpooned them from the canoes, or climbed onto the rocks to harpoon them.

Another Northwest Coast technique was to sit in a canoe and quietly watch where a seal dived. If the animal had not been disturbed, it was likely to rise again near the same spot, and the Indians paddled swiftly to that spot, hoping to harpoon the seal as it rose.

The Kwakiutl sometimes waited for a night when the moon was new and when there was phosphorescent plankton in the water. The phosphorescence revealed the movements of the swimming seals. The seals might even be attracted to the canoe if a paddle was swirled in the water to disturb the plankton.

The Eskimos used a greater variety of techniques. In the spring, the Alaskan Eskimo hunter paddled out to the edge of the broken ice. A small sled was fastened to the top of the kayak so that the vessel could be pulled across the larger floes. He waited at the edge of the ice and shot or speared the seals as they swam past.

All through spring, seals commonly slept or sunned themselves on the ice. The Greenland hunter crept up to them on his belly and imitated them by wagging his head and grunting. The Alaskan Eskimo hunter crept up to them wearing a long white mitten on his left hand and knee protectors made of white bear or dog skin. He carried a scratching tool, a stick with seal claws attached, and occasionally he scratched on the ice as if he were a seal digging a hole. The hunter of the central Arctic used similar techniques but disguised himself by dressing in sealskin clothing.

Seals were frequently speared in the spring as they came up through holes in the ice to deliver their young. After the pup is born, the mother seal digs a den in a snow bank, with an exit to the water at one end. The Eskimos used their sled dogs to find these dens, then quickly broke into them. The mother seal would usually escape, but the pup might be drawn out with a hooked stick. Sometimes a line was fastened to the hind flipper of the pup, which was then thrown into the water and forced to dive repeatedly until its cries brought the mother within harpooning distance.

An unusual technique was used in Greenland. A hole was made near a larger hole where seals came up to sun themselves. One hunter lay on a sled at the edge of the hole where the seal was to come up. A second hunter placed the tip of a harpoon in the smaller hole. As the reclining hunter saw the seal approaching, he signalled to his partner, who harpooned the animal through the smaller hole.

In summer the Greenland Eskimo paddled out in his kayak to reach the seals. He tried to approach them from leeward and with the sun behind him. When he was close enough, he threw his harpoon, using a throwing board. A bladder was attached to the harpoon line. When the seal rose again, it was speared.

Another unusual technique, called the "clapper hunt," was also used in Greenland. A shoal of seals in a creek was surrounded by hunters in kayaks. The hunters clapped their hands, shouted, and threw stones at the seals to make them dive. In order to breathe, the seals had to rise again, but they were forced to dive until they were exhausted and could easily be speared.

The Alaskan Eskimos often used nets, perhaps because fish were also important in their diet. In September, they set nets in the water near rocky points and peninsulas where the seals were likely to pass on their way into a bay. The nets were made of rawhide, about sixty to ninety feet long and nine to twelve feet wide, with a mesh large enough for the seal's head to enter. The nets were held up with floats made of wood or of inflated bladders, and sinkers of bone, ivory, or stone were attached to the bottom. The hunter watched the net from his kayak and clubbed the seals as they became trapped in the net.

In winter the seals dug their breathing holes in bays where the ice was smooth and thin. There were often so many breathing holes that it was difficult for a hunter to determine which ones were being used at any time. The Copper Eskimos preferred hunting in large groups so that more of the holes could be watched; they used dogs to locate the holes. Each hunter waited at a hole and speared the seal as it rose to breathe, then quickly dug away the snow and hauled the animal up.

The Eskimos sometimes used a small device consisting of a bone rod with a knob on one end to indicate the approach of a seal. The rod was thrust into the ice near the hole, so that the seal struck it when it rose to breathe. Some Eskimos, however, felt the device tended to frighten seals away.

If the hunter was alone and expected a long wait, he built a snow wall to keep off the wind, sat on a stool next to the breathing hole, and placed a smaller stool under his feet. His harpoon was kept nearby, resting on two forked pieces of ivory thrust into the ice.

Several hunters might wait together near a large hole in the ice, so that an entire herd of seals could be harpooned when they came up to breathe.

In midwinter the Alaskan Eskimos netted seals by digging four holes around the breathing hole. A pole was used to set a square net under the breathing hole. When the seal rose, it became entangled in the net.

In some western areas in winter, nets were set under the ice near rocky points. Holes were dug about ten or fifteen feet apart, and a pole and a long cord were used to pass the net under each of the holes. (The same technique was widely used for catching fish.)

Deer. Deer are found throughout most of temperate North America, white-tailed deer in the eastern forests and the center of the continent, mule deer in the generally more open country of the west. They are probably as common today, except in urban areas, as they were centuries ago.

The diet is extensive: fruits, nuts, grasses, mushrooms, herbaceous plants, and the bark and leaves of many trees and shrubs. Deer feed at dawn and dusk. If the night has a full moon and a clear sky, feeding may go on into the night. If there should be several days of stormy weather, deer will spend the time in shelter and then feed voraciously when the weather clears. After feeding, the animal retreats to cover, preferably somewhere with a good view. Bucks in particular prefer an uphill spot for spending the day.

Deer generally travel on fixed trails, which lead from one refuge to another, either thick cover or gullies. Different trails may be used in different seasons. They cannot travel well in thick snow and tend to "yard up" in such conditions—forming small herds to trample the snow down and eating only what they can reach in this area.

An unsuspicious deer tends to feed for a minute, twitch its tail, raise its head, and then feed again. When a deer is nervous, it begins to snort and stamp, and its tail is raised more slowly. It may also swing to windward of its intended trail. If spooked, a white-tailed deer travels a considerable distance, generally uphill, whereas mule deer will only run to the other side of a nearby ridge. Light snow and rain seem to make deer less cautious—or perhaps simply unable to hear and smell very well.

One of the least complicated but most arduous ways of hunting deer was to track the animal until it became exhausted and could be approached and shot. Deer are vegetarians and need to graze often and to rest in order to digest their food, so in spite of their ability to move swiftly for short distances, they become exhausted if followed for a long time. In the Eastern Woodlands, deer were tracked on snowshoes in the winter, and at other times of the year they were tracked and brought down with dogs.

The Indians of southern Quebec set branches across the trails used by deer in winter. The deer were forced to travel in the deeper snow, where they were an easier prey for the waiting hunters.

Some California tribes used the relay method of hunting: chasing a deer to another waiting hunter, who in turn chased it to another.

The Navaho also used the relay method. Men stationed themselves at various points along a deer trail. The deer were driven along the trail, and a smoke signal was made to notify the waiting hunters. As the first deer ran by, the first hunter gave a wolf call to frighten the deer, and the other hunters did likewise as the deer ran past, until it was exhausted and could be easily killed. The method was most commonly used to capture deer alive; the animal was then strangled and skinned for the "sacred buckskin" used for ceremonial purposes.

The Navaho also sometimes waited in a tree or on the ground where deer were accustomed to sleep, then shot them as they approached.

A common technique in the Southwest was for one group of hunters to drive the deer to other hunters who waited to shoot them.

The Hopi formed a circle around a herd of deer. Other hunters got into the circle and drove the deer to the perimeter where they were shot.

In the Southwest and the Eastern Woodlands, a very common method of hunting deer was to light the grass or undergrowth on fire in a great circle around the deer. Others might follow the first group of hunters, lighting places that had been missed and making sure that the fire did not spread outwards. The deer panicked and tried to get out of the circle, but as they found escape impossible, they huddled in a group at the center, making them an easy target. Other tribes simply set a wall of fire, driving the deer to waiting hunters.

In the Eastern Woodlands, hunters sometimes carried torches and encircled the deer, then walked towards the center of the circle, though without setting fire to the undergrowth.

Disguises were commonly used by a lone hunter. The disguise consisted of the skin from the head and neck of a deer. Twigs were arranged inside the skin so that it dried in its original form. The antlers might be left whole, or split in half and hollowed, or branches might be fastened in place. The Navaho even attached thongs, held in the hands, to make the ears wiggle, and imitated the deer's front legs by carrying poles with the lower ends carved to simulate deer's hooves. Sometimes an entire deerskin was worn, or the hunter might wear a buckskin coat. Other hunters painted their bodies. In some parts of the southeastern United States, the head was carried in one hand rather than on the shoulders. The disguised hunter imitated the movements of the deer; he lowered his head, pretending to browse, or imitated the bleating of a deer, until he was close enough to shoot. Such disguises must have been fairly lifelike, since cases have been recorded of one disguised hunter shooting another.

In the Southwest, the disguised hunter was sometimes accompanied by another person. The disguised hunter imitated the motions of a deer as he approached the herd, but he generally tried to stay behind cover. His companion waited further back in a spot where he could view the herd more carefully. From time to time the disguised hunter turned to watch his partner, who gave him directions.

A chute was sometimes used for deer in much of the western United States. In California it was customary to use a chute with hunters waiting at the apex, though sometimes a snare was set at the apex instead. On the western Plains, a pit was often dug at the apex, while on the Great Basin and in other parts of California a corral was used to hold the deer after they had fled down the chute.

The Zuñi and Cochiti built a fence of stakes when wood was available. Pits were dug at intervals, and the deer were led to the fence by men in disguises, working downwind from the deer.

The Shoshone made a chute of sagebrush, with a pit at its apex.

The Blackfeet dug pits fifteen to twenty feet wide. Willow poles were laid across, supported on vertical poles, then covered with grass.

The Navaho also used pitfalls. Several pits were dug along a deer trail. Each pit was slightly wider than the length of a deer, and four to six feet deep. A forked pole at one end of the pit floor held the deer suspended, and a stake in the center pierced the animal's heart. Sometimes several stakes were used instead of the forked pole. At other times the pit was dug six or seven feet deep and no poles or stakes were planted. A ledge was dug around the pit, and poles or sunflower stalks were laid lengthwise and crosswise, then covered with bark and dirt. Sometimes the deer were driven towards the pit, and sometimes the pit was just left and visited each morning.

In the Eastern Woodlands, a spring-pole snare was used, which caught the animal's leg and lifted it off the ground. These traps are briefly mentioned in the accounts of the early explorers, but any description of the actual mechanics of the trap seems to have been lost. However, the Kwakiutl of the Northwest Coast also used a spring-pole leg trap for deer. Perhaps this device bore a resemblance to the eastern form.

Hunters also often tried calling deer, sometimes with devices made from gourds or hollow branches—again, not described in detail. An Eastern Woodland technique was to hold a blade of grass between the first and second joints of both thumbs and blow on it to imitate the sound of a fawn.

Scents were also important. The Eastern Woodland hunter might live on nothing but bracken shoots for a few days, so that his odor was less likely to frighten the deer. It was especially important not to smoke tobacco before the hunt. A technique used in Virginia was to go to windward of the deer and rub a piece of angelica root (*Angelica atropurpurea*) between one's hands; the scent was supposed to draw the deer toward the hunter. The Miwok of California rubbed themselves with the root of *A. breweri*. The Ojibwa burned the flowers of Canada fleabane (*Erigeron canadensis*) to attract deer.

Antelope (pronghorn).   On the Great Basin and in the Southwest, antelope, like the other large herbivores, were sometimes hunted by tracking them to exhaustion, even though they are capable of fifty-mile-an-hour sprints. The Navaho sometimes ran down antelope by setting up a relay of men in order to catch the animal alive; after it was captured it was strangled to obtain "sacred buckskin."

Antelope were also frequently driven to other hunters waiting in ambush.

At other times they were hunted by forming a large circle of people that gradually closed in on the animals. When horses became available, these made the technique of encircling somewhat easier.

The chute and corral were used for antelope by many people on the Plains, the Great Basin, the Southwest, and in southern California.

The Pueblo Indians made a corral of tree trunks, and a chute of brush. Brush was also placed in piles that extended out from the main chute, often for ten miles or so. A fire was set behind the herd of antelope to drive them towards the chute, or boys followed the herd and howled like wolves to frighten the animals. When the antelope had entered the corral, the entrance was closed with more brush, and the antelope were shot with arrows.

The Navaho also used the chute and corral. Whenever possible, the corral was built behind a rise of ground to make it less visible. The corral was made of two semicircles of brush, preferably of cedar or pine boughs. An opening was left in the front and another in the back of the corral. The walls were about ten or twelve feet high and enclosed one or two acres of ground. The chute was built with walls as high, or nearly as high, as those of the corral, and it extended for anywhere between four hundred yards to a mile outwards from the entrance to the corral. Sometimes both sides were straight, but sometimes one side was semicircular, or at least semicircular at the end nearest the corral. At the end of the chute, more brush extended for another mile or two. These additional brush piles were placed at intervals of about five yards near the main chute, but about thirty yards apart further out. Sometimes a yucca plant was uprooted and turned upside down, and pieces of sagebrush were put on top of it to look like a person.

In earlier times, a semicircle of people drove the antelope towards the chute. When horses were available, usually two horsemen began the drive, and the antelope were only chased on foot after they had entered the chute.

When the horsemen had sighted a herd of antelope, they made a smoke signal to notify the people waiting at the chute. The horsemen carried torches and lit smoky fires to drive the antelope slowly towards the chute. When the animals were near the chute, one of the horsemen showed himself to the animals to make them run. More fires were lit if they began to run the wrong way. Sometimes the men also lit the brush piles that led out from the chute. When the animals were quite close to the chute, the horsemen began to chase them faster.

When the antelope had entered the chute, men ran across to form a line and prevent them from escaping. If any of the animals turned, the men crouched down and sprang into the air to frighten them. Eventually the antelope entered the corral itself, and old people who had been waiting near the corral stood in front of the entrance to prevent them from leaving.

The Blackfeet also used a chute, but combined with a pit instead of a corral. The pit was nine to twelve feet deep, twenty feet long, and six feet wide. The earth from the excavation was put down as a ridge all around the pit, and the tops of the ridge were lined with branches. The pit was built at an angle to the chute, in order to make the trap less visible. The chute was made of heaps of stones, with willows bent over them to form a fence.

When antelope were seen grazing inside the chute, old people and children hid behind the rock piles. Young people crept up behind the antelope, and as the animals began to move, the people behind the rock piles rose up and waved at the animals to keep them headed towards the pit. The animals ran down the chute, turned the corner, jumped over the ridge, and fell into the pit.

Disguises were commonly used for hunting antelope, as for similar animals.

Elk.   Elk were regarded as easy animals to stalk. They were tracked to exhaustion by certain tribes of northern California. Other Indians of northern California and the Plateau drove elk herds to waiting hunters, while the Yokuts also encircled them on foot. The Crow drove elk either over a cliff or into a corral. The Wiyot, another northern California tribe, drove them into a chute made either of of brushwood or simply of strips of bark tied from tree to tree. A clog snare was placed at the apex. Other California tribes hunted elk by using a disguise similar to that used for deer and other large herbivores.

Caribou.   Caribou were essential to the Eskimos and to most of the Subarctic tribes. Seal blubber was always appreciated, but the meat of caribou was preferred to that of seal. Caribou hides were required for clothing, tents, and other articles.

Caribou were usually present in scattered herds in winter, but it was difficult to hunt them at this time with bow and arrow, even with the aid of snowshoes, since they quickly fled. The creaking of the dry snow underfoot only increased the difficulty of approaching them.

But caribou gather into large herds twice a year as they migrate along fairly constant routes through valleys and across river narrows. During the autumn migration their meat was at its best, and their hides were most suitable for clothing, since at this time the skins were free from the holes caused by warble-fly larvae.

Sometimes—for reasons still not understood—caribou change the routes of their migration. For the Indians and Eskimos awaiting the arrival of the herds, such a change often meant starvation.

When migrating animals were sighted, the Eskimos often pursued them on water. Usually hunters waited in kayaks on the far shore as the animals approached a river crossing. When the caribou were well on their way across, the hunters paddled out to them and drove them upstream, allowing the current and the low temperature of the water to tire the animals. When the caribou began to show signs of exhaustion, the hunters paddled ahead of the herd and turned around. The herd was surrounded, while one or two hunters tried to drive their spears into the small of the animal's back. Some animals would be wounded sufficiently to reach shore and die. Those that died immediately were towed with a line fastened to antlers and jaw. Caribou that floated downstream were located later by the gulls that flew above them. Other people waited on shore for caribou that tried to escape and shot them with bows and arrows.

Usually this hunt was a community effort, but a similar technique might be tried with only one or two hunters in kayaks.

Another Eskimo method of hunting caribou was to build a wall across a ravine, and then to drive the caribou towards the wall, where they became trapped and could be shot.

An Alaskan Eskimo trick involved two men walking towards the herd, one man directly behind the other. The herd made a wide circle around the hunters, but in the meantime the hunter in back had dropped out of sight behind a boulder or any other sort of cover. When the herd reached this hidden hunter, he rose up and began to shoot at them. The herd turned back in the direction of the lead hunter, who also began to shoot at them, and the herd continued to run back and forth between the two hunters until several animals had been killed.

In early summer it was sometimes possible to simply run down the new-born fawns.

In the autumn, certain river crossings froze early, and a somewhat unusual method was to chase the caribou towards thin ice, where they would fall through and be unable to escape, making them an easy prey.

Snares of braided rawhide were commonly used by the Alaskan Eskimos. The snares were fastened to bushes at the end of a valley, and the caribou were driven towards them. The Eastern Cree often used toss-pole snares in winter, set up along caribou trails.

Eskimos also hunted caribou with a chute. The chute consisted of widely spaced piles of stones that looked, in silhouette, like men. A lump of sod was placed upside down on top of each of these cairns. Hunters waited with bows and arrows behind a low stone or sod wall at the apex.

Something similar to a chute, but consisting of a single fence, was used to guide caribou to river locations that the Eskimos regarded as more suitable for a hunt. This type of fence was more likely to consist of poles, with a piece of skin or bird wings attached to the top and allowed to flutter in the breeze.

The Subarctic Indians also used a chute or a combination of chute and corral, especially during migrations. Because they had more access to wood, their constructions were somewhat more elaborate than those of the Eskimos. The preferred location was a wooded area that opened onto a river, lake, or plain along one of the migration routes. The corral was a circular construction, often over a mile in circumference, with walls of logs and brush piled in any convenient manner. The entrance to the corral was only wide enough for a single animal to enter at a time. Sometimes a rear entrance was also left, with a snare hanging down across it. Other walls were built all across the corral, and rawhide snares were set either on standing trees or on poles leaned against other trees to form clog snares. The chute consisted of piles of brush set twenty or thirty yards apart across the open ground or ice, extending outwards for a mile or two.

The Indians camped on high ground where they had a good view of the entrance to the chute. When caribou were seen approaching, the hunters—which might include the entire camp—walked around the herd and approached it in a long crescent. The caribou fled down the two lines of the chute and into the corral, and the entrance was sealed with brush. As the animals became caught in the snares, they were speared or shot with bows and arrows.

A simpler type of chute was used by the Subarctic Indians during the summer. Poles were collected and prepared ahead of time, and when caribou were known to be abundant, these poles were set up to form the chute. A lump of moss was set on top of each pole, and a piece of skin was attached to blow in the wind. A small circular fence was set up at the apex, not to serve as a corral but to conceal the hunters who waited with bows and spears. Other hunters surrounded the herd and drove it down the chute.

Some Indians of the Subarctic even built permanent chutes in an hourglass fashion, in order to take advantage of both the spring and the autumn migrations.

A birch-bark "megaphone" was occasionally used in the Subarctic for calling caribou during the mating season. The device was similar to that used for moose, but smaller.

Moose.   Moose, like other animals, were frequently shot when they were accidentally encountered. Since moose often feed on the willows and other vegetation along river banks, they were often encountered by hunters travelling in canoes.

Moose were stalked at all times of the year. The task was made much easier if there had been a light snow overnight to reveal any recent tracks.

Moose usually feed in the early morning, before sunrise, and then sleep for a while. From midmorning until evening they rest, and then in the evening they begin to feed again. During their feeding periods they often make enough noise to hide the sound of the approaching hunter, and after that they are likely to be sleeping soundly enough to be approached. For the rest of the day they might be less easy to approach.

As with the hunting of caribou, the creaking of dry snow underfoot was a problem in approaching a moose. Loose snow and a good breeze to carry off human scent made winter hunting a lot easier.

If there had been a thaw, the surface of the snow might later freeze into a hard crust, making it difficult for the moose to travel, but easy for the hunter to approach it on snowshoes.

When the snow is crusted or deep, moose tend to "yard up," somewhat in the manner of deer, gathering in small groups and travelling on well established trails, again making the task easier for the hunter. A moose that could be forced out onto slippery ice was also an easy prey. Dogs were occasionally used in tracking and chasing moose.

Once a moose had been sighted, it was often possible to run it down over a period of hours. But as with other animals, this technique was considered to make the meat unpalatable. If a moose had been unintentionally frightened, it was likely to travel downwind in order to catch the scent of its pursuers. If the hunter lost a moose he had previously spotted, he would, therefore, be most likely to search for it downwind. However, if a bull and a cow had been spooked and separated, they were likely to rejoin later where they had first been seen, and so the hunters might simply lie in wait for them to return.

A common technique was what is sometimes referred to as "semi-circular hunting." Moose tend to wander about erratically while feeding, but, before going to sleep, cows in particular will often travel downwind for a few yards so that they can detect the scent of any predator following them. The Indians took advantage of this behavior. If they spotted moose tracks, they often turned aside from the trail and returned to it further on, since the moose would be most likely to expect hunters or predators along its own trail. The hunters thus made a series of semicircles along the moose's trail. If at some point they attempted to return to the trail and no longer found it, they knew it was likely that the moose had doubled back downwind in order to sleep. At this point the hunters also reversed direction, travelling in a series of smaller semicircles until the animal was located.

Moose were also frequently hunted by driving them towards other hunters. This technique was most effective on islands or peninsulas, where the moose's direction of travel was limited.

During the autumn mating season the bulls become quite belligerent, sometimes even oblivious to human presence. It was a common practice at this time for hunters to imitate the sounds of the animals. The central ridge was removed from a cow's shoulder blade, and the bone was swung back and forth through the bushes, or against the bark of a tree, to imitate the sound of the bull moose's antlers. Water was poured into a lake to imitate the sound of a urinating cow. The cow moose has a call which is a low grunt, sometimes described as being halfway between a "bark" and a "moo." The Indians attracted the bulls by imitating this sound, amplifying it by calling through a device made from a truncated triangle of birch bark about twenty inches long and equally wide, sewn at the edges to form a semiconical "bullhorn."

Snares were frequently set for moose, usually a clog snare, attached to a leaning pole. It was set up along a well-used moose trail, or even along man-made trails, since moose are likely to use these. In aboriginal times, snaring was probably the principal means of taking moose, even though the taste of the meat might be affected, and butchering the frozen carcass in winter presented some difficulties.

Chutes were rarely used, probably because moose are far less gregarious animals than other large herbivores. Pitfalls and nets seem never to have been used for moose.

Mountain sheep.　The Indians of the Southwest shot mountain sheep whenever they were encountered. In aboriginal times these animals were so numerous that they were often found on the flatlands, well away from the mountains that have now become the refuge of most species. Some tribes tracked them to exhaustion, but driving them to other hunters was a more common technique in the Southwest and the Great Basin. They were also surrounded or driven over cliffs. Disguises were frequently used, sometimes including stuffed buckskin "horns." The Shoshone pursued mountain sheep with dogs along mountain trails, bringing them to bay on rocky points where they could be killed. Other tribes of the Southwest crept above them and caught them with lassos; the animals usually expect danger from below, hoping to escape pursuers by climbing higher.

Buffalo.　Until the days of the white men, buffalo were seen almost everywhere in North America, but they were always more common on the Plains. A great many methods were used in hunting them.

In the Southwest, buffalo were often ambushed at water holes when they came to drink. In many areas, a single animal might be stalked by a lone hunter. The task was much easier if the animal was forced to travel on ice or snow, or driven into water. Snowshoes made it possible to stalk buffalo easily in winter, when the animal had to force its way through deep snow. The animal might also be chased to exhaustion, or chased by hunters in relay. But usually the Plains tribes did not allow an individual hunter to stalk buffalo, since he would be likely to drive away the rest of the herd.

An old Blackfoot trick was for men to dress in wolf skins and crawl on hands and knees towards the herd. Apparently wolves were less likely to disturb the buffalo than men.

Hunters often drove buffalo into a natural cul-de-sac when the opportunity presented itself.

The buffalo might also be surrounded on foot. It might even be possible to simply set up the lodges around the herd, locking them into a sort of "corral."

As with so many other animals, it was not uncommon to encircle buffalo with a ring of fire, forcing them into a tight mass where they could be easily speared. The Miami used a variant of this technique: they left a few gaps in the ring of fire, and hunters waited at these gaps for the buffalo to attempt to escape.

But probably the most common techniques, and certainly the most famous, involved some sort of a drive, usually in combination with a chute, and usually also involving a cliff or a corral at the apex.

Drives and chutes were used at any time of the year, but especially in late fall or early winter, when the buffalo had moved to high rocky ground suitable for such techniques. Also, at this time of year the buffalo were fat and provided better food. In the summer, however, they came down to the low flat lands where they were less easy to hunt.

The simplest technique was to drive the buffalo over a cliff, so that they would be killed by the fall. They might also be brought towards the cliff by someone disguised in the head and hide of a buffalo. If he caught the attention of the herd, they might be induced to walk towards him as he led them to the precipice. The same trick was sometimes tried without a disguise, simply relying on the buffalo's sense of curiosity.

Often, however, a chute and corral were used, and in flat country these would be necessary. Even though buffalo are very powerful animals, they are said to be uninclined to try to escape from an enclosure, at least if it has no gaps, so the corral did not have to be very strong.

The Blood and Piegan built their corrals at the base of a cliff. The corral might be made of logs, brush, or rocks. If the cliff was high enough that the animals were sure to all be killed, the corral might be omitted. The chute, consisting of two lines of rock piles or brush, was built at the top of the cliff. People hid along this fence, and one man went out, with or without disguise, and attempted to lead the herd toward the chute. As the animals approached, the people rose up, shouting and waving at the buffalo to keep them headed toward the cliff. Those that were not killed in the fall were shot while they milled about in the corral.

The North Blackfeet built their chutes on less steep ground. The corral was made of logs and built on high ground. Where the chute joined the corral, the ground was cut away to form a four-foot drop. When the buffalo had entered the corral, the entrance was closed with poles and robes.

The Cheyenne built a corral like that of the North Blackfeet, except that it might be constructed of brush. To ensure that the animals would stay within the frail enclosure, people stood around it and waved and shouted at the herd.

Another type of North Blackfoot corral was built at the bottom of a slope. A ramp of logs was built; forked uprights supported the main diagonal beams, and shorter logs were laid across these. Manure and water were spread on the ramp and allowed to freeze.

The Assiniboine built their corrals in a valley between converging lines of hills. Like the North Blackfeet, they used a ramp at the entrance. The corral was about five or six feet high, built of various materials. The chute extended for about a hundred yards, and widely spaced poles continued these lines for another two miles. A number of techniques were used to bring the herds to the chute: someone might imitate the sound of a calf in distress, or a grass fire might be started. Once the herd approached the chute, they might be led in by someone in disguise.

The Plains Cree also used a ramp before their corral, though they sometimes omitted the ramp and just sealed the entrance with poles and robes once the buffalo had entered.

After the introduction of horses and firearms, most of the techniques described above were abandoned. Instead, the herds were simply charged on horseback, or herded together and driven towards camp for slaughter.

Deadfalls, snares, and pits were rarely, if ever, used for buffalo.

Bear.   Polar bears were generally encountered by the Eskimo more or less by accident. If a hunter was travelling by dog sled and encountered a polar bear, he quickly cut loose his dogs. The dogs ran up to the bear and kept it at bay until the Eskimo could kill it with a spear or harpoon, or with a bow and arrows with heavy flint tips. Polar bears were also killed when their dens were located.

Many Indians, however, considered the bow and arrow too weak even for the smaller black bear. The Eastern Cree preferred to use a club.

Black bears and grizzlies were killed in their winter dens.

The black bear builds a den in a bank or under the roots of an upturned tree, placing moss and debris over the original entrance to leave a hole only about two or three feet wide. The animal hibernates soundly from early September to spring. The dens were located by noting the ice from the bear's respiration. The bear was driven out of the den, and as the sleepy animal came out it was killed with spears. A safer method sometimes used involved blocking the entrance with logs, noting the shape of the den, and determining the precise location of the sleeping bear. A spear was then driven down through the den and into the animal.

Grizzly bears, generally upland animals, leave an opening about a foot wider. They go into their dens later in the autumn, do not hibernate as deeply, and often leave the den several times during the winter to look for food. If hunters decided to attack one in its den, they had to be prepared for the likelihood that the grizzly would come out faster than a black bear would. Grizzlies were often entirely avoided by Indians. They are extremely powerful animals, and, unlike black bears, they may attack humans without provocation. There was also somewhat of a taboo against killing grizzlies.

In the Southeast, black bears often make their winter dens high up in the hollow of a tree. Hunters determined the general location of a den by claw marks on the surrounding trees, and they sometimes imitated the sound of a bear cub to induce the female bear to reveal her presence. Once the den was located, one hunter crushed a few cane stalks and climbed an adjacent tree. The canes were fastened to a long pole, set on fire, and pushed into the den, or they might be fastened to an arrow that was shot into the den. The flames caused the bear to climb down the tree and be shot by the other hunters.

Preservation of meat

In most of North America, meat was preserved by drying it over a fire to become "jerky." The meat was first cut into strips about three inches wide and about half an inch thick, with the cut going along the grain. (On the Plains, meat was first cut into large pieces, then each piece was cut in a spiral, again with the cuts mainly parallel to the grain.) The strips were placed on a scaffold so that they were a few feet above a slightly smoky fire. If flies were a problem, the smoke was increased. The meat was not allowed to become very warm, so it was only dried and not cooked. It was left on the scaffold for several days, until it had become dark and leathery but not completely hard.

Buffalo tongues were split lengthwise and similarly dried, and the fat along the spine was dipped briefly into hot fat before being smoked above a lodge fire. The organ meats of all types of animals, however, had to be eaten right away.

In the southwestern United States, where the air is generally drier, meat was dried with the aid of sun and wind, and the fire was omitted.

Meat dries to about a third of its original weight, so the process not only preserved the meat but made it easier to carry, an important consideration for nomadic people.

On the Plains, jerky was often turned into pemmican. The dried meat was roasted over a fire and pounded into powder or fine flakes. To this was added an equal weight of rendered fat or marrow, plus a small quantity of crushed dried juneberries or choke cherries. The fat was rendered by boiling it in water until the oil rose to the surface and the solid matter (to be discarded) sank to the bottom. The pemmican was packed as tightly as possible into folded rawhide containers. While jerky might only keep for a few weeks, pemmican could be stored for years.

In the Arctic and Subarctic, meat was preserved in winter simply by allowing it to freeze. Caribou were often left to freeze where they had been shot; the hunter might try to cover the carcass with stones or logs to discourage scavengers.

Tools and toolmaking

ike many Old World cultures, that of the Indians cannot be accurately described as "Stone Age," since it was just as much an age of wood, bone, ivory, and other materials. The digging stick used by nearly every Indian woman was made of wood, as were her husband's bows, arrows, and spears. His arrowheads and spearheads might be made of stone, but they might also be made of any other hard material.

Toolmaking required an extensive knowledge of materials and their properties, as one can easily confirm by trying to duplicate the handiwork of the Indians. In addition, certain preliminary tools were required to make other tools: not even the simplest spear shaft could be made without a knife to cut it to shape.

Stone tools

Stone was used to make a variety of tools: mauls and hammers, axe heads, adzes, hoes, knives, saws, arrowheads, spearheads, drill bits, and so on. Five principal techniques were used in their manufacture: chipping, pecking, and grinding were the most common techniques, but sometimes sawing or drilling was required.

Materials. A visit to any river bank, lake shore, or stony ocean beach should reveal several types of stone with potential tool-making value. In order to study these rocks, it would be best to break them in order to get a fresh surface. The first quality to consider is *hardness*: some stones are almost unbreakable, others (though perhaps not those found on a beach) almost crumble at a touch. We will also want to consider *grain size*: some stones, such as granite, look red or gray at a distance, but when held in the hand they can clearly be seen to consist of "speckles"—crystals—of red, black, gray, and white. Others have a homogeneous appearance, even when examined under a

lens. We also want to examine the *color*, though this can vary considerably in a single type of rock. Finally, we might want to consider the type of *fracture*. Does the rock break into thin plates? Does it break into irregular lumps? Or does it have a *conchoidal* fracture, the sort of rippled "clam shell" fracture one sees on thick pieces of broken glass?

A thorough understanding of rocks and minerals (rocks are mixtures of minerals) requires a lengthy study of textbooks, photographs, and especially specimens. It must be kept in mind, also, that rock types are not as clearly defined as plant and animal species; rock types, unfortunately, consist of grades between one form and another, and sometimes a specimen cannot be given a distinct name.

A geologist would consider whether a rock was igneous (formed of molten rock), sedimentary (formed from organic or inorganic sediments), or metamorphic (changed by heat or pressure from a previous type of rock). But this most basic set of distinctions has only indirect relevance to stone-working.

Let us return to our imaginary cobblestone beach and consider some of the types we are likely to find.

The most eye-catching type of rock (actually a mineral) will be snow-white, very hard, and heavy. This is igneous *quartz*, consisting of pure silica (silicon dioxide). It is usually found in this gleaming white form, though quartz can also be any other color, or even as clear and colorless as window glass. Igneous quartz often has a granulated appearance that makes it look somewhat like quartzite (a metamorphic quartz), but even in this form igneous quartz can be distinguished by the fact that it is pure white. There are other types of rock which are white, but these other types will usually be somewhat off-white and not as hard.

A very common type of rock is *granite* and its near relatives, diorite, gabbro, etc. The granitic rocks are gray or pink at a distance, but a newly fractured surface reveals a mixture of irregular crystals which are black, white, clear, or pink. Granite is fairly heavy and strong, and its fractured surface is rough and irregular.

Other very common rocks are as hard and heavy as granite, and chemically related to granite, but so fine-grained that they present a uniform appearance. *Basalt* is usually dark gray and often almost black. *Felsite*, on the other hand, is a creamy white. Though they are both fine-grained, they feel quite rough and almost never have a glossy appearance.

On a cobblestone beach we are less likely to see *sandstone*, which is highly variable but often of a golden color. When broken it looks very much like ordinary beach sand. Sandstone may be reasonably hard, though it might also be quite soft and crumbly. Sometimes it has a lightly banded appearance. It is a very common rock in the Southwest. As the name suggests, it is a sedimentary rock formed from sand. It is sometimes difficult to distinguish fine-grained sandstone from *limestone*, another sedimentary rock, but one which often contains fossilized shells.

Another common rock is *quartzite*, which looks like a cross between sandstone and white quartz and is usually a very pale gray or beige. Quartzite is metamorphosed sandstone, and it breaks with a cleaner fracture than sandstone. Quartzite feels smooth, while sandstone feels like sandpaper. Very hard quartzite may even have a conchoidal fracture.

An important rock that we are less likely to find on a cobblestone beach is *slate*, a fine-grained gray rock that breaks into flat plates. Slate is formed by the metamorphosis of *shale*, a sedimentary rock that breaks into far more irregular plates. Shale is quite soft, and it looks like—and is—simply hardened clay. A harder rock that sometimes looks like slate but also breaks into rather irregular plates is *schist*, which may be found on cobblestone beaches in the form of somewhat flattened dark gray disks. Schist often has a slight glitter from the mica it contains.

Gneiss is especially common on the Canadian Shield. It is a hard rock, somewhat like granite in appearance, but it consists of rather colorful bands, sometimes quite broad, composed of different materials.

One is also likely to find interesting specimens of *porphyry*, which is any rock composed of large irregular crystals in a "background" or matrix of finer rock. One might also find *breccia*, broken fragments of rock which have become bound in a finer matrix. *Conglomerate* consists of rounded pebbles in a fine matrix. None of these three has much value as material for tools.

Flint tends to be rather localized. Even though it is a chemical sediment, it is very hard and fine-grained. It was an especially prized rock all over the world because of its excellent conchoidal fracture. "True" flint is dark gray and usually found in the chalk beds of Europe, while *chert* is light gray or brown and is usually found as nodules in limestone beds. The distinction between flint and chert is controversial, but North American chert is also usually referred to as "flint." Good flint was mined in Illinois,

Stone tools

Ohio, New York, and at the tip of southern Ontario.

Obsidian looks like black or dark brown glass; thin pieces are transparent. It is only found in volcanic regions. It breaks with the same conchoidal fracture as flint. Obsidian is somewhat easier to work than flint and was always a highly prized material.

There are other materials which produce a conchoidal fracture. Some are closely related to flint, such as opal and the various forms of chalcedony (carnelian, agate, onyx, etc.), but none of these is very common. *Jasper*, however, is fairly common, at least in an impure form. It usually has a brick-red appearance. What I find distinguishing about it is that it is astonishingly difficult to break, and yet it was occasionally used to make arrowheads and other tools.

It is not always easy to give a name to a particular specimen. What was more important to the tool-maker was the properties of the available material, and these could best be determined by experimentation. The tool-maker did his best with whatever materials he could find in the local environment. Flint and obsidian, however, were also items of trade, so that tools were sometimes made from materials quarried hundreds of miles away. For reasons not fully understood, the best flint and obsidian were obtained from underground rather than from the surface. This may have been due to the fact that surface material has been subject to abrasion and therefore contains invisible fractures that prevent it from splitting evenly. Quarried flint, however, was often kept underwater or in damp soil before being converted into tools, which suggests that its water content had an effect on its working qualities.

Chipping

The earliest stone tools in human history were made by chipping, and even in primitive cultures that survive today, chipping is the most common technique in tool-making. The type of finished product was partly determined by the materials available. The cruder types of tools could be made from quartz, quartzite, basalt, or even from granite or related types of rock. But the finer products, some of which were so delicately crafted that they were reserved as ceremonial objects or gifts, were usually made of superior materials such as flint and obsidian. The various methods of manufacture are outlined below.

Simple percussion.   If we take a flat oval pebble, perhaps about six inches long, composed of any fairly hard type of rock, and knock two large opposing flakes off one end with another slightly smaller but harder pebble, we have, in a matter of seconds, created a duplicate of an early "hand axe." Such a tool might do a reasonable job of skinning and cutting up an animal, and one might even cut down a tree with it, especially if the wood had been well charred by fire. This tool has limitations, though. The material may be such that it will not form a fine cutting edge, and the angle of the cutting edge is likely to be rather broad, so that the tool has more of the effect of a wedge than of a knife.

But we can experiment further with such a tool. We could, for example, knock flakes off the entire surface of the pebble, so that—with luck—the finished product has a form more closely resembling a modern steel axe-head. The hand axe would then retain a fair-sized cutting edge without excessive bulk behind the edge, and the reduced width of the axe might allow us to create a finer angle on the cutting edge.

Such a tool might serve a variety of purposes. It could be used as an axe, an adze, a knife, a scraper, or a wedge, and most early hand axes were in fact such general purpose tools.

There would also be an interesting by-product of our labors. The chips broken from the pebble would have edges with quite a narrow angle. These chips would serve quite well for small cutting or scraping jobs, though they would not have the necessary weight required for use as an axe or adze. Chips broken off with a single blow were still being used as tools by various Indian tribes in the nineteenth century.

It is possible to make arrowheads by this simple method of percussion. Materials such as quartz, quartzite, and basalt can be smashed against a large boulder, and out of the many fragments there may be one or two that bear a resemblance to a future arrowhead. Suitable chips can also be found lying on the ground. An "anvil" stone is almost essential for these tough materials. The fragment is placed flatwise on the anvil and carefully chipped into shape. Work in such materials has rarely been described, but California Indians used an anvil stone for chipping quartz arrowheads.

The only real problem with such materials is that it is difficult to create a sharp edge. Quartz, quartzite, and basalt all vary considerably from one specimen to another. Basalt is usually worthless, unless it is so fine-grained that it has almost a waxy gloss, though it was by no means an uncommon choice of materials. Most quartz is also a very difficult material, though excellent artifacts have been made from clear quartz. Quartzite is far more likely to be of workable quality.

Flint and obsidian can also be worked in this manner, but these superior materials were usually reserved for more elaborate techniques.

Percussion with a striking platform.　The really well-crafted arrowheads, spearheads, and knives one sees in museum exhibits required a slightly more sophisticated approach. The material had to be of good quality; obsidian, flint, or one of the types of rock related to flint, was almost essential. Fine workmanship was also sometimes possible with quartz.

With a fair amount of practice, it is possible to duplicate these ancient techniques. The ideal starting point is to have an egg-shaped or slightly elongated boulder weighing about five pounds. The boulder is placed on one's leg, and the wider end is struck off at a right angle to the longest axis, using a hammerstone that is smaller but harder than the boulder. Some people prefer a disk-shaped hammerstone, others a somewhat pointed one, though almost any shape can be used. Quartzite seems to be a preferred material for hammerstones. Although it may seem to make the job easier, an anvil stone should never be used at this stage, because it tends to create an opposing force on the opposite side, resulting in an unpredictable fracture of the boulder.

With any luck, the boulder now has a nicely flattened end, a *striking platform*. This is, however, an idealized picture. Most boulders of either flint or obsidian are rather irregular in shape, and one must use one's own judgment to determine where to strike this initial blow. In any case, the striking platform should form a right angle with the sides of the boulder.

The next step is the most critical of all. The boulder is held in the left (preferably gloved) hand, and perhaps, if it is heavy, it is also resting on a pad placed on the left leg. The striking platform is upwards, and a smaller hammerstone is now used to strike off *blanks* all around the outside of the boulder—somewhat as if one were peeling a carrot. By a "blank" I simply mean a fragment of stone that has two more-or-less parallel faces, and very little distance between the two faces—a "slice," if you like. Several layers of blanks can be removed from a single core.

The blows should be roughly parallel to the main axis, though actually directed slightly towards the cortex (outer surface). The point of contact should be not far from the edge, of course. It is usually not necessary to use great force, but one should "follow through" with the blow and avoid the natural tendency to either curve the blow towards oneself or allow the hammerstone to bounce. It is necessary to strike off blades from a convex portion of the boulder; a blow to a concave portion will merely shatter the boulder.

If one is not successful in creating a nice flat blank, the result will be either a badly crumbled edge or an irregularly shattered boulder. In either case, it may still be possible to work with what is left. If after half a dozen blows one still does not succeed, it is quite possible that the stone is not of the right quality and should be discarded. In any case, if one has produced a very irregular lump of stone, any further work with it will be very difficult. If, on the other hand, one succeeds in producing one or more good blanks, then the rest is easy.

For an arrowhead, a blank one or two inches long, about half that wide, and about a quarter inch thick would be ideal. A spearhead would be considerably larger.

The blank must then be further shaped, first by further percussion and finally by a pressure technique, to be discussed later. A piece of leather is required, large enough to cover one's left hand, and it is a good idea to cut a hole for the thumb. The blank is placed on the ball of the thumb and held down *firmly* all over with the fingertips. If it is not held firmly, it is liable to crack in half at some time. At this point one will need a much smaller hammerstone, perhaps a bit smaller than a golf ball.

Beginning at one end of the blank, small flakes are chipped from all the way along one edge. Usually it is best if the direction of the blow is nearly parallel to the face of the blank, since this will tend to produce nice long flakes that will carry halfway across the face. These long flakes will help to reduce the thickness of the arrowhead. However, sometimes a blow as direct as this will knock off a good flake but also leave a crumbled edge on the resulting hollow. A few minutes of work will soon make apparent the proper angle, the necessary force, and so on. When the opposite end is reached, the blank is turned over, and work is begun on the other side of that same edge. When this edge is finished, the second edge is treated

in the same manner. If a "stemmed" arrowhead is desired, the base might be chipped somewhat at this point to reduce its width. The point will require more delicate treatment.

It is also quite possible to chip a blank by holding it pinched between the thumb and the bent index finger. This method reduces the area of support but makes it easier to deal with very small arrowheads.

The result should closely resemble a leaf-shaped, triangular, or stemmed arrowhead. However, the large chips taken out of each edge may have left the arrowhead looking rather uneven, and so it may now be necessary to go over the edges again, removing shorter and narrower chips.

A few refinements of technique might be worth mentioning at this point. When the initial blank has been removed from the boulder, it will have two different faces. The face created by the blow will be bulbar (convex), while the face nearest the exterior of the boulder will have longitudinal ridges caused by the removal of previous flakes (assuming that the blank in question is not part of the first layer to be removed). According to Knowles, the best type of blank will have two ridges caused by previous flakes. These two ridges ensure that the "center-line" of the blank is not unnecessarily high. A blank with a single high ridge in the center, on the other hand, is almost useless, because it is this particular region of the blank that is hardest to reduce by further chipping.

Knowles also stresses the technique of the "turned edge," a method used in Australia. The blank is first held with the ridged face upwards. A series of small steep chips is removed by striking down along one edge. The blank is reversed, revealing the area that has just been modified. This finely chipped edge, the "turned edge," then serves as a sort of "striking platform" for the removal of larger flakes. The process is repeated for the bulbar face. The result is a series of longer and flatter flakes.

Pressure flaking. The making of a finely crafted Indian arrowhead usually involved three stages: removing a blank from beneath a striking platform, chipping the blank into the right general shape, and finishing the arrowhead by pressure flaking. However, sometimes excellent arrowheads were finished without pressure flaking, while at other times small arrowheads were made entirely by pressure flaking after the removal of the initial blank.

Pressure flaking requires a special tool, a pointed implement made of antler (probably most often), bone, ivory, or even stone or hard wood. Copper points may have been used by some people, to judge from the deep indentations on some artifacts. (Nowadays a large soft nail works very well, if it is driven into a wooden handle and the head is sawn off and filed to a rounded tip.) This instrument might be of any shape. One common type had its working end shaped like a dagger with its tip snapped off, lens-shaped in cross-section, applied edge on to the edge of the arrowhead. Another kind had a tip in the form of an offset knob. The pressure flaker was often set into a handle, such as a long wooden rod that could be gripped between upper arm and chest for greater leverage. Some of the Eskimos used a pressure flaker with a handle like a pistol grip.

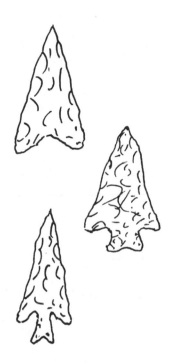

The arrowhead was held in the left hand and firmly gripped by the palm and fingertips, as for percussion flaking. The flaker was held nearly parallel to the plane of the arrowhead and pressed down, with considerable force, at a point near the edge. The entire process is much like percussion flaking, except that finer and more precise work can be done in this way.

Materials such as basalt, quartzite, and white quartz are usually too tough for pressure-flaking. On the other hand, since these are not such delicate materials, one can usually work them by percussion alone without having to worry about snapping the arrowhead in half.

It is interesting to note that Knowles' technique of the "turned edge" appears in North America among the Wintun of Oregon, as an aspect of pressure-flaking rather than percussion. After pressure-flaking one side, the arrowhead was rubbed with the antler pressure-flaker, creating a series of microscopic chips.

Arrowheads often had notches chipped in each side near the base, in order to provide a seat for the sinew binding. These notches were usually made with a tool that resembled a smaller and more finely tipped version of the basic pressure-flaker. It is easier to remove chips from alternate (left and right) sides of the notch, rather than to begin at the center. The "stemmed" type of arrowhead can equally be regarded, of course, as a sort of "notched" triangular arrowhead.

The basic steps I have outlined above were by far the most commonly used chipping techniques in North America. However, several less common techniques were also used at times.

Fire.   A few accounts of Indian stone-working suggest that fire was sometimes used. The Wyot of California, for example, are said to have heated obsidian in a fire and then let it cool, after which the stone broke into flakes. Modern experimenters seem to have had very little luck duplicating this method, and some of the accounts may well be fictitious.

Batons.   Some stone artifacts have large but quite flat depressions (scars) where the chips have been removed. Experiments have indicated that these conveniently flat chips resulted from the use of a baton of antler or even wood, rather that a hammerstone. Antler batons are know to have been used by some American Indians, though probably only for lighter work. The blank was struck with the baton in much the same way that a hammerstone was used, but the softer material of the baton tended to diffuse the force of the impact.

Turtlebacks.   A slightly different variation of the "striking platform" technique was used in the making of a "turtleback" or "tortoise stone." A large, somewhat flat pebble was chipped all over to remove the cortex. A small amount of material was struck off one end, creating a striking platform, and this platform was then struck to remove a large flake from one face. The resulting core, which was then discarded, gives rise to the name. The technique was used to some extent by North American Indians. It was also used in Europe, but was rejected in the late Paleolithic in favor of the faceted or cylindrical type of core mentioned earlier.

Hammer and punch.   The Cheyenne used a hard wooden mallet and a punch made from the tooth of some sort of marine mammal to remove chips from the blank. The blank was held in the left hand, the punch was held against the edge of the blank, and a second person struck the punch to remove the chips.

The Wintun used a similar technique to remove the initial blank from the core. The obsidian core was held in the left hand, the punch was held by the tips of the left index and middle fingers, and a stone was used to strike the mallet.

Ishi, the last of the Yahi Indians, also used a hammer and punch for large obsidian tools such as spearheads and knives.

Crutch tools.   The Aztecs used a pressure technique for removing the initial blank, as opposed to the final chips.

The tool required for this technique was a piece of wood about five feet long with an upper cross-piece about eight inches long. The tool was placed against the edge of a block of obsidian, the cross-piece placed against the chest, and by pushing downward the worker managed to force a blank to separate from the main block.

Certain western Indians used a similar technique. The tool required was a section of sapling thirty to thirty-six inches long and two or three inches thick. A half-inch-thick section of bone, antler, or walrus tusk, with either a pointed or a round tip, was inserted into the end and bound with rawhide. This tool, like that of the Aztecs, had a cross-piece at the other end so that it could be held against the chest. But there were also two stumps on the sapling. The highest stump helped to support a stone tied to the main shaft, and the lower stump was meant to receive a blow from a paddle-shaped club. The block of stone to be flaked was set into the ground, held between the feet, or bound between two sticks that one of the workers stood on. The bone tip was placed against an indentation that had been made in the block of stone. As one worker pressed down on the cross-piece, the other struck the lower stump, so that the blank was removed by a combination of percussion and pressure.

Chipping from tabular stone. Some unusually long or flat stone artifacts were made from tabular stone, i.e. stone that has formed in layers. Flint often forms layers instead of nodules, and obsidian splits into layers if the formation was created by several flows of molten rock, each hardening over the previous layer. Both types of tabular rock pose a problem, namely that the edges are often right-angled. It is difficult to strike a lateral chip from a blank with such squared edges. The solution is to strike off a projecting corner from somewhere on the blank. The resulting conchoidal edge will be thin enough to allow another chip to be struck off, and so on all the way along the rest of the edge.

This problem of "squared edges," incidentally, can occur with any sort of otherwise-workable stone. The problem occurs, for example, if one has struck an insufficiently strong blow, or if a projecting lump on one face has made that part of the edge too thick for a chip to fly off easily. The solution is to strike off chips from somewhere else along the edge, and then to continue striking off chips, one after another, until the problem area is reached. By removing these previous chips, the stone around the problem area becomes thinned or weakened enough for the lump or squared edge to be removed by a final blow.

Ground-and-chipped tools. Some extraordinary stone knives and projectile points from Mexico, as well as from Europe, the Middle East, and India, are quite large and symmetrical and have long, nearly identical flake-scars running across the blade from each edge. Such work is impossible by ordinary techniques, as anyone who has attempted to make stone tools can understand. To judge particularly from what is known of certain Egyptian knives, the technique employed for these artifacts began with the removal of a long blank, which was chipped roughly into shape. The tool was ground into a smooth and symmetrical form. A second flaking was then carried out, almost certainly not by direct percussion, but by a pressure tool, a baton, or a punch.

Pecking

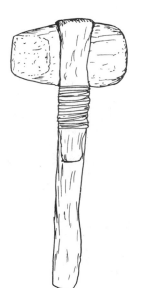

Pecking was a technique used for making adzes, axes, and mauls, as well as for metates and stone mortars and pestles. Adzes and axes were necessary for woodworking, and, as one might expect, they were common tools on the Northwest Coast. Chipped flint blades could cut wood, but they were somewhat fragile, and their irregular edges also caused problems.

Pecking was a simple process but a long one. Anywhere between several hours and several weeks were required to make a tool by this process. First a large pebble was selected, usually composed of a fine-grained igneous rock such as basalt or felsite. On the Northwest Coast, nephrite ("jade"), a very hard stone, was the preferred material. For an adze or axe, the stone would be fairly long and narrow, about two inches by three inches by six inches—shaped, in other words, somewhat like the future tool. It was held on the left palm and struck all over, using modest force, by a harder but smaller spherical hammerstone. The tool had to be fully supported along its entire length, or the hammerstone might crack it in half.

Pecking powdered or crumbled the surface of the stone, slowly reducing it to the desired shape. One end of the tool would be made thinner than the other, like the cutting edge of a modern steel axe. But the reduction of the cutting edge by this process could only be continued to a certain degree; usually the edge was finished by grinding.

Pecking might also be used to make a groove around

the middle of the stone, so that it could be fastened to a handle, though not all such tools were grooved.

The axe head might be bound into a split in the end of a wooden handle, but a better handle was made by tapering one end of the wood and bending it around the stone before binding it. Adze heads were similar to axe heads but were bound flat (rather than edgewise) to the top of an almost T-shaped handle; sometimes holes were drilled in the handle to hold the rawhide bindings.

Grinding

Axes, adzes, and hoes produced by pecking had their cutting edges smoothed and sharpened by grinding, and sometimes the entire surface might be finished by grinding. A slab of sandstone was the usual abrading material. The surface of the sandstone was dampened, and the tool was ground upon it by a circular motion, just as one sharpens a modern steel knife or axe. The sandstone was kept wet during the work.

Stone tools might also be chipped into form, rather than pecked, before being ground.

Slate breaks easily into thin plates. These plates could be chipped or sawn into the outline of the finished tool, and the edges would be finished by grinding. Many Eskimos used this process to produce knives, scrapers, and projectile points from slate.

Drilling

Drills with bits of flint, nephrite ("jade"), slate, or other stone were used to make holes in stone tools, but a more effective type of bit was tubular, made of wood, bone, or copper. In the latter case, it was not the bit that did the actual cutting, but an abrasive sand that was placed under the bit. Quartz sand was the most commonly used, but corundum sand enabled a worker to drill through virtually. any material. The ulo, a semicircular, chopper-like slate knife of the Eskimos, was often drilled so that its straight edge could be fastened to a wooden handle. Soapstone was drilled to make cooking pots and pipe bowls.

Sawing

Sawing was not a very common technique in stoneworking, but on the Northwest Coast and in the Arctic, boulders of nephrite, an extremely hard stone, were sawn to obtain the initial blocks for adze heads. The saws consisted of slabs of sandstone or sandy schist with a V-shaped cutting edge.

Metal tools

Metal tools were probably first made in the New World by the Old Copper Culture of the Great Lakes about 4,000 B.C. These people used pure native copper, hammering it into projectile points, knives, axes, chisels, and ornaments. Later a number of cultures in the southeastern United States, Mexico, Central America, and South America began to use metals and to develop far more refined techniques.

An important advance in metalworking began with the understanding of hardening and annealing. When a metal is hammered, it becomes harder, and eventually it may become too hard to be worked. If the metal is heated to a temperature slightly below the melting point, the grains realign and the metal is easier to work; the metal is then slowly cooled. Far better work could be done if the metal was treated to this process of alternate hammering and annealing.

Copper, iron, and other metals sometimes occur in a pure form in nature. The pure copper of the Old World was largely worked out by the end of the Bronze Age. Pure copper can still be found in the New World, but even in early prehistoric times there were only a few places where it could be found in any abundance. In North America, the principal sources were the south shore of Lake Superior and, much further north, the Copper and Coppermine Rivers. Copper from the Great Lakes supplied the metalworkers of both the Old Copper Culture and of the southeastern United States. The only major source of pure iron, however, is meteorites.

Most metals occur far more frequently as compounds: oxides, carbonates, and sulfates. Many of these compounds do not even have a "metallic" appearance, and it was probably not a simple step to recognize their value. A compound ore cannot be merely hammered into shape. The metal must be heated to convert it to liquid form and thereby separate it from the other elements. Some compounds require lower smelting temperatures than others; oxides are easier to work than carbonates or sulfates. Advanced metalworking began with the art of smelting.

Although we have a fair understanding of the general history of New World metallurgy, we do not know a great deal about the actual technology. We do know that the Indians of Peru smelted copper in clay furnaces. These furnaces consisted of vertical clay cylinders, three feet high, with several holes in the side, set on hillsides where there was a strong uphill wind. The furnaces were filled with a mixture of crushed copper ore (oxides and carbonates) and charcoal. Platforms around the base held more charcoal. Both the mixture and the charcoal on the platforms were set on fire, allowing the copper to melt and run down to the bottom of the furnace. The wind supplied oxygen, and the cylindrical shape of the furnace caused a vacuum or "chimney" effect, drawing in more air as the heated air rose. Very similar types of furnaces were used throughout the Old World in fairly recent times, though a bellows was used to provide oxygen.

A technique used by some (though not necessarily all) Mexican Indians was to put a mixture of ore and charcoal in a shallow bowl and use a blowpipe to supply air to the burning mixture. The liquid metal ran out through a tap directly into a mold.

New World metallurgy was in many ways highly advanced. Copper, gold, and silver were worked, and a number of alloys were produced. The most important alloy, produced only in South America, was bronze, a combination of copper and tin. Bronze is harder than either of its constituents. Perhaps the apogee of New World metallurgy was lost-wax casting: a clay core was shaped, coated with wax, provided with wooden supporting pegs, and surrounded with more clay; the wax was melted out to leave a mold that could be used to cast intricate hollow works of art. New World metallurgy was usually applied to the production of ornaments rather than tools, probably because obsidian was widely available.

The Indians never learned how to smelt iron ore, though tools were sometimes hammered out of meteoric iron. The Eskimos and the Indians of the Northwest Coast had a few tools of smelted iron before white explorers arrived, but these tools had probably been brought in trade from the Old World via the Bering Strait.

Bone, antler, ivory, horn and shell

Bone decays eventually and leaves no trace, so it was probably used more often than archaeological sites suggest. Bone was used as often as stone for projectile points, especially on the Plains and in Canada. Good stone is absent from many parts of North America, and bone was a reasonable substitute. Bone projectile points lacked the weight and sharpness of stone, but bone is an easier material to work than most kinds of stone. For some devices, such as needles, bone is superior.

The simplest way to make a bone arrowhead, for example, was to smash any sort of bone until conveniently shaped pieces were obtained. These could be further broken into the required outline and then ground on a rough-grained rock to form a cutting edge.

It was also possible to take advantage of the natural shape of bones. Various leg-bones of deer and other animals could be sharpened to be used as awls for making holes in skin or bark; the ulna, a long thin bone in the forelimb, only needed to have the tip snapped off and sharpened. The scapula of the same animals provided a hoe blade. A section of rib could be placed edgeways on a stone and tapped with another stone until it fell into two halves, and then it could be chipped and ground into the shape of a projectile point or knife blade. The leg bones of birds and small mammals provided a cylindrical arrowhead; the shaft fitted loosely and fell away, harpoon-like, while the arrowhead remained in the animal.

The Eskimos had some more elaborate techniques. They used flakes of sandstone to saw across the bones, or they used nephrite adzes to chop it. Antler could be worked by the same techniques. Ivory, from teeth and tusks, can likewise be worked, but it is a difficult material. Nevertheless, the tips of walrus tusks were the standard material for a harpoon head; a ground slate blade was often fitted into a slot at the end. Fresh bone and ivory both shrink a little as they dry, so a stone blade set in a carefully cut slot would require no glue.

Bone, antler, and ivory split more easily after they have dried out, but fresh material is better for any task requiring cutting or bending. These materials were also softened by soaking them in urine, often for several weeks, or by boiling them in water. It is conceivable that Indians and Eskimos used a steaming technique common in the Old World: the material was wrapped and soaked for a long period and then held over a fire. (Steam is hotter than boiling water.)

For either very fine or very large tools, the surface of the bone was cut with pointed or edged "gravers" of flint or other stones, which were kept sharp by re-chipping. After the blank was cut out, it was finished by abrasion.

The front teeth of beaver or porcupine were bound to a wooden handle to form a tool used for scraping wood.

The entire skull, minus the lower jaw, was used in a similar manner.

The horns of buffalo, bighorn sheep, and mountain goat were carved, boiled, and bent to form ladle-sized spoons.

Shell was not a commonly used material, but adzes were made, on both the east and west coasts, by sharpening the edge of a large mussel or clam shell, and Nootka whalers used harpoon blades made from the California blue mussel. Arrowheads were also occasionally made from shell. Spoons were often made by chipping and grinding one end of a clam shell to form a short stem that could be inserted in a wooden handle.

Woodworking

A great many things, from hooks to houses, were made of wood. Wooden tools included digging sticks, hoes (either partly or completely made of wood), adze and axe handles, wedges, drills, and fire kits. Wooden weapons included clubs, throwing sticks, spears, and arrows (again either partly or completely wooden), spear throwers, and bows. For fishing one needed hooks, traps, and wiers.

Wood, however, required stone tools to carve it. Wood needed to be chopped, split, cut, gouged, and scraped, requiring axes or adzes, wedges, knives, chisels, and scrapers.

After carving a wooden tool, a common method of hardening it was to hold it over a fire. This is sometimes described as heating or charring, but it is actually somewhere in between—perhaps "roasting" is a better word. If the wood actually charred (blackened) a little, no harm was done, but the charring needed to be scraped off. The earliest spears were simply cut from a sapling, the tip carved and scraped to a point and hardened over a fire.

Modern methods of woodworking, either for carpentry or for cabinetmaking, involve first sawing the log lengthwise into parallel boards, with little regard for twists in the grain; the more expensive woods are sometimes treated with more regard to structure. Then the boards are cut transversely into various lengths. For cabinetmaking the boards are then selected by size, planed to form a flatter surface, and cut into the required outline. The ends are cut to form various joints, unless a simple butt joint is to be used. The pieces are then put together with glue and screws, the assembled product is sanded, and finally a protective coating of some sort is applied.

Indian methods of woodworking were quite different.

Often a de-barked sapling required little further preparation. For the finer products of Indian woodworking, such as snowshoes or canoes, the major steps included splitting, steaming, bending, and sometimes oiling or fire-hardening.

A tree to be split would first be examined by removing a section of bark to determine whether the grain ran in straight lines. Often the grain of a tree has a gradual twist that makes it unsuitable for splitting. The tree would also be examined to make sure there were few or no knots in the trunk.

If the tree was suitable, it would be cut down with axes. If it was fairly large, a fire was lit all around the base, sometimes with a ring of clay plastered on further up the trunk to prevent the fire from spreading too far. The wood was slowly removed by alternately burning and chopping.

A small section of sapling could be split by a single wooden or bone wedge driven in from one end, but a larger section of trunk might require two or more wedges. One wedge was driven in at the narrower (top) end, with the blow delivered parallel to the grain. A second wedge was set into the side of the crack, or, in other words, at right angles to the grain. The first wedge would then be removed and struck into the log further along, creating a groove in line with the first crack. Both wedges would be struck with a mallet until a lengthy split had begun. The wedges would then be moved down to the ends of the cracks and hammered again, until the log fell in half. The process was repeated to quarter the log.

After the log had been quartered, it could be further divided to form boards or splints. The boards could be split from the wood either parallel to the radius or parallel to the growth rings. The brittle (and perhaps rotten) heartwood might be discarded.

An important rule in splitting wood is that each section must always be split into two sections of equal thickness, then each of these likewise divided, and so on. If one attempts to split off, for example, only a third of the wood, the split will run to the side rather than to the far end.

If a narrow piece of wood is being split in half but the split threatens to run to one side, the thicker side should be pulled into a sharper curve.

Eskimo woodworking involved a few further refinements. In order to split a driftwood log, such as might be used for a kayak gunwale, grooves were incised along the log before the wedges were inserted. Adzes, knives, and scrapers were used to finish shaping the wood. In order to assemble various pieces, holes were drilled, and braided sinew was passed through the holes, wrapped around the pieces of wood, and tied. Sometimes a single length of sinew cord ran from one joint to another. A second common technique of assembly was to drill holes and hammer in "treenails," sharpened lengths of very dry wood or antler. The holes would be placed at various angles to each other to counteract any stresses that might pull the nails out of the holes.

Very similar techniques appear on the Northwest Coast. But the great boards that formed the covering of Northwest Coast houses were not made by splitting logs into halves and quarters. Instead, the boards were split directly out of the living tree.

Many Indians were familiar with the mortise-and-tenon joint, which involves reducing the width and thickness of one end of a board and inserting it into a rectangular hole in the side of another board. The mortise-and-tenon joint appears on most snowshoes, in kayaks, and in the plank houses of the Northwest Coast. (It was also the principal joint in good furniture-making in our own culture not long ago.)

The scarf joint was used to connect long pieces of wood end to end. Scarfing involves making a diagonal cut—straight, zigzag, or sinuous—to remove one end of a piece of wood and fitting the wood to another piece of wood cut in matching (reverse) fashion. A simple straight scarf was commonly used to join the two ends of a piece of wood bent into a hoop, and the same joint appears on the frames of many snowshoes.

Kerfing appears on Northwest Coast wooden boxes: a three-sided slot was cut across the grain to reduce the thickness of the wood, which was then steamed and bent to form the corner of the box.

Fresh wood was bent, tied, and left to retain its form. Wood might also be bent after prolonged soaking. More often, hot water was used to make the wood flexible. The wood might be inserted into boiling water, or the water might be poured over the wood. Pieces of wood might be left in a covered pit with fire-heated rocks and any sort of wet material; variations on the technique included building a fire on top of the pit, or pouring water into the pit through a hole or tube. After the wood had been soaked or steamed, it was bent into shape, tied, and left to dry.

Bows and arrows

Bows and arrows were used to a varying extent throughout North America for hunting and warfare. Harpoons were the principal weapons for sea mammals in the Arctic. Spears (thrust, not thrown) were used more often than bows for caribou, since the killing usually took place at short range. In the Southwest, rabbits were usually killed with throwing sticks. But in most areas, bows and arrows were used far more often than other types of weapon.

Bows

Almost any type of wood was used to make bows, since the Indian had to make use of local material unless he could obtain a better wood through trade. Some woods were regarded as superior. Osage orange was highly prized but only available in the central United States. Yew was also considered valuable (the English longbow was made of yew), but tree-sized yews only grow on the West Coast. Ash, hickory, and oak were frequently chosen. After that came the other hardwoods, in no particular order of preference. Softwoods other than yew were generally regarded as too brittle, though cedar and juniper were popular in some areas.

Bows varied considerably in length. The Plains Indians used a bow that was sometimes less than three feet long, while the bows of the Eastern Woodlands were often six feet long. South American bows were sometimes twelve feet long, for no apparent practical reason. Theoretically, the best length for a bow is about four feet (assuming a two-foot arrow), since the greatest pulling force is obtained with a bow that is twice the length of the arrow. But other factors also applied. Some woods, especially conifers, will not bend very much without cracking, and a longer bow would not have to be bent very far in order to draw the string back two feet. Shorter bows, on the other hand, were

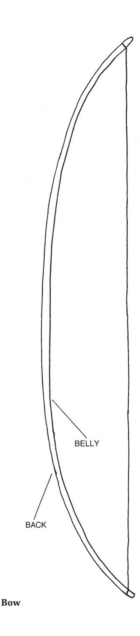

BELLY

BACK

Bow

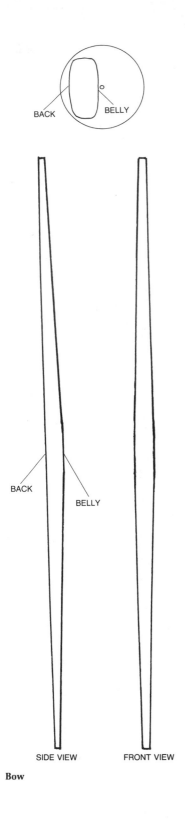

BACK　BELLY

BACK

BELLY

SIDE VIEW　FRONT VIEW

Bow

easier to wield on horseback or in thick brush, and the tendency of the wood to crack could be reduced by applying a backing of sinew.

Bows were usually made from saplings about two and a half or three inches thick. The sapling was split in half (or into quarters, if it was fairly thick) with wedges, or merely chopped or scraped to remove half the wood. The inner side of the wood became the belly of the bow, and the outer side became the back. The wood was usually trimmed to a slightly rounded rectangular cross-section. The back was cut flat and preferably followed the grain of the wood. The belly, however, was often cut away at a slight angle from grip to tip. The grip might be narrower or wider than the limbs, and it was more or less square in cross-section, but it was never distinctly offset as in the modern bow.

The wood was then scraped, rather than cut, to a uniform finish. The bow was carefully bent from time to time to see if each limb bent to the same curve and with the same strength; if not, the limbs required further shaping. One or two nocks were cut into each tip to hold the bow string.

After that the bow was well rubbed all over with animal fat (probably to prevent the wood from cracking by drying too quickly), and further coats were applied throughout the life of the bow. The bow was left to dry for several weeks or months, sometimes suspended a few feet above the fireplace; if the bow was strung very much before the wood had completely seasoned, it would acquire far too much of a curve. When the bow was ready to be used, the grip might be spirally bound with a narrow strip of rawhide.

Rawhide, intestines, and plant fibers (nettle, Indian hemp, etc.) were sometimes used to make bowstrings, but the most frequently used material was the sinew from the back and legs of deer or other animals (see chapter 13, "Cordage"). The only problem with sinew is that it tends to stretch in wet weather, so in wet areas plant fibers were preferred. The Ojibwa often used the hide from a snapping turtle's neck, cut in spiral fashion; this material was less likely to be affected by the weather.

Several kinds of knots were used to fasten the string to the bow, but usually the lower end of the string was fastened more or less permanently with a timber hitch, and the upper end was fastened—though only when the bow was in use—with two half-hitches.

The cross-section of bows varied considerably. Many

had round bellies and flat backs, and some were oval or completely round. Others even had flat bellies and round backs, an impractical design that removed the wood's strength where it was needed most. The wood of evergreen trees tends to be brittle, and so it was often cut so that the bow was quite wide from one side to the other, but narrow from back to belly, thereby reducing the stress of one fiber against another.

The earliest bows, as well as bows made in emergency situations, were made of unsplit saplings, but they were rather brittle. Some bows were made by chopping out a section from a large standing dead tree, but saplings provided stronger wood. California Indians sometimes used the roots of willow.

In both the east and the west, bows were often composed of a single piece of wood with no additional material. West of the Rockies, however, many bows were backed with sinew, which both prevented the bow from breaking and greatly increased its pulling power. In this way smaller bows could be made, especially useful for hunting or fighting on horseback. Glue was made from boiled rawhide chips, hooves, antler tips, or fish skin, and applied over the slightly roughened back and sides of the bow. Then strands of sinew were laid over the glue, parallel to the length of the bow and working from the grip to the tips. Several more layers of glue and sinew were applied until the entire mass was about a quarter of an inch thick. Each layer was allowed to dry before the next was applied. The glued bow was temporarily bound with a spiral of bark. As the glue and sinew dried, they shrank, so that the bow bent forward when it was not strung.

The Eskimos usually did not glue sinew to the backs of their bows, but they braided sinew in an elaborate fashion and fastened it to the tips. Eskimo bows were also often made of more than one piece of wood, or even of antler.

Not even the best-made bow could be guaranteed not to break at any stage, and the job was a lesson in patience. Cold weather also made a bow more brittle. So an Indian usually had several bows in various stages of construction.

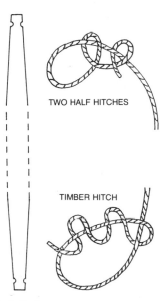

TWO HALF HITCHES

TIMBER HITCH

Knots for bow

Arrows

It was often said that a good arrow was harder to make than a good bow.

Arrow shafts were made from the shoots—sometimes split into quarters—of almost any kind of tree, though

Arrow

serviceberry was probably the most popular. The stems of reed (*Phragmites communis*) and cane (*Arundinaria* spp.) were also used as arrow shafts. The shoots were peeled, tied in bundles to straighten them, and then left to dry for several months. They were then further straightened by being held over a fire (or a fire-heated stone) and bent into shape with the fingers. Sometimes special tools were used to straighten the shafts. A piece of bone, antler, or wood might have a hole drilled into it, and the resulting tool was used to "wrench" a shaft into shape.

A notch in a stone blade could be used to scrape the shaft, and grooved sandstone pebbles, often in pairs, were used to make the surface more uniform. Finer-grained stones finished the sanding. A deep notch was cut or sawn at the front of the shaft to hold the point, and a shallow V- or U-shaped notch was cut into the back, either on the same plane as the front notch or perpendicular to it, to hold the arrow in place on the bowstring. The nock (the portion of the shaft around the back notch) was sometimes carved flat, flaring, or bulbous.

"Blood grooves," straight, sinuous, or zigzag, were often cut along the sides of the shaft. Their actual function is unknown, though they were sometimes said to allow blood to flow from wounds.

The feathering came from the wings, or sometimes the tail, of hawks or other large birds. Usually three feathers were used, though arrows with two feathers were by no means uncommon. All the feathers were supposed to come from the same wing of the same bird. Each feather was split lengthwise and the pith scraped from the midrib of the larger half of the feather. The top and bottom of the feather were then cut away, and the barbs peeled from the rib for half an inch or so at each end. (Unlike the modern arrow, the Indian arrow did not have a "cock feather," one designed specifically to be uppermost.)

The feathering was bound on with strands of sinew, held in the mouth until soft. The back of the shaft and the feathering were held in the left hand, and the front of the shaft was held between the upper left arm and the chest, or resting on the left elbow. The sinew was wrapped around the projecting back midrib, wrapped back over itself for a few turns to hold the end of the sinew in place, and then closely wound around the rest of the projecting midrib. It was considered easier to turn the shaft with the left hand than to wind the sinew around the shaft with the right hand. The end of the sinew was tucked under the last few turns and pulled tight. More sinew was wrapped in the same manner at the other end of the feathering, though sometimes a single piece of sinew was used for both ends, with a wide spiral running between the barbs. The feathering was finished by trimming a fraction of an inch from the edges with a knife.

In general, the feathering on Indian arrows was longer but narrower than on modern arrows. The only function of feathering is to hold back the end of the arrow to prevent it from tumbling in flight, and the long vanes on Indian arrows sometimes created unnecessary drag.

Finally the point was fastened on. The head of an arrow has two functions: its weight provides inertia to prevent the arrow from tumbling in flight, and its sharp edge allows the arrow to penetrate the quarry. Arrowheads were usually made from stone or bone, but many other materials were also used: antler, horn, ivory, hard wood, shell, beaten copper, or even the claws of reptiles, birds, or mammals.

The arrowhead was fastened to the shaft in the same manner as the feathering: shaft and point were held in the left hand and twirled while wet sinew was wound around the shaft.The starting end of the sinew was covered by a few more turns. As it reached the arrowhead, a few more turns were made diagonally over each notch in the stone, and the sinew was then continued back to where it began, with the end tucked through the last few turns. The sinew shrank as it dried and held the arrowhead firmly. No glue was necessary, though animal glue or resin was sometimes put into the shaft notch before the head was inserted and bound.

Arrowheads were not always meant to stay on the shaft. Sometimes a looser binding of sinew or bark was used instead, since an arrowhead without its shaft was more likely to stay in the wound.

Poison was sometimes used on arrowheads. Two very common substances were rattlesnake venom and rotten liver, often used in combination.

Some arrows, particularly for small game, did not have true arrowheads. The shaft itself might be left blunt or cut to a point. In other cases, a large knob was carved at the tip, and the rest of the shaft was cut to a smaller diameter. Indians of the Southwest often tied a cross of tiny twigs to the end of the shaft. Nor did all arrows have feathering.

Arrows were carried, with the points downward, in a quiver, which was usually a roughly rectangular piece of buckskin, rawhide, or fur, folded in half lengthwise and sewn. A stiffening rod was sometimes sewn to the outside.

A strap (baldric) was fastened to both ends so that the quiver could be held on the back, with the strap passing over the left shoulder and the chest.

Quivers were made in a great variety of styles. Many Indians used the entire fur of a small animal, some Eskimos used a salmon skin, and the Indians of the Northwest Coast used an elongated cedar box. Quivers were also made with separate compartments for bows, arrows, fire kits, and other paraphernalia.

Shooting

The archer usually protected his left wrist with a bracer, a band of rawhide fastened with thongs.

Several different methods were used for releasing the arrow. Most often the nock of the arrow was pinched between the thumb and forefinger. A far more powerful method was the "Mediterranean" release, also used in modern archery: the first and second fingers pulled back the string, and the nock was held loosely between the two fingertips.

The bow was held vertically, diagonally, or horizontally. The arrow might be on the left side of the bow, as in modern archery, or on the right. The string was usually pulled back to the full length of the arrow shaft, but the nock of the arrow was held at the chest rather than at the cheek.

Traps

Trapping was sometimes more effective than hunting as a means of killing animals. A trap worked "around the clock," whereas a hunter's bow or spear was only effective when it was carried by the hunter and when he was near his quarry. Also, the hunter's presence was likely to scare off the game.

A trap, in the strictest sense of the word, is an animal-catching device that operates without human presence. The two basic types were snares and deadfalls. Pitfalls can also be regarded as traps, though they were used far less frequently, and other kinds of traps were used for fish. Nets and chutes, on the other hand, usually required an operator.

Traps were used most frequently in areas of thick undergrowth, where animals tend to travel on fixed trails and are therefore less likely to avoid a suspicious arrangement of sticks and logs. Deep snow increases the tendency of animals to use fixed trails. A combination of thick undergrowth and deep snow is found in the Subarctic, and it was the Indians of this region who relied most extensively on traps to provide food.

Snares were used for a wide variety of animals throughout North America, though mainly in the Subarctic. Deadfalls in the north were used mainly for beaver and bear. Deadfalls were also used in the north for fur bearers (weasel, lynx, fox, etc.) in prehistoric times, though they were used for this purpose far more often in the days of the fur trade. Stone deadfalls were used in the Southwest and the Great Basin for rodents, rabbits, coyotes, and foxes.

Snares

A snare is basically a noose with a slip knot, often fixed to a triggering device. The material for a finer snare was hair, baleen, or plant fiber. Stronger snares were made of

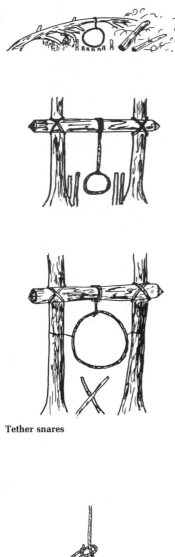

Tether snares

Double slip knot

sinew or rawhide. Snares were usually built across an animal's trail and required no bait.

Tether snares. The simplest type of snare was the tether snare, merely a noose fastened to a branch, a horizontal or vertical pole, or the trunk of a tree. Twigs or fine breakable cords were used to hold the noose open. Brush or twigs were placed under and beside the snare to dissuade the animal from going around it; the more elaborate this fencing became, the more it approached the form of the chute, described in Chapter 2. The tether snare was used to a varying extent nearly throughout North America.

Small tether snares were used for grouse, prairie chickens, ptarmigan, waterfowl, and smaller birds. For grouse and similar birds, the noose was about four inches wide and set about four inches above the ground. Sometimes a wall or ring of brush was set up, and snares were set at various points along this wall. Seeds, buds, or fruit might be scattered as bait. Snares for smaller birds were either laid on the ground or set on natural or artificial perches, so that the birds became entangled by the feet.

Tether snares were also used to some extent for rabbits and hares. In that case, the snare was about four inches wide and two or three inches from the ground or snow, though if the snow was loose the snare might be touching the surface. The snares were effective if the rabbits were driven into them and quickly removed, but tether snares left overnight were far less effective, since the animals could chew the cord and escape. (Nowadays the problem is solved by using wire.)

In the Arctic and Subarctic, much larger tether snares were used for deer, caribou, moose, and bear. The noose might consist of inch-thick braided rawhide. The snare was often set on trails used by the quarry, though they were also set up inside the walls of a caribou corral. For deer or caribou, the noose was about two and a half feet wide, and the bottom of the noose was two or three feet from the ground. A snare for moose was anywhere between three and six feet in diameter and about three feet from the ground. Often a double slip knot was used, so that the noose would stay tight when the animal began to struggle. A tether snare for bears was hung from a heavy horizontal log tied between two trees; the noose was about two feet wide, and the bottom of the noose was about three feet from the ground.

Another very simple type of snare (though not really a trap) was the pole snare, a loop of cord fastened to the end of a long pole. The pole snare was slipped over the heads of spruce grouse, very unwary birds, as they perched on branches.

Clog snares. The clog snare, similar to the tether snare, was used in the Subarctic for caribou, moose, and bear. Instead of being tied to a fixed pole or tree, the noose was fastened to a log that was leaned against the trunk of a tree, or to a sapling which could be pulled out of the ground. When the animal was caught in the noose, it could still travel, but its flight was impeded by the log or sapling. Since the device was not stationary, the cord was less likely to break. A very strong cord was still necessary, however.

Clog snare

Sometimes the clog snare was designed so that the line from the noose passed over a heavy branch. Then when the log fell, the noose was pulled upward and the animal was suspended.

Spring-pole snares. The spring-pole snare consisted of a noose attached to a sapling or pole which was bent over and held in place by a trigger mechanism. Snares of this sort were used to a varying extent in the Arctic, the Subarctic, on the Northwest Coast, and in the Eastern Woodlands.

The Indians of the Subarctic used the spring-pole snare mainly for snowshoe hares, and to a lesser extent for grouse and ptarmigan. Hares were trapped mainly in winter, when they leave distinct trails. A sapling was broken to form a horizontal bar about a foot above the trail, and a log was put on its top to hold in in place. A second sapling, on the other side of the trail, was stripped of branches and bent over to form the spring pole, and the noose was fastened to its tip.

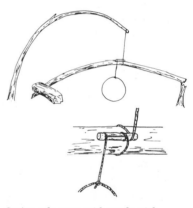

Spring-pole snare with toggle stick

The noose was held in place by one of two types of triggering devices. Sometimes a *toggle stick* was used, roughly half an inch wide and four inches long. The snare cord was tied to both ends of the toggle stick, wrapped once around the horizontal sapling, and hooked under the toggle stick, which was placed on top of the sapling.

The spring-pole snare might be held in place by a *knot* rather than a toggle stick. When the hare was caught and it began to tug at the noose, the knot was released and the spring pole lifted the hare from the ground.

The bent sapling (the spring pole) for either of these types was usually of spruce, birch, or willow. Birch tended to freeze and become less flexible in winter, and some

Spring-pole snare with knot

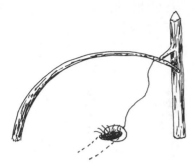

Spring-pole snare with stump

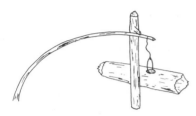

Spring-pole snare with stump

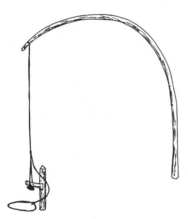

Spring-pole snare with loop

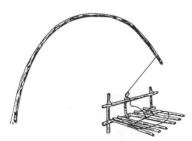

Spring-pole snare with tread bar

trappers felt that spring-pole snares in general were less effective in winter.

A less complicated type of spring-pole snare was sometimes used in the Arctic, on the Northwest Coast, and the Eastern Woodlands, for grouse, rabbits, groundhogs, marmots, and a few other animals. In the Eastern Woodlands, a pole with the *stump* of a small branch was planted in the ground. The tip of the spring pole, with noose attached, was placed under the stump. When the animal ran into the noose, its struggles pulled the tip of the spring pole away from the stump, and the spring pole lifted the animal from the ground. The trap was set up on trails or at the entrance to a burrow. When used for grouse, the noose was placed upright on a log and held in that position by a small flat stone.

The Kwakiutl of the Northwest Coast used the stump release for both large and small animals. Instead of hooking the tip of the spring pole directly under the stump, the Kwakiutl tied a *loop* in the noose cord and hooked this loop over the stump, letting the rest of the cord and the noose fall to the ground. Bait might be placed within the noose.

The Kwakiutl built another type of spring-pole snare for deer. This more elaborate trap used a *tread bar* as a release mechanism. Two sticks with downward-projecting stumps were planted in the ground, and a horizontal stick ran between these stumps. A second horizontal stick was placed below the first. This stick was held a few inches off the ground by a bent "kicker" stick, which was tied to the noose cord. More sticks were laid against the lower horizontal stick, and the noose was placed on top of these. When a deer stepped on the trap, the kicker and spring pole were released, and the noose suspended the deer by the leg.

A spring-pole leg snare for deer was also used in the Eastern Woodlands. This eastern snare was only vaguely described by the early explorers, but perhaps it resembled the Kwakiutl form.

Toss-pole snares. The fourth major type of snare was the toss-pole snare, similar to the spring-pole snare, except that an inflexible pole was used instead of a bent sapling. The toss pole was placed in the fork of a vertical sapling. The heavy butt end of the pole was furthest from the noose, so that the vertical sapling acted as a fulcrum, and the tip of the toss pole pulled up the noose. In other words, the energy of the toss-pole snare was derived from gravity rather than elasticity.

Toss-pole snares were used mainly in the Subarctic, and the principal quarry was again the snowshoe hare, but bears and smaller fur-bearing animals were also caught with snares of this type, and the Kwakiutl used a type of toss-pole snare for deer. The type used for hares had a toss pole six to eight feet long, placed in a fork about three feet from the surface of the snow.

The toss pole, like the spring pole, was often triggered by a toggle stick or knot, but sometimes a *rear support*, a vertical pole planted under the heavy end of the toss pole, was used instead. When the animal struggled in the noose, it pulled the toss pole away from the supporting post.

The Kwakiutl sometimes built a larger version of the rear-support toss-pole snare for deer, though the noose was laid flat on the ground, and some sort of bait was placed inside the noose.

Deadfalls

A deadfall is trap that uses a heavy object, usually a log or a flat stone, to kill the animal. Though not shown in the illustrations, deadfalls made of logs also had vertical stakes enclosing and guiding the fall log, and usually additional fall logs were leaned against the principal fall log. The entire trap was generally enclosed in a U-shaped pen of closely-set vertical stakes, forcing the animal to approach the bait by going under the fall log.

Most deadfalls required bait: fish, meat, or skin for carnivores; fruit, seeds, or other plant material for herbivores. For beaver, a common bait was a small poplar sapling, cut and planted vertically. Beaver and almost any other animal were also strongly attracted to beaver castoreum and especially beaver oil. Castoreum is a pleasant-smelling yellow fluid found in the two castor glands, which are near the anal openings of both male and female beavers. Beaver oil, a foul-smelling cream-colored fluid, comes from the two oil sacs, also near the anal opening.

Snares were usually built on trails, but deadfalls were usually built by the side of a trail, by the entrance to a burrow, or wherever the animal was likely to pass.

Samson-post deadfalls. The samson-post deadfall was the simplest type and was used nearly throughout North America, mainly for smaller animals. In most of North

Samson-post deadfall

Lever deadfall with toggle stick

Lever deadfall with loop

Lever deadfall with vertical bait stick

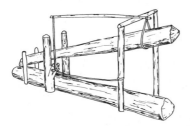

Lever deadfall with trip-string

America, it was used almost solely for fur bearers. It usually consisted of three working parts: an oblique log or stone, a vertical prop, and a horizontal bait stick projecting from under the vertical prop. Sometimes the horizontal bait stick was omitted, and often a horizontal log or flat stone was placed under the oblique log or stone.

A very simple deadfall of this type was used for rabbits by the Indians of the Southwest. A flat stone was laid on the ground, and an oblique flat stone was supported at one end by a vertical stick. Instead of a horizontal bait stick, a kernel of dried maize was placed under the vertical prop.

The Indians of the Southwest used a similar trap for coyotes and foxes. Blood was smeared on the vertical prop, or meat was tied to it, and a round pebble was placed under the prop.

Lever deadfalls. Many types of deadfall were constructed with a horizontal lever on top of a vertical fulcrum.

One type of lever deadfall had a *toggle-stick* release. This trap was commonly used for rodents and rabbits in the Great Basin and the Southwest, though apparently restricted to those regions. Again, a flat stone was used instead of a fall log. The lever rested in a vertical forked stick, and a string led from one end of the lever to the toggle stick, which was twisted around the vertical stick. The toggle stick was held in place by a long bait stick, to which bait (fruit, seeds, etc.) had been fastened. A flat stone was leaned against the lever, and the other end of the bait stick rested against the underside of the stone, either where the stone touched the ground or an inch or two higher.

Other lever deadfalls had a *loop release*: a fall log rested on one end of the lever, and a cord ran down from the other end of the lever to a stump on a vertical stake.

In the Subarctic, a common version had separate strings for lever and bait. The bait was tied to a loop of string, which was placed on the stump. The second string ran from the end of the lever and was also tied in a loop and hooked onto the stump. When the animal pulled off the bait, it also pulled off the loop holding down the lever. In this type of trap, as in most Subarctic lever deadfalls, the lever extended into the trap from the right or left corner of the entrance, rather than from the middle.

A type of lever deadfall used for bear in the Subarctic had its lever held in place by a *vertical bait stick*, notched at each end but on opposite sides. The lower notch fitted into a matching notch in a planted stake, and the end of the lever fitted into the upper notch of the bait stick.

The Kwakiutl built a lever deadfall with a *trip-string release*, basically an elaboration of the stump release. A cord ran down from the lever to a short stick placed in two adjacent notched stumps, but the string then continued horizontally to the fulcrum. This trap required no bait, since the animal released the fall log by trying to walk under it. The Nootka used an almost identical type of trap.

Tread-bar deadfalls. The tread-bar deadfall was used most often for beaver in the Subarctic and on the Northwest Coast, but it was sometimes used for muskrat, bear, and fur bearers, and the Ojibwa also used it for rabbits and grouse. In a sense, the tread-bar deadfall was a vertical form of lever deadfall. It consisted of a vertical lever ("kicker"), a horizontal fulcrum, a fall log, and a tread bar, plus a framework of vertical poles to hold it all together. The fall log was held up by a loop of cord which hung from the upper end of the lever. The lower end of the lever pressed against the tread bar. When the animal stepped on the tread bar, knocking it out of place, the lever swung up and released the fall log.

When used for beaver, the trap was often built on top of a dam. The entrance of the trap was about a foot wide and faced the pond. A poplar sapling was stuck into the dam behind the trap as bait. Bait was also used for most other animals, though it was not essential to the operation of this type of trap.

Tread-bar deadfall

Fishing

Fish were an important source of food, particularly along the coasts and in much of the Subarctic and the Eastern Woodlands. Along the Northwest Coast, fish were the mainstay of the economy.

Pacific salmon live in the ocean most of the year, but they congregate in large schools to migrate up rivers and spawn at various times from spring to autumn, and fishing methods were timed to their arrival. After spawning, they float downriver, dead or half-dead, but they were also harvested in large quantities at this stage. (Pacific steelheads, however, return alive, like most other fish that ascend rivers to spawn.) Saltwater fishermen could take advantage of the tides in constructing traps.

Freshwater fish also "migrate," from lake to river, or from deep water to shallow water, when they spawn. Northern fish move to deeper water in the wintertime, and many fish feed less in midsummer. But freshwater fishing was generally less dependent on seasonal changes in the behavior of fish.

There were many methods of catching fish. A hook and line might do the job, or one might use a gorge instead of a hook. Among other devices to catch fish one at a time were spears, harpoons, and even bows and arrows. Far more productive methods involved such things as weirs, traps, and nets, and even poisons were used on occasion.

Hooks and gorges

Hooks were widespread but not used a great deal, sometimes only if other implements failed to work. The Indians of the Northwest Coast generally used hooks for halibut and cod, but hooks were useless for salmon on their spawning run, since they stop feeding at that time. Hooks were also used for trolling behind a boat. Cod were caught in Alaska by jigging through holes in the ice; the fish were

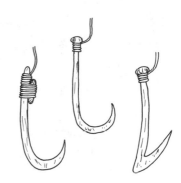

One-piece hooks

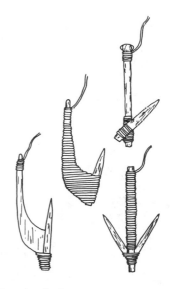

Two-piece hooks

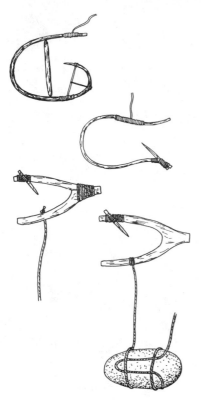

Northwest Coast hooks

Gorges

attracted by a lure, and a four-pronged hook was pulled upward to snag the fish as they milled about.

Most hooks in early times were cut from a single piece of bone, antler, shell, or wood, and they were usually unbarbed. The hook might be gouged out of a flat piece of bone, or a series of drill holes might be made in the bone to form the outline. It was also possible to take advantage of the natural shape of bones, such as the nose bone of a deer or moose. Two antler prongs provided a simple hook, and so did the fork of a sapling. After the blank was cut out, it was carved or abraded into a more precise shape, and a groove or knob was carved at the top of the shank to hold the line.

The Mohave of Arizona made fishhooks by steaming (alternately soaking and bending) the spines of a type of barrel cactus, *Ferocactus wislizeni*, and bending them into shape.

For unknown reasons, the composite V-shaped hook became more popular in late prehistoric times. This hook was made with a straight shank, usually of wood, though bone, ivory, and stone were also used, and a bone pin was lashed to the bottom of the shank at an angle, sometimes fitting into a slot cut for the purpose. Other hooks, usually made for jigging, had two or more pins radiating upwards from the bottom of the shank.

Northwest Coast Indians made two unusual and rather large types of hook for halibut and other fish. One type was made from a conifer knot, steamed in a plugged kelp bulb or wrapped in bundles to steam in a pit filled with seaweed. The next day it was bent into shape and left to dry on a form made of pegs stuck into a board. The final shape had either flaring or inward-curving ends. Because it was made from a knot, it was heavy enough to sink. Another type of halibut hook was V-shaped, made of either one or two pieces of wood, with an added barb. It was designed to float slightly above a stone weight which could be easily detached.

Gorges were used throughout North America. Usually these consisted of a straight or slightly curved bone dowel, sharpened at both ends. The line was fastened at the middle, and the bait was impaled on the gorge. The fish swallowed the bait and the gorge, and tension on the line caused the gorge to turn sidewards and catch in the fish's stomach.

A type of gorge made in southern California looked more like a hook, except that it was almost circular. To make this gorge, a piece of abalone shell was chipped and ground to a disk shape, a hole was bored through the center and enlarged with a conical stone file, and finally one side was worn away to create the point. The tip of the gorge was intended simply to hold the bait, not to impale the fish. Again it was intended that the device be swallowed by the fish, not caught in its lip like a hook.

Sinkers (not always necessary) were made from any hard material and attached to the line or the shank.

A great variety of baits were used, including grubs, strips of meat, and small dead fish.

Artifical lures were usually fish-shaped, carved from wood, bone, or ivory, though sinkers and hooks often acted as "lures." Lures were used more often with spears than with hooks; the lure was jiggled at the end of a separate rod and line.

Spears, harpoons, and arrows

When fish were visible and not too far below the surface, a spear was used. One simple type, very widespread, consisted of a long bone blade heavily barbed on one or both sides, lashed to a slotted wooden shank. Many Indians of the southeastern United States made spears by cutting barbs into the end of a pointed cane stem (*Arundinaria* spp.), and the Indians of Virginia stuck a shaft into the hollow end of a horseshoe crab tail.

A more efficient device was the leister spear, consisting of two prongs with one or more barbs on each inner side, and usually a shorter prong in the center. The center prong pierced the fish, and the outer prongs and barbs held the fish in place.

Spear-fishing was often made easier by erecting a makeshift sunshade, cutting down the glare from the surface of the water.

Fish were often speared at night. The fish were attracted by a burning torch, or by a fire built on the riverbank, on a platform built over the water, or on a clay hearth in a boat. Sometimes a mat was placed vertically before the fire and the fisherman to prevent his moving shadow from frightening the fish.

The problem with an ordinary spear in water was that the shaft tended to lever the head out of the quarry. One solution was to use a harpoon, a spear with a detachable head. In addition, one could carry a bag of harpoon heads and thereby carry many weapons with little bulk.

The head of the harpoon might be held in place by friction, or a breakable string might be used. A cord was

Simple spears

Simple harpoon

Leister

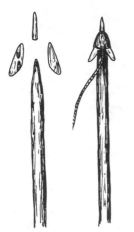

Harpoon with separate barbs

Two-pronged toggle harpoon

Toggle harpoon

used to pull in the fish. The cord was tied around the head, or through a hole in the head, and the other end was fastened to the shaft. More often, both the head and the shaft were fastened to a much longer line which was held coiled in the left hand.

Harpoons were used in many parts of North America, though the Eskimo used them more frequently for sea mammals.

One common type had a barbed head of bone, ivory, or antler. The base might be flattened to fit into a slot in the shaft, or it might be cylindrical and hollow to fit over the rounded tip of the shaft.

Sometimes this head was slotted to receive a slate, flint, or shell blade. This blade, rather than the bone or ivory head, then became the cutting edge. An Eskimo variation of this two-piece head, used for seals rather than fish, was slightly crescent-shaped; the bottom of the crescent acted as a barb or toggle and turned the head cross-wise in the quarry. Seal harpoons often had a detachable bone fore-shaft between the head and the main shaft.

Harpoons were sometimes made with separate barbs. A central bone point might be used to pierce the quarry, or the barbs might be designed to receive a blade, as with previous types. Two curved prongs were fitted parallel to the central part and wrapped in place or covered with pitch.

On the Northwest Coast, harpoons with multiple shafts and smaller heads were used for trout, salmon, and sturgeon.

The toggle also appears in a much simpler type of harpoon, merely a sliver of bone tied at a slight angle at the tip of a shaft. Harpoons of this type often had two prongs, with a bone head at the end of each prong.

The bow and arrow were not often used for fish, but sometimes arrows were designed with multipronged bone or ivory heads, and harpoon-type arrows were also used.

Weirs and traps

Weirs are walls built across a shallow river or beach. Wooden weirs were made of vertical and horizontal poles (often willow), either woven or tied together. Other weirs consisted of low walls of boulders; gaps between the stones allowed water to run through but were small enough to hold back the fish.

Some weirs consisted simply of a straight fence running across a stream. The weir blocked the movement of fish on their spawning runs. At other times, fish were chased towards the weir by people wading downstream. Other people waited at the weir to harvest the fish with spears, dip nets, or baskets.

Stone weirs on Arctic rivers were parallel straight rows. One wall was built right across the river, while each of the other walls had a gap in the middle to allow fish to enter. When the fish had congregated at the last wall, they were taken with spears.

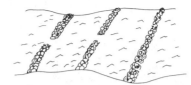
Stone weir

Another type of weir was the tidal trap, which was often crescent-shaped, built below the high-tide mark in estuaries and bays. When the tide went out, the water flowed through the rocks or poles, and the fish were left stranded.

A slightly more elaborate type of construction was the keyhole trap, consisting of a straight or V-shaped fence with a gap in the center. The gap formed the entrance to a square or oval pen, or a series of pens. Unable to get through the main fence, the fish would swim into the enclosure, where they could be taken by dipnet or spear. The keyhole trap bears a curious resemblance to the chute-and-corral device for catching mammals, and the Blackfeet used the same word for both constructions.

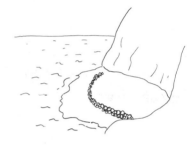
Tidal trap

A very common device was the basket trap, usually consisting of a long cone with a smaller truncated cone or funnel set in for an entrance. Basket traps were anywhere between four and twenty feet long. As the name suggests, they were actually elongated openwork baskets, woven with either simple twining or wrapped-warp twining. For freshwater fish, such a trap was usually placed at the central gap in a weir, particularly where there was a fast current to force the fish into the trap and hold them there. To catch salmon migrating upstream, a weir was built across the river, and a basket trap with short wings was placed downstream to catch the fish as they fell back from the weir.

For shallow water, the basket trap might be tied to stakes planted in the river bed, but for deeper water the trap was sometimes weighted with rocks and let down on a line with a float.

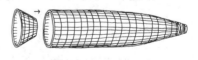
Keyhole trap

Nets

Nets were made from a long line of almost any sort of cordage. The cord was held by looping it onto a shuttle, a flat stick with a deep notch at each end. The line was tied to a stake and knotted together in rows, using the shuttle as a "needle," alternating from left to right with

Basket trap

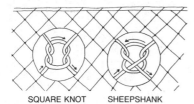

SQUARE KNOT   SHEEPSHANK

Square knot and sheepshank

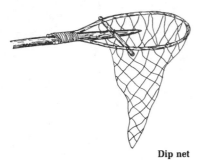

Dip net

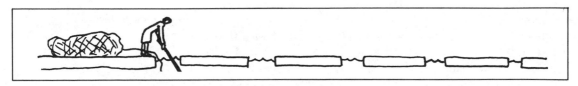

Gill net

either a sheepshank or a square knot—the same two knots that have been used for fishing nets worldwide for thousands of years. Before each knot was tied, the cord was wrapped around a rectangular gauge to maintain an even size of mesh. The finished netting was bound on the edges with a stronger cord, and a heavy rope ran through the top edge.

Conical nets were made in a similar manner, but starting at the center with two square meshes and one triangular mesh. The rest of the net was continued in a spiral of rectangular meshes. A "trumpet"-shaped net could also be produced, by increasing the size of the meshes and by adding extra meshes.

Dip nets were commonly used to take fish out of weirs, but where fish were plentiful they could be dipped straight out of the water. One popular design had a rim with its ends bound parallel to the shaft, with further support provided by a cross-piece over the projecting tip of the shaft.

Seine nets were large rectangular nets with floats along the top edge, and weights along the bottom, to be drawn around schools of fish.

One of the most popular types of net was the gill net, used along rivers and lake shores. Gill nets were used in many areas in aboriginal times, but they became even more common when white people began to sell cheap cotton and nylon versions. The mesh was large enough for a fish to put its head in, but when it did so, the gills caught in the net. Except for the size of the mesh, the gill net was similar in construction to the seine net. Floats of wood or bark were tied at even spaces along the top, and stone weights (often grooved) were likewide tied along the bottom.

One end of the main rope of the gill net was fastened to a bank, and the other end, pointing towards the center of the river, was held by a post, or by an anchor stone and a larger float. The net could also be set without a boat, by attaching it to the apex of a "V" of long poles, which was pushed out across a river. Eddies in bends along rivers were considered good places to put a gill net. If the river was narrow enough, the net could even be fastened to opposite banks.

Setting gill net under ice

In winter, holes were chopped in the ice, about ten feet apart. The net was fastened to a long cord, the other end of which was tied to a pole which was pushed under the ice. Another pole pushed the horizontal pole from one hole to another. When the last hole was reached, the net was pulled up and the net thereby drawn under the ice. A pole was pushed into the river bottom, or merely into the ice, at each end of the net. It was drawn up again the next morning through the first hole, leaving the long line under the water so that the net could be easily reset.

Poisons

In ponds or shallow slow-moving streams, poisonous plant material was sometimes added to the water. California Indians, for example, used the crushed nuts of buckeye (*Aesculus californica*), the entire crushed amole or soap plant (*Chlorogalum pomeridianum*), and the entire crushed turkey mullein (*Eremocarpus setigerus*). The stunned fish rose to the surface, some were harvested, and the rest recovered and swam away. Apparently the poison did not render the fish inedible. Other fish poisons included Indian hemp, pokeweed, Indian turnip, walnut bark, and devil's shoestring.

Preservation of fish

Fish were usually preserved by being split in half, cleaned, and sun-dried or smoked, just as meat was preserved. The flesh of larger fish was gashed slightly to allow quicker drying. Small fish could be smoked without being split or cleaned. Salmon roe was sun-dried or smoked. In several western areas, dried fish was pulverized to make a sort of pemmican. Fish were frequently frozen in wintertime. Some northern tribes suspended or buried fish and allowed it to decay as a delicacy.

Shelter

Many kinds of houses were built by the North American Indians, but three major categories can be discerned. In most of Alaska and along the Northwest Coast, houses were rectangular, with post-and-beam construction. Over the greater part of the continent, most houses were conical or domed with a circular ground plan. In much of the Eastern Woodlands and in more southern regions, houses were again rectangular.

Both the northwestern rectangular and the circular style seem to have been developed from Siberian prototypes. Both types often had a floor below ground level, as one might expect of houses developed in a northern land. The rectangular style of the east and south was probably developed in Mexico or Central America.

Many Indians built two or more types of houses. The winter house was designed primarily to keep out the cold. The summer house might be cooler and less smoky. Many Indians moved to the shores of rivers, lakes, and oceans in the summer, where fish and shellfish were plentiful and the wind kept the mosquitoes and blackflies away. Other types of dwelling were built for hunting trips or general travel, and still other types were purely makeshift: a lean-to, a windbreak, or a hole dug in a snowbank. Nomadic tribes used dwellings that could be easily transported.

Arctic and Subarctic

Winter houses of the Alaskan Eskimos and northern Athapaskans were made of vertical logs. These houses were about sixteen feet wide and about twenty feet long, and usually two families shared a house. The floor was usually dug down one to three feet below ground level, and a ditch was dug outwards from one side of the floor for the entrance tunnel. A heavy log, notched at the top, was planted vertically in each corner, and the four main beams ran around the tops of these posts. A similar structure was built in the center of the floor: four taller posts were planted in either a square or a rectangle to support the four ridgepoles. Once this support structure had been built, more vertical posts were planted to fill in the walls, and other poles ran from the ridge poles to form the roof. A gap along the center of the ridgepoles served as a smoke hole and window. The same sort of post-and-beam construction was used to form the entrance tunnel. The entire house was then covered with a thick layer of moss, though the Koyukon used four outer layers: moss, bark, turf, and finally dirt. A fire was usually built in the center of the floor, but seal-oil lamps were used in areas where wood was scarce.

Another type of Alaskan winter house had the same kind of structure for the walls, but the roof consisted of horizontal logs (cribwork) that overlapped at the ends and sloped inwards to form a squat four-sided pyramid.

The winter house might be used as a year-round residence, though some tribes built a separate but similar house for the summer, sometimes using boards or bark for the walls, and the entrance tunnel might not be dug quite so far underground. A few other groups used conical tents of caribou hides in the summer.

In northern Alaska, a common type of dwelling was built in the form of a squat dome, with a framework like that of the Ojibwa wigwam. The covering consisted of a layer of loose caribou hides or two strips of sewn hides. This domed structure was mainly used as a summer dwelling or for summer travel. However, the Nunamiut, nomadic caribou-hunters, lived in a dwelling of this sort year-round; they used two layers of hide, one with the hair side facing outwards, and a layer of de-haired hides on top of this, followed by a layer of snow on top of both.

Across the central Arctic, the principal winter dwelling of the Eskimos was the igloo, made of blocks cut from the hard, wind-packed snow with a machete-like ivory knife. The blocks were three or four feet long, about two feet wide, and about six inches thick, cut from the snow either vertically or horizontally. Usually two people were required for the construction, one to cut the blocks and the other to bevel them and fit them into place from inside.

The blocks of the first row were bevelled mainly on their vertical sides. When the first row was in place, a deep slanting cut, reaching to the ground, was made through several of the blocks, so that a large wedge-shaped

Alaskan house

section could be removed. The space thus created provided a seat for the next few blocks. All the remaining blocks were bevelled on four sides, so that they would fit together to form an ever-shrinking spiral right to the top of the igloo. The last block or two were rather irregular in shape.

An igloo designed for hunting trips was only about five feet high, but one designed as a family residence was ten or twelve feet high and twelve to fifteen feet wide, so the builder had to stand on a large block of snow in order to complete the igloo.

A bench of snow was built all around the inside, except where the entrance tunnel would be. Whenever possible, the igloo was built on a slope, so that the benches could be cut directly out of the snow bank.

When the dome was completed, the builder let himself out by cutting a hole for the entrance. Any gaps remaining between the blocks were filled with chunks of snow or with handfuls of loose snow. A tunnel, in the form of an elongated dome, was built out from the entrance hole.

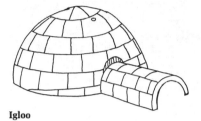

Igloo

A small hole was cut near the top of the igloo for ventilation. Just over the entrance an arched or square hole was cut for a window. This hole was filled with a pane made of a slab of ice or of seal intestines sewn together. The entire igloo was then usually covered with a thick layer of loose snow.

Snow is a good insulator, and igloos remained warm with nothing more than the heat from human bodies and a small oil lamp. Some eastern Eskimos improved their igloos by fastening caribou hides to the inside of the roof. Cords were tied to the hides and run through the wall to the outside, where they were kept in place with toggles. The hide lining kept a layer of cold air next to the snow blocks and prevented them from melting quite so quickly. But in any igloo the snow would eventually start to melt, and as it refroze it formed ice, a poor insulator, so the igloo might need to be abandoned and a new one built.

In many cases the igloos were multiple structures. One or two small domed structures were built in the middle, side, or end of the tunnel to serve as storerooms. Often two or three igloos were built in contact with each other, with holes cut between them for access, or the igloos were built separate but with the entrance tunnels joining onto each other.

Other winter houses of the central and eastern Eskimos were built of stone, whalebone, or turf, with roofs of whale ribs, driftwood, or flat stones. Houses of the central Arctic had a circular ground plan, while in the east the ground plan took the form of a rounded triangle. It is quite likely that stone or turf houses were more common in the central Arctic in prehistoric times.

The summer dwelling of the central and eastern Eskimos was a wedge-shaped tent with a covering of caribou hides, built in any manner that would take advantage of the scarce supply of wood for the frame.

A common type of dwelling in the western Subarctic was the wedge-shaped lodge, or double lean-to, which varied considerably in its manner of construction. Two forked posts supported the ridge pole, and other poles ran from the ridge pole to form a series of inverted V's. Sometimes the two supporting poles were omitted, and two diagonal poles were fastened along each side for bracing, leaving the doorway at the end less obstructed. The end walls were usually vertical. The frame was covered with bark or logs, though the ridge was left slightly open as a smoke hole.

Across most of the Subarctic, the principal dwelling throughout the year was the conical lodge, a crude relative of the Plains tipi, with a diameter of ten to fifteen feet. The lodge was usually built with a foundation of four poles. Forks were left on one or more of the poles so that they could be placed together at the tips, or they were tied with willow bark, spruce roots, or strips of rawhide. Other poles were placed in the crotches of the foundation poles to complete the conical framework. The cover consisted of caribou or moose hides, sometimes sewn together to form two large strips; tall rectangles of spruce bark; rolls of sewn birch bark; or a thick layer of conifer boughs with the tips pointing downwards. More poles were added to keep the cover in place.

Northwest Coast

Along the Northwest Coast, the principal type of dwelling was a massive post-and-beam structure covered with planks. The wood came from various conifers, though western red cedar (*Thuja plicata*) was the preferred species in British Columbia. In aboriginal times, most timber was taken from driftwood rather than from live trees.

The type of house built on the central coast of British Columbia was thirty or forty feet wide and up to a hundred feet long. The ridge pole might be three or four feet thick,

Subarctic lodge

and the other main timbers were not much narrower. The main vertical members all had a U-shaped notch cut into the top. The four corner posts rose nine or ten feet above the ground, but they were buried for another three feet. On each side of the house, a beam ran from front to back on top of each pair of corner posts.

The ridgepole, the heaviest element, was supported at the front of the house by a short beam, which in turn rested on two posts ten to twelve feet high. At the rear of the house, the ridgepole was supported on a single post. A long notched lever, a fulcrum, and a vertical lifting pole were used to raise the ridgepole, and various types of shoring were used to hold the ridgepole whenever the lever needed to be adjusted. Sometimes the ridgepole was raised along a pole slanted against the post. Some houses had two ridgepoles, with or without a beam below them.

Northwest Coast house

The wall planks, set horizontally, performed no supporting function and could easily be dismantled. Widely spaced pairs of narrow poles were set into the ground between the corner posts to hold the planks. The lower planks overlapped slightly and were held in place by loops made of cedar withes tied to the poles. The higher planks were set edge-to-edge and tied, with the same material, directly to the poles. A doorway was left in front, and a mat was hung up for a door.

Pole rafters were placed from the ridgepole to the side beams on each side of the roof, with a slight gap between each rafter, and horizontal poles were tied on top of these. Then layers of planks, running from the ridgepole to the side beams, were placed on top of the rafters. The first layer of roofing planks was widely spaced, and the second layer covered the gaps. The planking was not fastened down, though stones were placed on the boards if a high wind threatened to do any damage. Except in bad weather, a gap was left in the boards to allow smoke to escape.

Further north, the Tlingit, Haida, and others built a similar house but with a few more sophisticated touches. The principal members were less massive, and the vertical members were rectangular in cross-section. The posts supporting the ridgepole did not form part of the front and back walls, but were planted slightly closer to the center of the house. The planks for the siding were set vertically rather than horizontally, fitting into slots cut into other planks that ran along the bottom of the house and along the top of the eaves. Quite often, most of the floor was several feet below ground level, and boards covered the bottom and sides of the pit. The doorway was often a hole cut through a totem pole.

The coastal Indians of Washington, Oregon, and northern California also built plank houses, usually simpler and smaller than those described above.

All these houses were primarily winter dwellings. Summer houses might be built in the same style but on a smaller scale. Often the planks from the winter house were removed, transported downstream to the summer campsite, and set into the waiting framework of the summer house. Other summer houses were covered with bark instead of boards.

Plateau

The principal winter dwelling on the Plateau consisted of a circular pit twenty to forty feet wide and about five feet deep, covered with a roof in the shape of a flattened dome. After the pit was dug, four heavy bracing logs, notched at the top, were planted about fifteen inches deep around the center. Four long rafters, planted about two feet deep outside the pit, ran across the top of the braces. The rafters did not quite meet at the top, so that space was left for what would become the entrance hole. Eight smaller rafters were laid against the four main rafters. Horizontal poles, spaced a foot or two apart, were placed over the twelve rafters. Willow withes were used to tie all parts together at the junctions, and sometimes the rafters were also notched before being fitted into the notches at the tops of the vertical braces.

Plateau winter house

Once this framework had been created, it was entirely covered with poles or split wood, except for the square opening at the top. The poles were in turn covered with pine needles or dry grass (in wetter areas, cedar bark was used instead, with the inside of the bark facing upward), and then with the earth that had originally been dug from the pit.

A series of deep notches was cut into a heavy log to form a ladder, planted near the center of the pit and extending up through the entrance hole. The fireplace was in the center of the pit, and a slab of rock protected the base of the ladder.

These houses were said to be very warm. Their only disadvantage was that debris tended to fall from the roof whenever someone outside climbed up the side of the house to reach the entrance hole.

The principal summer dwelling on the Plateau was a wedge-shaped lodge, similar to that used in the western Subarctic, but covered with either rush mats or cedar bark.

Plains

The conical tipi was perfected by the Plains Indians.

In the days before horses, the Plains tipi had a diameter of only about ten feet, and sometimes the cover was made in two halves so that each half could be packed on a dog. Only about seven or eight buffalo hides were required for these aboriginal tipis; later tipis might require twenty or more hides. In the early days, when the Plains were sparsely inhabited, tipis were used largely—perhaps solely—for summer hunting trips.

Generally speaking, the tipis of the eastern Plains and the Prairies had a three-pole foundation, while the tipis of the western Plains had a four-pole foundation. Three-pole tipis were more stable.

The three-pole tipi, described below, consisted of poles, a covering, and an interior lining.

The poles were made of cedar (preferably) or pine saplings. For the larger nineteenth-century tipi, the poles were two to four inches thick at the base, and fifteen to thirty feet long. Approximately thirty poles were required. The branches and bark were removed from each sapling, and the lower two feet were scraped to taper to a point. The poles were set up in conical fashion, turned occasionally, and left to dry so that they would remain straight when they were used inside the tipi.

The covering consisted of tanned buffalo hides cut and sewn together in any way that would allow them to form a semicircle. The center of the curve was somewhat flattened, since the back of the tipi was slightly less oblique than the front. Two smoke flaps projected from near the center of the straight edge, and on the inner corner of each a pocket was sewn to receive the poles that adjusted the flaps. A cord ran from the lower corner of each flap. A small triangle was firmly sewn between the smoke flaps, and a double cord was sewn to this triangle. Holes were punched along most of the straight edge of the cover to receive the ten to twenty pins that held it in place on the poles.

On some tipis there was no real door or doorway, and one simply lifted the covering below the pins in order to enter or exit. On other tipis the doorway was an oval hole

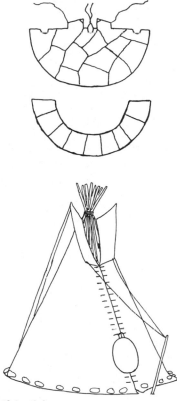

Plains tipi

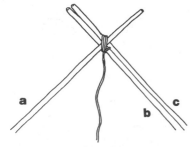

Cheyenne tipi foundation poles

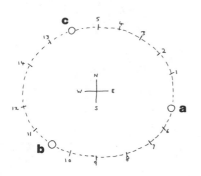

Arrangement of tipi poles

(actually two half-ovals) cut in the hide below most of the pins, with the bottom of the oval about a foot above the ground. The door itself, which hung from the doorway, was a piece of hide, fastened at the top to a horizontal pole or stretched on an oval or rectangular frame.

The interior lining was a semicircular strip, about six feet wide, also made of sewn buffalo hides.

Methods of erecting the tipi varied somewhat. The Cheyenne technique was fairly typical. They began by laying the hide on the ground with the inside up. In order to determine where the three foundation poles should be tied, they were placed on the hide so that two poles ran along the straight side, and the third ran down the center. The end of a long cord was wrapped several times around the junction and knotted. The three poles were raised and spread out to form a tripod, though at this point the poles were not placed as far apart as they would be when the cover had been put in place. The base of pole *a*, the tallest, pointed nearly east, but slightly south of where the door would be (facing away from the the prevailing westerly wind); pole *b* pointed slightly west of south; and pole *c* pointed slightly west of north.

All but three of the remaining poles were placed in the crotches of the three foundation poles, in the order shown, and the cord was wrapped four times around the poles by holding the end and walking clockwise around them. The rest of the cord was spiralled loosely down the northern pole and fastened to it with a half-hitch, though in very windy weather the cord would be run directly from the crotch of the poles to a stake in the center of the floor.

The doubled cord between the smoke flaps was fastened along one of the remaining poles with "cross-gartering," and the cover was lifted with this pole, draped over the frame, and fastened together with dogwood pins about the size of a pencil. Two shorter poles were inserted into the top corners of the smoke flaps.

The cover now hung loosely on the frame. The three foundation poles were moved further out and planted in holes dug a few inches into the ground, and then the other poles were moved out and planted, so that the hide was taut on the frame. Since the tipi tilted slightly backwards, the ground plan was not circular but oval, with its long axis from east to west.

The lining was fastened around the inside of the poles. Rainwater running down the poles was caught by the lining instead of dripping onto the floor. The lining also helped to keep the tipi warm, by deflecting the cold air currents brought in by the rising current of warm air above the fire.

If the tipi was new, a smoky fire of sagebrush or rotten wood was lit inside and left to burn for a day or two.The smoke impregnated the cover and ensured that it would remain pliable even after repeated soaking and drying.

Further east, on the Prairies, tipis were sometimes used in the summer, but the winter dwelling was the "earth lodge". The sod was removed from the ground to provide a round pit about forty feet wide and a foot deep. Four heavy posts, notched at the top and about ten or fifteen feet long, were planted in the center to form a square ten feet wide, and four beams rested on their tops. A circle of twelve notched posts, each about six feet long, was planted just inside the circumference of the pit, and beams rested on the notches. A brace slanted down from the top of each of the six-foot posts to the edge of the pit, and slabs of wood were leaned against the entire circumference of this wall. A box-like entranceway of logs ran out from the side of the dwelling. The framework was completed by running logs, three or four inches thick, from the central beams to the wall, leaving a four-foot smoke hole in the center. The entire structure was covered with a layer of willow mats, a layer of grass, and a thick layer of earth.

On the southeastern Prairies, large thatched lodges were built, somewhat in the shape of an old-fashioned beehive.

Prairie earth lodge

Great Lakes

The Ojibwa built conical, wedge-shaped, and rectangular lodges, but their principal winter dwelling was the dome-shaped wigwam or waginogan. This type of dwelling was also used to a large extent through a great part of the Eastern Woodlands.

Wigwams were usually about ten or fifteen feet long and either hemispherical or slightly elongated. Poles of hornbeam, tamarack, oak, or other wood, about two inches thick and ten to twenty feet long, were planted about one to three feet apart in a circle or oval. The tops were bent together, with a considerable amount of overlap, to form two series of arches at right angles to each other. The cordage used to tie the framework was either the untreated inner bark of the basswood tree or twisted rope made from this bark. The poles were also tied together at every point where the arches crossed each other. Additional poles were tied horizontally all around the walls and over the roof, again about one to three feet apart.

The cover consisted of birch, ash, or pine bark, cattail mats, or (rarely) tanned hides. Quite often two materials were used, such as cattail mats or ash bark for the sides and birch bark for the roof. Ash or pine bark was removed from the trees in large rectangular sheets in the springtime, flattened and dried, then tied to the framework through holes punched in the corners of the bark. Birch bark was treated in a similar manner, but the squares of bark, each about a yard wide, were sewn together with basswood bark to form long rolls, with the seams at a right angle to the grain of the bark. A pole or slat was sewn to each end of the roll, and the rolls were fastened to the framework with cords tied to their ends. Some of the rolls were fastened to the roof along the shorter axis, and a second layer was fastened over the length of the roof.

A hole was left in the center of the wigwam to allow smoke to escape. The rectangular entrance, in the middle of one of the narrower sides of the wigwam, was covered with a door made from a hide with a pole sewn onto the lower edge. The lodge was completed by passing a few cords completely over the roof and fastening them down to stakes near the base of the walls. The furniture consisted of beds made of parallel poles placed across two longer poles, which in turn were supported by short forked posts planted in the ground.

The rectangular summer lodge was constructed in the same manner as the domed lodge, except that it had vertical walls and a peaked roof, somewhat like a modern house. The ridgepole was supported at the back by a tall forked pole in the middle of the back wall, and in front by a shorter forked pole rising from the top of the rectangular door-frame. The covering was elm, cedar, or birch bark.

Eastern Woodlands

Houses of the type most frequently built in the northern half of the Eastern Woodlands had a rectangular ground-plan and are known as "longhouses." These were usually multi-family dwellings, and some of them were a hundred and fifty feet long, though most were less than half that length. Most houses were about twenty feet high and about twenty feet wide.

Two parallel rows of poles were planted in the ground,

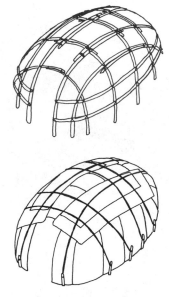

Great Lakes wigwam

four or five feet apart, bent over, and tied in pairs to form a series of arches. Horizontal poles, also about four or five feet apart, were tied to these arches.

The covering consisted of elm or ash bark. The bark was removed in six-foot-long rectangles, and the roughest parts of the outer surface were hacked off. It was stacked and weighted down until it became permanently flattened. Holes were punched in the edge of the sheets, which were then tied to the framework in overlapping rows, with the grain of the bark running horizontally along the walls and vertically over the roof.

More poles were fastened vertically over the bark covering of the walls. The poles were planted about four or five feet apart and tied, through the bark, to the inside arches. Poles were also fastened to run along the roof, with other poles crossing these at right angles.

Some houses differed from the above by having rafters separate from the wall posts. Each rafter consisted of a pole bent into an inverted V.

Eastern Woodlands longhouse

The inside of the house had a foot-high bark-covered platform running along each side, crossed by partitions to form living and storage compartments. Another platform, not quite as wide, ran along the wall several feet higher.

In the southeastern United States, summer houses had a rectangular ground-plan, vertical walls, and a ridged roof. The walls were filled in with vertical poles, and horizontal canes or poles were tied across these, forming a foundation for a coating of mud mixed with grass or moss. Horizontal poles were also tied across the roof, which was completed with several layers of cypress bark or with a thatching of grass or palmetto fronds. Winter houses were communal and resembled the Prairie earth lodges.

California and the Great Basin

A variety of conical, domed, or bullet-shaped lodges were built in California, the Great Basin, and much of the Southwest. These dwellings had a covering of bark, boards, soil, or thatch. Thatching sometimes consisted of bundles of grass twined together at one end with cord or bark to form large rectangles or "skirts," which were then tied to the framework. A few horizontal poles were tied over the completed thatching as reinforcement. Another type of thatching consisted of cattail leaves or rushes laid between three widely spaced pairs of poles; each pair of

Great Basin thatched house

Navaho house

poles was tied together every few inches to pin the leaves in place, and the completed mat was lifted and tied to the framework of the house. On the Great Basin, a far more primitive type of dwelling was often used, consisting of nothing more than a three-pole foundation and a layer of brush.

Southwest

The very earliest inhabitants of the Southwest lived in pit dwellings with a conical roof. The Navaho and Apache, rather late arrivals, also lived in conical pit dwellings, at least in the winter. The central pit of the Navaho house was dug down about a foot but was narrow enough to leave a "bench" around the outside. Over the pit were leaned three heavy logs, forked at the top to interlock as a tripod. On the east side, two longer parallel logs, about four feet apart, were leaned against two legs of the tripod. These two parallel logs formed the top of the slanted entranceway. Several feet out from the pit, but between these two logs, two forked posts were planted, and a horizontal pole was placed in the forks, forming the actual doorframe. Many smaller poles were leaned against the tripod to leave as few gaps as possible. A series of parallel horizontal poles covered the two slanted logs of the entrance way, though a gap was left at the top of the house for a smoke hole. The entire structure was given a thick coating of mud.

The summer dwelling of the Navaho was a three-sided lean-to, built in any convenient manner.

The Anasazi and many later inhabitants of the Southwest lived in huge multi-story dwellings known as "pueblos". Even though these dwellings were quite large and impressive, they were structurally quite simple.

The walls of the pueblo were made from a variety of materials, depending on what was available. The western pueblos often had walls made of slabs of sandstone, with smaller stones to fill the cracks. The stones were cemented together with adobe, a naturally occurring mixture of clay and sand. Further east the walls might be made of adobe mixed with pebbles or dry grass, built up gradually like a huge pottery vessel. (Some later pueblos were made of adobe brick, but brick-making was introduced by the Spanish.) Other eastern pueblos had a double wall of vertical poles, with adobe packed between the two rows of poles. Walls of all types were given a final plastering of adobe, so they all looked alike when they were finished.

The foundation of the roof consisted of widely spaced peeled cottonwood logs, set a few inches below the top of the wall. Willow rods were laid transversely over the logs, and several layers of grass and brush were laid over the willow rods. The grass and brush were in turn covered with a thick layer of adobe. Most of the roof of one story became the floor of the next.

For protection against enemies, the lower story of the pueblo had no windows or doors. A ladder was used to reach the entrance hole (which also served as a smoke hole) in the roof, and another ladder was used to descend into the rooms. The walls of other stories had T-shaped doorways, and the windows were small holes in the walls. Some windows were paved with selenite, a slab-like form of gypsum.

Pueblo

Clothing

In most parts of North America, clothing was made from tanned hides, with or without the hair, though the Indians of the Northwest Coast made clothing out of cedar bark, and in the Southwest clothing was made from cotton woven on a loom.

Most clothing was simple and untailored, and in aboriginal times many Indians went naked or nearly naked much of the time, though fur robes were used throughout North America in cold weather. Only the Eskimos and some of the Subarctic Indians made clothing carefully tailored to fit the entire body.

When hide or fur was sewn, it was usually done by punching a hole with a bone awl and inserting a thread of sinew. The usual stitch was the common spiral stitch, also known as an overcast, overhand, or whip stitch. The running stitch was also used.

Arctic

In summer, Eskimo men of the central Arctic wore an outer parka of sealskin, with the hair facing outwards, and an inner garment of either seal or caribou skin, with the hair facing outwards. The body of the parka was made in two pieces, front and back, with the back piece continuing to form a hood. The shoulder seams ran across the front of the shoulders rather than on top, and the sleeves were sewn on separately. There was no opening in the front of the parka, so it was pulled on over the head. The thread, made of sinew, was sewn with a delicate eyed ivory needle rather than an awl.

Summer trousers consisted of an inner and an outer pair, of the same materials as the parkas. These trousers were quite baggy and only reached to a little below the knee. Footwear consisted of knee-length boots or "mukluks," worn over socks of hide or woven grass.

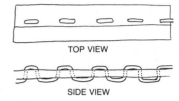

TOP VIEW

SIDE VIEW

Running stitch

Spiral stitch

Eskimo parka

Winter garments for men were the same, but made entirely of caribou skin.

Women wore clothing similar to that of the men, but the parka had a rounded flap in front and a longer flap behind. The hood, and often the back, was made much larger for carrying children.

Women's trousers varied somewhat. Some Eskimo women wore short trousers that only reached halfway down the thigh. Under these they wore leggings that reached from the middle of the thigh to just below the knee. The leggings were kept in place by a cord fastened to the top of the trousers. Other women of the central Arctic wore knee-length trousers, extending down over extremely baggy hip-length boots.

Both men and women also wore mittens, which were attached to a thong that ran up the inside of the sleeves and around the back of the neck.

Subarctic

In the Subarctic, men wore a shirt that was cut and sewn very much like an Eskimo parka except that it had no hood. The shirt was made of tanned caribou or moose hide and reached to midthigh or the knees. The summer shirt had the hair side out, though the hair was shaved off, and the winter shirt was worn with the hair left on, facing inwards. In very cold weather both shirts might be worn at once. A thin belt was worn around the waist. Shirts were also made of the woven skins of snowshoe hares.

A man's lower garments consisted of a breechcloth, leggings, and moccasins. The breechcloth was a rectangle of tanned hide about a foot wide and three to five feet long, passed between the legs and folded over a thong belt. Leggings were fastened by thongs to the same belt. Each legging was made from a long folded rectangle of hide with a seam running down the outside of the leg. The seam was sewn several inches from the edge of the hide, so that the border could be cut into a fringe. A garter, usually sewn in place, was tied around the legging just below the knee.

Fur caps were sometimes worn in the wintertime, but often the headgear simply consisted of a strip of fur wrapped around or over the head.

A woman's dress was virtually identical to a man's shirt, except that it reached to the ankles. Under the dress a long skirt was worn, consisting of a rectangle of hide

Subarctic shirt

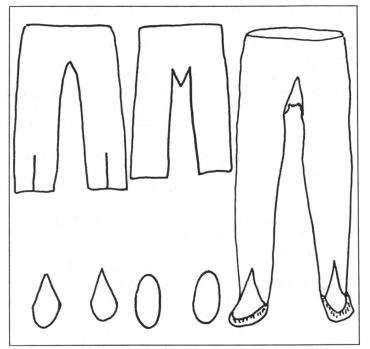

Western Subarctic trousers

attached to a belt but left open at the front or side. Leggings were also worn, but they only reached down to the knees.

In the western Subarctic, both men and women often wore trousers with attached footwear: a diamond-shaped gore was sewn into a slit at the front of the ankle to form an instep, and an oval piece of hide was sewn on below to form the sole.

Both sexes wore moccasins, which often had high cuffs, and mittens were worn in the wintertime.

Northwest Coast and Plateau

Men on the Northwest Coast often went about completely naked. When they did wear clothing, the principal item was a blanket of woven cedar bark, made with three straight edges and a convex lower edge.

Inner bark was taken from western red cedar (*Thuja plicata*) or western yellow cedar (*Chamaecyparis nootkatensis*), the latter supplying a softer fiber. The Kwakiutl soaked the bark in salt water for up to a month, beat it over the edge of a paddle with a whalebone implement that had longitudinal grooves on the lower edge, and hung it up to bleach and dry. The dried bark was separated into two layers, and the innermost layer was divided into bun-

Northwest Coast blanket

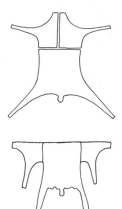

Plains poncho

dles half an inch thick and saved to make the blanket. Other tribes used similar techniques: sometimes the inner bark was separated into two layers as soon as it was removed from the tree.

The weaving was done on a loom-like device consisting of a grooved horizontal bar tied between two stakes. The wefts (horizontal threads) were of tightly spun yellow-cedar bark, twined across the bundles in rows half an inch apart. The Tsimshian and Tlingit used a similar loom and a similar weaving technique to produce blankets of mountain-goat wool.

Conical rain-capes, with a hole in the center for the head, were produced in the same way, except that the "loom" consisted of two poles planted in the ground, leaning together so that they almost touched at the top. No horizontal bar was needed.

Some tribes made rain capes that consisted of a long rectangle with a square hole in the center, but these were essentially mats, plaited rather than twined, and made from strips of unbeaten bark.

Conical caps, made of twined spruce root or plaited cedar bark, were often worn in rainy weather.

Moccasins, breechcloths, and leggings were rarely worn on the Northwest Coast, except in the north, where clothing was often the same as that of the Subarctic Indians. Most Indians of the Northwest Coast wore no footwear at all, even in the snow.

A woman's basic item of dress was a skirt, also made of beaten and shredded cedar bark. The bundles of bark were doubled, hung over a waist cord, and held in place with one or two rows of twining, but below these rows the bark simply hung down loosely, "hula skirt" fashion.

Clothing on the Plateau was basically the same as along the Northwest Coast. The inner bark of cedar was used to make shirts, mats, and capes, but other materials were often substituted: the entire shredded bark of big sagebrush, silverberry, orange honeysuckle, greasewood, and white clematis, and the shredded inner bark of willow. Indian hemp was often made into cord for twining these materials.

Plains

Clothing on the Plains was very much like that in the Subarctic, except that tailored shirts were rare until late historical times. The basic dress for men was a breechcloth and moccasins. A poncho was sometimes worn in cold weather and on ceremonial occasions, especially on the northern Plains. This poncho was cut from two entire skins of deer, antelope, or mountain sheep. The hair was removed. Each hide was cut into three parts, and the six pieces were sewn together, though the sides were not sewn up. Buckskin leggings were also worn in cold weather and on ceremonial occasions, as well as for protection when travelling.

Women wore a dress made of two elk hides, with the tail uppermost. The tail and outer leg portions were folded over to form a yoke. The sides of the dress were sewn up, and another seam ran along the top of each shoulder, but there were no seams at the armpits. Under the dress, women wore a skirt and knee-length leggings, like those of the Subarctic.

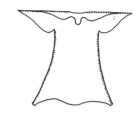

Plains woman's dress

Canada-United States border

In a broad area from the Rockies to the Atlantic, in the northern United States and Canada, women wore a dress with detached sleeves. This dress was a tube-like garment of deer skin, sewn with a seam up each side, and extending from the underarms to below the knees. It was held up by a leather thong over each shoulder. Each sleeve was conical, reaching from wrist to shoulder, and sewn with a single lower seam that only extended up to the elbow. The two sleeves were attached to each other by cords across the back and front. Naskapi women of Labrador, however, made the two sleeves in one piece, like a very short cape, with a hole in the center for the head. New England women wore a single sleeve on the right arm, fastened around the neck, with the left arm covered by a fur robe. The usual skirt and leggings were worn under the dress.

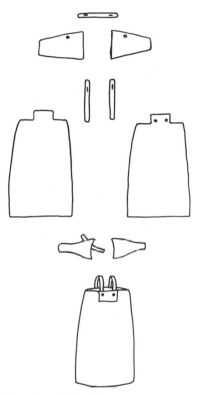

Dress with detached sleeves

Prairies and Eastern Woodlands

Men's dress on the Prairies and in the Eastern Woodlands was very simple in aboriginal times. The basic items were the breechcloth and moccasins, with a fur robe for cold weather. Shirts and ponchos of any sort were rare or nonexistent in prehistoric times. Leggings and moccasins were occasionally worn.

Women wore a skirt made of a deer hide, wrapped around the waist so that there was a slit at the left thigh. The single sleeve, mentioned above, was also worn.

California and Great Basin

Men in California and the Great Basin often went naked, though sometimes a tanned hide was wrapped around the hips. Usually no footwear was worn, but moccasins were sometimes used when travelling.

Women wore a two-piece skirt, with the back piece wider than the front. Sometimes the skirt was made of buckskin, but often it consisted of shredded plant fiber that hung loosely, like the Northwest Coast skirt. The fiber of the California skirt usually consisted of the inner bark of maple or other trees, but grass, reed, and other materials were also used. Sagebrush bark was often used in the Great Basin. Robes of woven rabbit-skin were common in both areas.

Southwest

Men and women of the Southwest wore clothing of woven cotton. (Wool was only used after sheep were introduced by the Spanish.) Men wore a breechcloth between the legs, and on top of this they wore a short kilt wrapped around the waist.

Women wore a long rectangle of cotton cloth, wide enough to be wrapped once around the body from armpit to knee. The two top corners were pinned together over the right shoulder, and a braided cloth belt was worn around the waist.

In early prehistoric times, footwear consisted of sandals. Often these were made of hide, but plant material was more common. Yucca and other fibers were plaited or twined to form a rounded rectangle for the sole, and cords were variously fastened to hold the sandal onto the foot. Moccasins eventually replaced sandals, and pueblo women wore a long spiral of buckskin over the tops of the moccasins and up the leg as far as the knee.

Cotton cloth was also woven in Mexico, but it was reserved for the nobility. Poorer people wove cloth out of agave fiber.

Weaving

The weaving of cotton and other clothing fabrics is similar to plaiting in basketry. Woven fabric has horizontal threads called wefts, which cross alternately over and under a set of vertical threads called warps. Each row of weaving is the opposite of the previous row: if the weft goes over a warp in one row, it will go under that same warp in the next row. The fabric, if examined closely, appears to have a "checkerboard" pattern. Many variations on this basic pattern are made possible by skipping certain warps and wefts, by using more than one weft thread, and by using colored threads.

Twining, which uses pairs of wefts, twisting around each other after each warp, is also possible on more primitive loom-like devices, though ironically, not on the true loom. (Plaiting and twining are described in more detail in Chapter 14, "Basketry and Pottery.")

Plant and animal fibers were woven in many parts of North America with a variety of loom-like devices, some of them extremely simple in design. Mats and blankets could be woven with nothing more than a horizontal bar or cord from which to suspend the warps, though each stitch required a separate set of movements on the part of the weaver. Cotton clothing was made practical only by the development of the true loom, which was used in the Southwest, Mexico, Central America, and South America. The true loom may also have been used in the Southeast for weaving inner bark. The principal characteristic of the true loom is that it allows an entire row of weaving to be completed with a single set of movements.

Cultivated cotton (*Gossypium hirsutum*) was harvested in the autumn. The seeds were usually picked from the fiber by hand, though sometimes the fiber was spread between two blankets, beaten with a stick to loosen the seeds, and then scraped from the blankets. The bundles of fiber were then roughly straightened out (drawn parallel) with the fingers and spun with a spindle. Before the spindle was used, however, the fiber might be placed on the thigh and brushed with the flattened hand to produce a loosely twisted thread or "roving."

The spindle consisted of a rod with a disk or flywheel jammed on about a third of the distance from the bottom. Spindle rods might be only a few inches long or several feet long, but the type used for spinning cotton usually measured from one to two feet. The disk was usually made of wood, though many other materials were also used, and more primitive spindles simply had a short stick tied across the rod.

Several inches of fiber were wrapped tightly around the rod just under the disk, and the next few inches were brought up to the rod just above the disk. There were several ways of manipulating the spindle. The Hopi worker usually sat on the ground with his legs folded

Hopi spindle

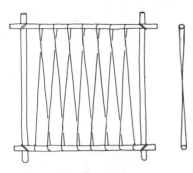

Temporary weaving frame

Top or bottom selvage cord

under him (clothmaking was a male occupation in the Southwest), rested the bottom of the spindle on the ground, and placed the other end on his right thigh. The line of fiber was held taut in the left hand, and the spindle was rolled forward on the thigh. Since the line of fiber and the spindle rod formed a slight angle, the fiber was not only rolled onto the rod but also twisted slightly at the same time. The worker guided the thread with his right hand so that it built up in a cone around the rod, just above the disk.

Every once in a while, the worker jammed the spindle between his foot and the ground and went over the extended thread to untangle any kinks that were beginning to form. He also wound the half-formed thread up around his left hand and spun it again to form a tighter thread.

Eventually all the fiber was spun onto the rod, but the thread was likely to have a rather loose and irregular twist, so it was slipped off the rod and completely respun at least once more. The finished product was still a lot thicker and more irregular than what we usually think of as cotton thread.

Larger pieces of fabric were woven on the "blanket loom." The warp thread was first set up on a temporary frame, then removed and fixed to the loom.

The frame consisted of four heavy poles placed on the ground and tied together to form a rectangle.The warp thread was tied near one corner and then stretched back and forth between two opposite poles. Each line of thread crossed the previcus one, so that the warps actually formed a series of elongated figure-eights.

When the frame had been filled, a doubled selvage cord was twined along the top and bottom (i.e. the near and far ends) of the warp, on the outside of the frame. This cord might be twisted several times before passing over and under each loop of the warp. These selvage cords held and separated the rows of warp, and when the fabric was finished they served to reinforce the edge. A loose pole was placed alongside each selvage cord, and another cord was wrapped in a spiral around the pole and the selvage cord.

The heddles were inserted. The first heddle was simply a long horizontal rod placed *between* the two rows of warp threads just above the line where the warps crossed to form the figure-eight. The second heddle was also a horizontal rod, but it was placed in *front* of all the warps just below this line, and fastened to the foremost line of warps with a spiralled cord. If a complicated pattern was to be created, several more heddles might need to be added. The ends of all the heddles were loosely tied together to prevent them from falling out.

The foundations of the loom needed to be set up. A long horizontal log was suspended from the ceiling, and a similar beam was fastened to the floor, or stakes were planted in the floor. These were often permanent fixtures of the house.

The four original poles of the frame could now be dismantled and pulled out from the warp threads. The warp, end rods, and heddles were ready to be attached to the loom foundation.

The lower end pole was simply tied to the floor log or stakes. The upper pole, however, needed a means of adjusting its tension, so instead of being directly attached to the ceiling log, it was tied to an intermediary pole, which in turn was attached to the ceiling log with a wide spiral or zigzag of cord. This last cord could be loosened or tightened at any time.

The last step before the actual weaving began was to attach one or more selvage cords between the end poles on each side. These selvage cords would strengthen the left and right sides of the finished fabric.

No true shuttle was used to hold the mass of weft thread, though sometimes it was strung back and forth along a stick and looped around notches cut near the ends. Often the weft thread was kept as a ball, just as it came from the spindle.

Weaving was always done from top to bottom. The worker pulled one heddle forward and laid the weft thread in place underneath it from one side to the other. When he reached the three selvage cords at the sides, he passed the weft in and out of them, using any of various stitches. He then pulled forward the other heddle, reversed the weft thread, and laid another row in place.

A "weaving sword," a long flattened stick, was used to beat the weft tightly into place and to help separate the warps. A wooden comb was also used to even up the stitches.

By the time the fabric was nearly completed, the last few inches of warp would be hard to separate, and there were two solutions to the problem. One solution was to remove the heddles and put in the last few stitches one at a time. The other solution was to weave half the fabric, reverse the loom, and weave towards the first half, though in that case it would be the middle rows that needed to be put in a stitch at a time.

Heddles

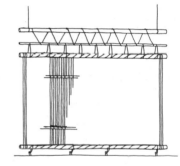

Side selvage cords

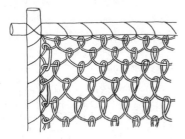

Knotless netting

Rabbit-skin weaving

The skins of rabbits and hares, with the hair left on, were used in most of North America for blankets and sometimes even for coats and mittens, but the material was not given the same sort of treatment as other types of furs. The two principal techniques used were "knotless netting" and twining. Rabbit skin required no tanning, since it is thin enough to be flexible. The only disadvantage was that the hair tended to fall out.

In the Subarctic, snowshoe hares were skinned by cutting off the feet and then either slitting across the back legs and peeling the skin off like a glove, or by making a slit up the belly. The skin was cut into a long spiral about an inch wide, then loosely twisted by inserting the end into the split end of a stick which was rolled on the thigh (or fastened to the middle of a stick which was twirled like a propellor). The twisted hide was hung up to dry for a few days.

A rectangular weaving frame was built, consisting of two vertical poles and two horizontal poles. A strip of rabbit skin was bound all around the inside of the frame, using a bark cord that spiralled all around the skin and the pole. The rest of the rabbit-skin strips were woven back and forth across this frame, using a technique called "knotless netting." When one strip ran out, another strip was tied to its end.

Coats were made by the same process, except that holes were left for the sleeves. The sleeves were woven in the same fashion, but the square frame was not used. Instead, a piece of buckskin was rolled around a stick to form a thick bundle, and a piece of cord was tied around one end. The skin strips were woven downwards from the string to produce the tubular sleeve.

The technique of knotless netting, incidentally, was also used to make bird-skin blankets and rawhide-thong bags.

In California, the Great Basin, the Southwest, and in some areas further east, rabbit-skin blankets were usually made by a twining process. As in the Subarctic, the skin was cut across the hind legs and peeled off upwards to include the skin of the head, then cut into a spiral about an inch wide. The end of the strip was pushed through one of the eye holes, so that the skin became a large link in a chain of such strips. The chain of skins was hung up to dry, and eventually the ears were snapped off.

The chain of skins was strung back and forth on a four-sided vertical frame, though sometimes the bottom pole of the frame was omitted. Cord made of twisted Indian hemp or yucca was then twined across the rows of skins, with a gap of anywhere between one-half and four inches between the rows of cord.

Other techniques were also used. Pueblo Indians cut the skins only a quarter of an inch wide and twisted them around a yucca cord before twining them in the above manner. Eastern tribes sometimes braided the strips together and then sewed the lengths of braiding together. Others sewed the skins in a patchwork technique, without cutting them into spirals, though this technique is probably fairly modern.

Moccasins and mukluks

Dozens of distinct types of moccasins were made, but they fall into two general classes, soft-soled and hard-soled.

Soft-soled moccasins were especially characteristic of forest areas. They were the ideal footwear to use with snowshoes. In the northern Subarctic, moccasins often had large ankle flaps that could be turned up to keep out the snow, and some even had tubular tops like those on boots. Soft-soled moccasins usually had the main seam running down or around the instep, though a few in the west had the seam running along the side of the foot from toes to heel. Right and left moccasins were usually interchangeable.

Hard-soled moccasins were more suited to the Plains and the Southwest, where the terrain had a lot of rocks, thorns, and sharp grass. Some of the Apache designed their moccasins with turned-up toes for further protection. Hard-soled moccasins had the main seam running all around the foot, joining the upper part to the sole. The two parts were usually made of different materials: tanned hide for the top, and thicker rawhide for the sole. Hard-soled moccasins were usually made with distinct lefts and rights.

The most common material for moccasins was tanned deer skin, but many other kinds of skin were also used, from salmon to buffalo. The sewing thread was usually split deer sinew, but the coarser sinews of caribou, moose, and buffalo were also used. Thread from twisted cedar bark and other plant fibers was not uncommon; plant-fiber

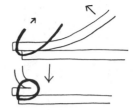

Modified spiral stitch

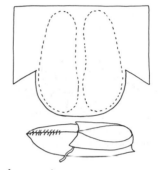

Simple moccasin

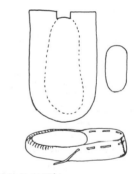

Eastern moccasin

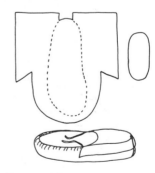

Eastern moccasin

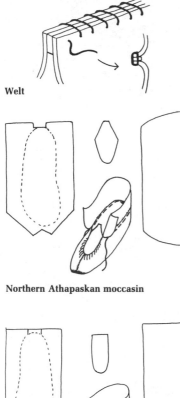

Welt

Northern Athapaskan moccasin

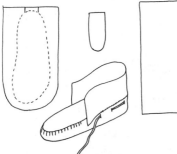

Northern Athapaskan moccasin

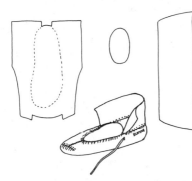

Iroquois moccasin

thread was weaker and more difficult to insert through the holes in the hide but less likely to stretch and fall apart in wet weather.

The tools required were a knife to cut the hide and an awl to punch holes for the thread. The awl was often a sharpened deer ulna, but awls were also made from thorns or hard wood.

Usually the hair was removed from the hide, and the hair or "grain" side became the outside of the moccasin. If the moccasin was intended for winter wear, however, the hair might be left on, and this grain side became the inside of the moccasin.

Most moccasins were sewn inside out, then turned "outside out" to be worn.

The most common stitch was the spiral stitch, with the edges of the hide overlapping each other or pressed face to face. A modified spiral stitch was used to join the soles of hard-soled moccasins to the upper part. The running stitch was used for joining a cuff to the main body of the moccasin. Superior moccasins had a welt, a long strip of hide, sewn into the seam so that the stitching was less exposed.

Many moccasins had a puckered seam where the vamp (instep) was attached to the main piece. A puckered seam required that the holes in the vamp be only half as far apart as the holes in the main piece, though, of course, there were the same number of holes in each piece. To help make the puckering uniform, three "basting" stitches were first put in: one at the middle of the seam, and one at each end.

A rawhide thong was usually laced through the top edge of the moccasin to hold it onto the foot.

In cold weather, moccasins were worn with a padding of rabbit skins, muskrat skins, dried grass, or dried moss. It was a common practice to remove moccasins in wet weather and travel barefoot, since they tended to fall apart in the presence of moisture, especially if sewn with sinew.

Several types of moccasin are shown here. The type shown first is the simplest and probably represents the style from which most others developed. Other types eliminated the pointed toe and heel and added cuffs. Cuffs made as part of the main piece required less sewing, but cuffs made from a separate piece added strength to the back of the moccasin and also took advantage of smaller pieces of hide.

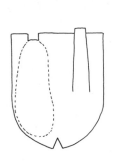
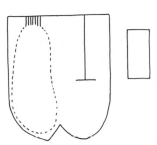
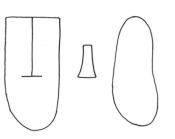

Sioux side-seam moccasin

Shoshoni side-seam moccasin

Sioux hard-sole moccasin

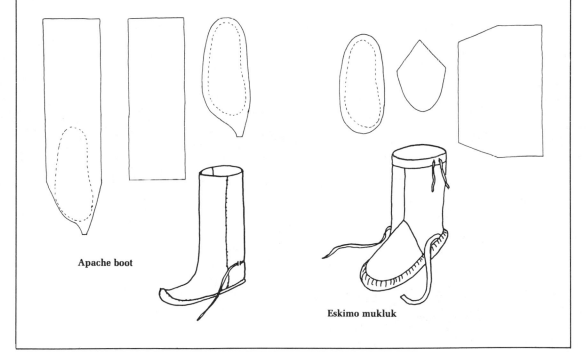

Apache boot

Eskimo mukluk

Medicine

Medical problems in aboriginal times included wounds, sprains, broken bones, burns, and minor skin ailments. Rheumatism and arthritis affected the old. Smoke-filled lodges caused sore eyes. Toothache was fairly common. Women had problems with menstruation and childbirth. Respiratory and digestive ailments sometimes occurred, and intestinal worms were a common problem.

The "civilized" ailments of heart disease, arteriosclerosis, and cancer were rare in aboriginal times.

Very few viral or bacterial diseases existed in prehistoric times. It was white explorers and settlers who brought many of these diseases, which played a great part in the destruction of aboriginal culture. A genuine cure for viral and bacterial ailments requires vaccines and antibiotics. Indian medicine, therefore, like most other forms of "folk medicine," was least effective in dealing with problems of this sort, though some forms of treatment alleviated congestion, fever, diarrhea, and other symptoms.

The North American Indians did not usually regard physical problems as distinct from spiritual problems. Some tribes had herbalists as well as shamans, but in many tribes the two roles were combined. Even when a physical remedy was applied, the cause of the ailment might still be ascribed to evil spirits, acting in response to sorcery or a breach of taboo. This approach was not entirely illogical; modern medicine also recognizes that there is a complex interrelationship between "mind" (or at least "brain" or "attitude") and "body" in the causes and cures of illness. Of course, a shaman whose skills were purely spiritual might be less successful than one who also used more mundane techniques.

In many respects, Indian medicine was quite effective. Willow, poplar, and wintergreen (*Gaultheria procumbens*) contain salicates related to acetylsalicylic acid, commonly known as aspirin, and these materials were used for the same purpose of reducing fever and pain. Pipsissewa, spiraea, and black, yellow, and cherry birch also contain salicates, though these plants were used less frequently. Cherry bark contains hydrocyanic (prussic) acid and is still used as a cough suppressant. Coniferous trees such as balsam fir, pine, and cedar contain volatile oils used to reduce nasal and pulmonary congestion, and the menthol in various mints served the same function. Tablets and ointments of pine and mint oils are used for similar purposes today. The resin from coniferous trees was also used as an antiseptic application on wounds, and the inner bark was mashed as a poultice. Oak, raspberry, sumac, dogwood, alumroot, and many other plants contain astringent ingredients such as tannin, serving to reduce the flow of blood and other fluids. Many herbs are rich in vitamins, minerals, and purifying agents and acted as general tonics. Witch hazel is still used for sore muscles, pennyroyal as an insect repellent, and raspberry as a treatment for diarrhea. Many of the herbal remedies used today, or the related synthetic drugs, were actually adopted from Indian medicine. Other medicinal plants, such as willow and yarrow, were equally popular in early European folk medicine.

The "doctrine of signatures" sometimes had an influence on Indian medicine, as it did on the medicine of many Old World cultures. According to this theory, plants bear a resemblance to something else related to the ailment. A plant with long twisted roots, for example, might be used to treat snakebite. Milkweed and other plants with milky juice were used to cure breast problems.

Plants were gathered when they contained the largest quantity of the active ingredient. Inner bark was gathered in the spring, when it was full of sap and easier to remove. Leaves were usually picked just before the plant was in bloom, and the roots of annual plants were dug at the same time. The roots of perennial plants were gathered in the autumn, while they were storing various substances for winter. Many plants were dried for later use, though in some cases the active ingredients would evaporate or decay eventually. Some plants were only used in their dry form.

Like us, the Indians distinguished between infusions and decoctions. Infusions are prepared by adding a substance to water, which is usually boiled just before the plant material is added, though lukewarm or cold water is sometimes used. Decoctions are prepared by boiling a substance in water. Infusions and decoctions can extract different ingredients from the same plant material.

Some plants were far more important than others. The conifers (including juniper and yew, which actually have berries rather than cones) were used to treat colds, wounds, inflammations, burns, sore eyes, rheumatism, headaches, and insect bites. Willow bark was extensively used for fever and pain. Cherry bark was widely used as a sedative. Yarrow, milkweed, calamus, sagebrush, and several members of the mint family were each used for a variety of ailments throughout North America.

Many Indian herbal remedies—often the most valuable—were potentially toxic and had to be used in moderation. Of those mentioned below, the most dangerous plants are yew, blue flag, Mexican tea, bloodroot, black cherry, dogbane, Indian hemp, and jimsonweed. Pitcher plant is said to be toxic. Members of the buttercup family (*Ranunculus*, *Anemone*, etc.), arum family (such as Jack-in-the-pulpit and skunk cabbage), and milkweed family (including butterfly weed) are all toxic in varying degrees, especially when raw or undried. All parts of coniferous trees contain volatile oils, which served many useful purposes but are nevertheless toxic and even abortifacient in large doses. Horsetail is also poisonous in large doses.

Non-herbal Indian medicine also resembled modern practices. Inflamed tumors and abscesses were lanced. Arrowheads and bullets were removed whenever possible. The Ojibwa made a bulb syringe out of a bladder and quill for washing out wounds. A number of tribes are known to have sewn up major wounds, and minor amputations were sometimes performed. Dislocated limbs were pulled back into place. Fractures were held immobile with wooden splints. The Ojibwa heated birch bark and bound it around a fractured limb, and the bark hardened as it cooled to act as a cast. The Haida used the bark of lodgepole pine as a cast or splint, and other tribes used other kinds of wood or bark. Decayed teeth were struck out, and snakebites were treated with sucking and binding.

The sweat bath was regarded almost as a panacea, though it was used most often for rheumatism and fever. A sweat lodge was usually a small domed structure with a framework of arched poles and a cover of hides or bark, though sometimes a patient simply sat under a blanket. Rocks were heated in a fire and rolled into the lodge. Water containing medicinal plant material was sprinkled on the rocks to form steam, or the plant material was laid on the rocks and plain water was sprinkled on both the plants and the rocks. The sweat bath was usually followed by a plunge into cold water.

Certain tribes were more skillful in medicine than others. Several early observers regarded the Ojibwa as particularly knowledgeable, and this tribe certainly used a large number of herbal remedies.

Cuts and sores

Minor cuts and sores were treated with antiseptic or astringent lotions or washes. More serious wounds were treated with poultices held in place with strips of buckskin or inner bark. The Ojibwa used a needle and deer sinew for sewing up major wounds. A great many herbal remedies were used.

The pulverized leaves of yarrow (*Achillea* spp.) were used across North America as a poultice for cuts and wounds. The crushed leaves of plantain (*Plantago major*), an alien species, were frequently used as a poultice on sprains and sores. The chewed or powdered roots of alumroot (*Heuchera* spp.), though not a very common plant, were applied to wounds in several areas across North America. Coniferous trees were more widely used than any other plants for the treatment of cuts and sores. Balsam fir was the most commonly used conifer in eastern North America, but the pitch, the mashed inner bark, and the needles of pine, cedar, juniper, tamarack, hemlock, and spruce were also applied to wounds.

The Ojibwa used many other plants as poultices for cuts and sores, including the crushed roots of cattail (*Typha latifolia*), the chewed inner bark of trembling aspen (*Populus tremuloides*), the crushed buds of balsam poplar (*Populus balsamifera*), the chewed roots of white oak (*Quercus alba*), and the chewed roots of Canada anemone (*Anemone canadensis*).

Several other plants were used in northeastern North America. The crushed rootstock of yellow pond lily (*Nuphar advena*) was used by a number of eastern tribes as a poultice for cuts, sores, and bruises. The crushed roots of spikenard (*Aralia racemosa*) and wild sarsparilla (*A. nudicaulis*) were often used as a poultice on sores. Many eastern tribes crushed the roots of the poisonous blue flag (*Iris versicolor*) as a poultice for wounds. The Menominee dried and powdered the roots of eastern skunk cabbage (*Symphocarpus foetidus*) and sprinkled it on cuts. The Meskwaki pounded and moistened the inner bark of slippery elm (*Ulmus rubra*) as a poultice for cuts. The Mohegan and Delaware made a decoction of the roots of wild indigo (*Baptisia tinctoria*) and applied it to cuts and sores. The Rappahannock used sphagnum moss (*Sphagnum* spp.) as an absorbent on wounds; the plant contains iodine and was also used on wounds in Europe during World War I. In the southeastern United States, the Choctaws boiled the roots of sweet gum (*Liquidambar styraciflua*) and applied the liquid to cuts and wounds.

Spiderwebs were used on the Northwest Coast to stop bleeding, and wounds were bound with strips of bittercherry bark (*Prunus emarginata*). Strips of the inner bark of yellow cedar (*Chamaecyparis nootkatensis*) were used as tourniquets. The rotten stems of devil's club (*Oplopanax horridum*) were burnt to ashes and mixed with fish oil or spruce pitch as a lotion for sores. The leaves of the western skunk cabbage (*Lysichitum americanum*) were used on the Northwest Coast as a poultice for sores.

In the Plateau region, cattail fluff (*Typha latifolia*) and the shredded inner bark of willow (*Salix* spp.) were used as absorbent dressings on wounds.

The Kiowa, Zuñi, Blackfeet, and Ojibwa sprinkled the spores of mature puffballs (*Calvatia* and *Lycoperdon* spp.) on cuts to stop the bleeding. The spores of clubmoss (*Lycopodium* spp.) were used by the Blackfeet and Potawatomi for the same purpose. The Blackfeet also used the pitch of alpine fir (*Abies lasiocarpa*), the chewed leaves of pasture wormwood (*Artemisia frigida*), and the chewed roots of locoweed (*Astragalus canadensis*) on cuts and wounds.

The Omaha and Ponca pounded and boiled the roots of a type of anemone (*Anemone* sp.) as a poultice for wounds. The Sioux, like some of the eastern tribes, dried and pulverized the rootstock of yellow pond lily (*Nuphar advena*) as a poultice for cuts. The Illinois and Miami made a poultice of the inner bark of white oak (*Quercus alba*). The Illinois also mashed and soaked the roots of a type of buttercup (*Ranunculus* sp.) as a poultice.

In California, the crushed roots of western jimsonweed (*Datura meteloides*) were used as a poultice on cuts, wounds, and bruises. An infusion of the crushed root was drunk as an anesthetic when a fracture needed to be set. The crushed leaves of yerba santa (*Eriodictyon californicum*) were used as a poultice by the Miwok. The Cahuilla Indians used moldy acorn meal on cuts and sores; the mold may have had a penicillin-like antibiotic effect.

Many tribes of the Southwest split and soaked the pads

of prickly pear cactus (*Opuntia* spp.) as a poultice for wounds. The Hopi and the Apache used the pitch of various pinyon pines (*Pinus* spp.) on cuts and sores. The Hopi sprinkled the dried and ground leaves of spectacle pod (*Dithyrea wislizeni*) on wounds, and the Apache boiled mesquite gum (*Prosopis juliaflora*) as a wash for cuts and wounds. The Pima and Papago used the dried and powdered roots of canaigre (*Rumex hymenosepalus*) on sores.

Burns

A number of eastern tribes used the pitch or boiled inner bark of balsam fir (*Abies balsamifera*) on burns. The inner bark of tamarack (*Larix laricina*) was also used as a poultice.

The crushed leaves of plantain (*Plantago major*) were extensively used in the east as a poultice for burns.

The Algonquin boiled the inner bark of pin cherry (*Prunus pennsylvanica*) to a jelly as a poultice.

The Meskwaki and Cree crushed the roots of blue flag (*Iris versicolor*) as a poultice for burns. The Meskwaki also used the leaves of Canadian wormwood (*Artemisia canadensis*) or the leaves of thimbleweed (*Anemone cylindrica*) as a poutice.

The Rappahannock made a decoction of the pith of red sassafras (*Sassafras albidum* var. *molle*) and used it as a wash for burns.

The Potawatomi used the fresh leaves of green-stemmed Joe-Pye weed (*Eupatorium purpureum*) as a dressing for burns.

The Thompson of British Columbia burned the stems of horsetail (*Equisetum* sp.) and sprinkled the ashes, sometimes mixed with fat, on burns.

The pitch of digger pine (*Pinus sabiniana*) was used as a salve in California.

In the Southwest, the Hopi crushed the roots of cattail (*Typha* sp.) and mixed it with fat as a salve for burns, while the Zuñi crushed the entire yarrow plant (*Achillea millefolium*) and mixed it with water as a poultice.

Skin problems

Across North America, animal oil (including fish oil) or vegetable oil was rubbed on the skin to prevent sunburn in summer and frostbite in winter.

The Ojibwa made an infusion of the inner bark of witch

hazel (*Hamamelis virginiana*) as a lotion for skin problems in general. A decoction of the twigs was used by the Menominee as a lotion for sore muscles, and the Potawatomi used the twigs in the steam bath for the same purpose.

The Meskwaki used a thick decoction of the inner bark of white ash (*Fraxinus americanus*) for itching skin, the Alabama used a decoction of the inner bark of prickly ash (*Xanthoxylum americanum*), and the Pomo of California used a decoction of willow bark (*Salix* sp.).

A number of plants were used to treat poison-ivy infections. The Ojibwa boiled the young bark of red-osier dogwood (*Cornus stolonifera*) as a poultice. The Potawatomi crushed the entire spotted touch-me-not plant (*Impatiens capensis*) and put the juice on skin irritated by either poison ivy or nettles. The Mohegan and Penobscot made an infusion of the leaves of sweet fern (*Comptonia peregrina*) and bathed the skin with the liquid to treat poison-ivy infections. The Menominee used the juice from the leaves of wild lettuce (*Lactuca canadensis*). On the Plains, the Cheyenne dried and crushed the leaves of milk vetch (*Astragalus nitida*), and the Omaha crushed the fruit and leaves of smooth upland sumac (*Rhus glabra*) as a poultice. Poison-ivy infections and other skin problems were treated in California with an application of the crushed leaves of gum plant (*Grindelia robusta*). Indians of the Southwest used a tea of manzanita berries (*Arctostaphylos* spp.) as a wash for poison-oak infections.

Boils were also treated with specific remedies. The Ojibwa crushed the roots of spikenard (*Aralia racemosa*) or wild sarsparilla (*A. nudicaulis*) as a poultice for boils. The Menominee crushed the roots of thimbleweed (*Anemone virginiana*) as a poultice. The Potawatomi used a splinter of the inner bark of slippery elm (*Ulmus rubra*) to lance boils; the splinter was left in the boil, and a poultice of the inner bark was placed around the boil until it healed. The Blackfeet pulverized the bulbs of glacier lily (*Erythronium grandiflorum*) as a poultice for boils. They also used a poultice of the leaves of western mugwort (*Artemisia ludoviciana*). The Sioux crushed the leaves of yellow dock (*Rumex crispus*), an alien species, as a poultice for boils. The Navaho chewed the entire horned euphorbia plant (*Euphorbia brachyera*) and applied it to the skin.

The Rappahannock put the sap of red mulberry (*Morus rubra*) or the sap of milkweed (*Asclepias syriaca*) on the skin to cure ringworm and warts. Several Plains tribes used the crushed leaves and stems of jewelweed (*Impatiens* spp.) to cure rash and eczema. The Thompson of British Columbia applied an infusion of the entire plant of virgin's bower (*Clematis ligustifolia*) to the skin to cure rash and eczema.

As a mouthwash for canker sores and sore gums, the Ojibwa used a decoction of the roots of canker root (*Coptis groenlandica*). The Ojibwa also chewed the fruits and flowers of smooth sumac (*Rhus glabra*) to heal mouth sores. The Blackfeet used an infusion of the roots of prairie smoke (*Geum triflorum*) for canker sores and sore throat.

Colds

Sweat baths were often used to cure colds and fevers. Conifers and other plants were added to the water that was poured onto the heated rocks. Quite a number of plants were used for treating colds.

An infusion of the inner bark or roots of the various willows (*Salix* spp.) was used almost throughout North America as a treatment for colds, fevers, and coughs. The related poplars (*Populus* spp.), as noted below, were also used in the east.

Many tribes used an infusion of yarrow leaves (*Achillea* spp.) for colds and fevers. The Ojibwa also placed the leaves on hot coals and inhaled the fumes.

The leaves of wild mint (*Mentha arvensis*) and most other members of the mint family were used almost everywhere as an infusion drunk for colds.

The roots of calamus (*Acorus calamus*) were used by many tribes of the eastern Subarctic, the Plains, and the Eastern Woodlands for colds. The root was either chewed or made into a tea. The Potawatomi dried and powdered the root as a snuff for nasal congestion.

Material from coniferous trees was widely used in the Subarctic and the Eastern Woodlands to treat colds and coughs. The trees used included balsam fir, spruce, cedar, juniper, pine, hemlock, tamarack, and even the rather toxic yew. Tea was made from the resin, needles, inner bark, or branches. The branches were also used in the sweat bath, or they were burnt so the smoke could be inhaled, and the inner bark was also used as a chest poultice. Conifers in other parts of North America were used in very much the same way.

An infusion of the leaves of Labrador tea (*Ledum groenlandicum*) was sometimes used by the Ojibwa and other

Subarctic tribes as a remedy for colds. The Ojibwa also had several other remedies. A tea of wintergreen leaves (*Gaultheria procumbens*) was used as a remedy for colds. A decoction of the roots of Seneca snakeroot (*Polygala seneca*) was used for colds and coughs, and an infusion of the leaves was used for sore throat. A weak decoction of dried dogbane roots (*Apocynum androsaemifolium*) was sometimes used for colds and sore throat.

The Delaware made a tea of thimbleweed roots (*Anemone cylindrica*) to treat lung congestion.

On the Plains and Plateau, the various species of sagebrush (*Artemisia* spp.) were frequently used for colds and sore throat. The roots and leaves were chewed, or a tea was made from any part of the plant.

The Navaho chewed the roots of black root (*Lithospermum incisum*). Several tribes of the Southwest chewed the roots of canaigre (*Rumex hymenosepalus*) to treat coughs and colds, and a decoction of the root was used as a gargle for sore throat. The Pima drank a tea of elderberry flowers (*Sambucus* spp.) for colds, fever, and sore throat.

Coughs

Other plants were used primarily to relieve the coughing and sore throat associated with colds and other viral ailments. Many eastern tribes drank an infusion of the inner bark of various species of cherry (*Prunus* spp.) as a sedative for coughs. Black cherry (*P. serotina*) was used most often; this species contains more of the active ingredient, prussic acid, than other types of cherry. The infusion was also used as a gargle for sore throat. The Ojibwa drank an infusion of the leaves of staghorn sumac (*Rhus typhina*) or a decoction of sarsparilla roots (*Aralia nudicaulis*). They used a decoction of the inner bark of slippery elm (*Ulmus rubra*) as a gargle, and an infusion of the roots or bark of northern prickly ash (*Xanthoxylum americanum*) was used by the Ojibwa as a drink or gargle for sore throat.

The Ojibwa dried the entire wild bergamot plant (*Monarda fistulosa*), boiled it to extract the oil, and inhaled the fumes of the oil to relieve bronchitis. The Natchez drank an infusion of the roots of butterfly weed (*Asclepias tuberosa*), also known as pleurisy root, as a remedy for bronchitis. The Omaha chewed the roots of the same plant to relieve bronchitis and other respiratory ailments.

In California, a tea of gum plant leaves (*Grindelia* spp.) was used to treat bronchitis and whooping cough.

Fever

Other herbal remedies were used specifically to reduce fever. An infusion of the inner bark of willow or poplar, as previously mentioned, was used in many areas. A decoction of the inner bark of flowering dogwood (*Cornus florida*) was widely used in the eastern United States to reduce fever; in the nineteenth century, it was used specifically as a remedy for malaria. An infusion of the dried leaves of Joe-Pye weed (*Eupatorium purpureum*) was used in much of the eastern United States as a treatment for typhoid fever. Infusions of the roots, leaves, and stems of other species of *Eupatorium* were used to treat fever in general. The Rappahannock drank an infusion of the roots of red sassafras (*Sassafras albidum* var. *molle*) to treat fever and rash associated with measles. The Cherokee treated fever with an infusion of the leaves of feverwort (*Triosteum perfoliatum*). Many eastern tribes regarded an infusion of the roots of pitcher plant (*Sarracenia purpureum*) as a cure for smallpox fever. The Pima drank a strong decoction of sunflower leaves (*Helianthus annuus*) for fever. They also used a decoction of the entire Mormon tea plant (*Ephedra* spp.).

Stomach and intestinal problems

Calamus (*Acorus calamus*) was widely used in central and eastern North America for digestive problems; the root was chewed, or an infusion of the roots was drunk. Infusions of wild mint (*Mentha arvensis*), wild bergamot (*Monarda fistulosa*), horsemint (*Monarda punctata*), and other members of the mint family were used across North America as a cure for stomachache and intestinal gas. An infusion of the roots or berries of the various species of raspberry (*Rubus* spp.) was used across the continent as a cure for stomachache and diarrhea. Several tribes of eastern and central North America used a tea of the inner bark or roots of willow (*Salix* spp.) for stomachache. A tea of the inner bark of various species of oak (*Quercus* spp.) was widely used in the east to treat diarrhea.

The Ottawa and Ojibwa also drank a decoction of the entire geranium plant (*Geranium maculatum*) to cure diarrhea. The Ojibwa drank a decoction of red-osier dogwood stems (*Cornus stolonifera*) or an infusion of the inner bark of panicled dogwood (*C. paniculata*) as a treatment for dysentery. A decoction of the roots and flowers of Philadephia fleabane (*Erigeron philadelphicus*) was used by the Ojibwa for stomachache; the Cree used Canada fleabane (*E. canadensis*) for diarrhea. The Ojibwa, Rappahannock, and others drank a tea of dandelion roots (*Taraxacum officinale*) as a treatment for stomachache and as a diuretic, laxative, and general tonic.

The Meskwaki drank a tea of the root bark of black cherry (*Prunus serotina*) for stomach trouble and as a sedative.

The Creek and Choctaw drank the oil from boiled red cedar berries (*Juniperus virginiana*) as a cure for dysentery. The Alabama drank a tea of boneset leaves (*Eupatorium perfoliatum*) for stomachache.

The Catawba drank a tea of the roots of butterfly weed (*Asclepias tuberosa*) for dysentery.

An infusion of a small portion of the toxic blue flag root (*Iris versicolor*) was extensively used in the east, especially by the Iroquois, as a powerful cathartic and purgative.

In many parts of western North America, the roots and leaves of various types of sagebrush (*Artemisia* spp.) were chewed or made into a tea as a cure for stomachache.

In California, stomachache was treated with a tea made from the crushed roots of yerba mansa (*Anemopsis californica*).

In the Southwest, a tea made from the leaves of creosote bush (*Larrea mexicana*) was used to treat stomachache and diarrhea. A tea of mesquite leaves (*Prosopis juliaflora*) was also frequently used. Other common remedies for stomachache in the Southwest included infusions of the powdered leaves of Rocky Mountain beeweed (*Cleome serrulata*), infusions of the root of western chokecherry (*Prunus serotina* var. *virens*), infusions of manzanita leaves (*Arctostaphylos* spp.), and decoctions of the leaves of blue gilia (*Gilia longiflora*). The Pima drank a tea of elderberry flowers (*Sambucus* spp.) for stomachache, as well as for colds and fever.

Worms

The North American Indians usually killed intestinal worms by taking a vermifuge for several days, then expelled them by taking a laxative.

The Indians of Quebec steeped a small portion of the root of the poisonous blue flag (*Iris versicolor*) in water as a vermifuge.

The Ojibwa combined the roots of black cherry (*Prunus serotina*) and wild plum (*P. americana*) to make a decoction that was drunk to get rid of worms. They also used a decoction of the roots and flowers of wild bergamot (*Monarda fistulosa*).

The Penobscot used an infusion of Indian hemp roots (*Apocynum cannabinum*). The Mohegan used an infusion of blackberries (*Rubus hispidus*) or an infusion of the leaves of spearmint (*Mentha spicata*) or peppermint (*M. piperita*). The Potawatomi drank an infusion of swamp milkweed roots (*Asclepias incarnata*) to get rid of tapeworms. The Cherokee used a strong decoction of the roots of pinkroot (*Spigelia marilandica*).

A decoction of the seeds of Mexican tea (*Chenopodium ambrosioides*) was widely used to kill worms in the southeastern United States. The plant is native to Central or South America but was introduced to North America in pre-Columbian times.

Kidney and bladder problems

Many tribes across North America drank an infusion of various species of horsetail (*Equisetum* spp.) to treat kidney and bladder ailments.

A decoction of the roots of blue cohosh (*Caulophyllum thalictroides*) was used extensively in the east for urinary and genital problems in both men and women. Several eastern tribes also used a tea of the leaves of Joe-Pye weed (*Eupatorium purpureum*) or boneset (*E. perfoliatum*) to treat urinary and genital problems.

The Ojibwa made a tea from the roots and stalks of dogbane (*Apocynum androsaemifolium*) as a kidney medicine; the Potawatomi used a decoction of the green fruit as a diuretic. The Ojibwa also made a diuretic tea from the roots of slender nettle (*Urtica gracilis*) or the related wood nettle (*Boehmeria cylindrica*), and a tea from the roots and stalks of red currant (*Ribes triste*) was used as a cure for kidney stones.

The Natchez drank a tea of milkweed roots (*Asclepias* sp.) for kidney and bladder problems. The Blackfeet made a tea from Rocky Mountain juniper seeds (*Juniperus scopulorum*) or from the roots of wild black currant (*Ribes americanum*).

Several tribes of the Plateau region made a tea from bearberry leaves (*Arctostaphylos uva-ursi*).

Rheumatism

Sweat baths were very widely used as a remedy for arthritis and other forms of rheumatism, and animal grease was often rubbed on affected joints.

An infusion of the leaves or berries of wintergreen (*Gaultheria procumbens*) was used by a number of eastern tribes as a remedy for rheumatism. Willow (*Salix* spp.) and poplar (*Populus* spp.) roots and inner bark were used to a varying extent across North America, as infusions, poultices, or in the sweat bath.

The Algonquin chewed the inner bark of prickly ash (*Xanthoxylum americanum*) to make a poultice or drank a decoction of the roots. They also drank a decoction of white cedar fronds (*Thuja occidentalis*) to relieve rheumatic pains.

The Ojibwa used a decoction of the roots of balsam fir (*Abies balsamifera*) in the steambath as a treatment for rheumatism, or they drank a decoction of the branches of hemlock (*Tsuga canadensis*).

Several eastern tribes drank a tea from the twigs, needles, or roots of yew (*Taxus canadensis*), a rather poisonous plant, to treat rheumatism. The infusion was also sprinkled on hot stones in the sweat bath.

An infusion of the roots of bloodroot (*Sanguinaria canadensis*) was used by several tribes in the Mississippi region; the plant is quite toxic.

In California, a tea of yerba santa (*Eriodictyon californica*) or sagebrush leaves (*Artemisia* spp.) was used. California Indians also used the twigs of pinyon pine (*Pinus edulis*) and Douglas fir (*Pseudotsuga taxifolia*) in the sweat bath as a treatment for rheumatism.

The San Carlos Apache heated the twigs of greasewood (*Covillea tridentata*) and applied them to rheumatic joints. The Pueblo Indians baked the fruit of buffalo gourd (*Cucurbita foetidissima* and *C. digitata*) and rubbed it on the body to relieve rheumatic pains. The Maricopa heated the fresh twigs of creosote bush (*Larrea mexicana*) and applied them to parts of the body affected by rheumatism.

Toothache

In North Carolina, bad teeth were knocked out with a hammer and punch, and the Ojibwa are also reported to have struck out infected teeth. Undoubtedly other tribes did the same.

In many parts of eastern North America, the roots or crushed inner bark of prickly ash (*Xanthoxylum* spp.) was placed on aching teeth. Several eastern tribes made a decoction of the roots of goldthread (*Coptis groenlandica*) as a mouthwash for toothache as well as for sore gums and canker sores. The Meskwaki made an infusion of the root bark of panicled dogwood (*Cornus paniculata*) and held it in the mouth to ease toothache. The Meskwaki also used a decoction of geranium roots (*Geranium maculatum*) as a mouthwash for toothache and sore gums, or they put the root hairs of eastern skunk cabbage (*Spathyema foetida*) on an aching tooth. In Pennsylvania, the root bark of tulip tree (*Liriodendrum tulipifera*) was heated and placed on an aching tooth. The Alabama put a piece of goldenrod root (*Solidago* sp.) in a tooth cavity. The Miwok of California also used goldenrod; they held a decoction of it in the mouth for a few minutes, then spat it out.

The Plains tribes chewed the rootstock of calamus (*Acorus calamus*).

The Miwok of California also chewed the stems of goldback fern (*Pityrogramma triangularis*) to soothe aching teeth.

In the Southwest, the Pima heated a fresh twig of creosote bush (*Larrea mexicana*) and placed it in the cavity of an aching tooth.

Eye problems

The Eskimos protected themselves against snow blindness by wearing wooden or ivory goggles with a single horizontal slit in front of each eye.

Sore eyes were treated with various washes. Many eastern tribes used an infusion or decoction of the roots or root bark of raspberry (*Rubus* spp.) or rose (*Rosa* spp.) as a wash for sore eyes. Other popular applications in the east included an infusion of the roots or inner bark of various sorts of dogwood (*Cornus* spp.), an infusion of the roots of goldenseal (*Hydrastis canadensis*), and the raw juice of Indian pipe (*Monotropa uniflora*). The Ojibwa also put the pitch of balsam fir (*Abies balsamifera*) or a decoction of the root of a type of alumroot (*Heuchera* sp.) on sore eyes. The Potawatomi used an infusion of the inner bark of chokecherry (*Prunus virginiana*). The Illinois and Miami bathed sore eyes with an infusion of the inner bark of white oak (*Quercus alba*).

The Blackfeet used an infusion of the leaves and flowers of yarrow (*Achillea millefolium*). They also used an infusion of the roots of prairie smoke (*Geum triflorum*) or of the entire snowberry plant (*Symphoricarpus albus*). Other Plains tribes used an infusion of the leaves of Indian currant (*S. orbiculatus*).

Mesquite (*Prosopis juliaflora*) was a common remedy in the Southwest. The sap was applied directly to the eyes, or an infusion was made from the powdered leaves.

Headache

Several tribes across North America drank an infusion of the roots or inner bark of willow (*Salix* spp.), or applied poultices of the scraped and moistened inner bark to the head to cure headache. A tea of wintergreen leaves (*Gaultheria procumbens*) was a very popular eastern remedy for headache. The Ojibwa sometimes burned the needles of white pine (*Pinus strobus*) and inhaled the fumes, or crushed the needles as a poultice. They also used the needles of white cedar (*Thuja occidentalis*) or the needles and berries of eastern red cedar (*Juniperus virginiana*) as a tea, or crushed them as a poultice.

The leaves of mint (*Mentha* spp.), bergamot (*Monarda* spp.), pennyroyal (*Hedeoma* spp.), and other members of the mint family were widely used as infusions for headache.

The Montagnais crushed the leaves of common buttercup (*Ranunculus acris*) and inhaled the fumes. The Meskwaki drank a tea made from the roots of thimbleweed (*Anemone cylindrica*), another member of the buttercup family, to relieve headache.

The Pawnee crushed the roots (corms) of Jack-in-the-pulpit (*Arisaema triphyllum*) as a poultice applied to the temples to relieve headache.

A tea of mesquite leaves (*Prosopis juliaflora*) was often used in the Southwest.

Insect bites

To ward off insects, many Indians used an application of bear grease on the skin. The Subarctic Indians used human urine as a "shampoo" to get rid of lice.

Indians of the Subarctic burned sphagnum moss (*Sphagnum* spp.), rock tripe (*Umbilicaria* and *Gyrophora* spp.), anemone (*Anemone* spp.), and other plants to keep biting insects away. The Cree burned dried Canada fleabane (*Erigeron canadensis*) to get rid of fleas and gnats. The Ojibwa used the leaves of plantain (*Plantago major*) as a poultice for bee stings, and they used the leaves of yarrow (*Achillea millefolium*) as a poultice on spider bites.

In the Eastern Woodlands, the Rappahannock kept dried pennyroyal leaves (*Hedeoma pulegioides*) in the house to repel fleas. The Cherokee crushed the roots of goldenseal (*Hydrastis canadensis*), mixed them with bear fat, and spread the mixture on their skin as an insect repellent.

The Blackfeet crushed the flowers of pineapple weed (*Matricaria matricarioides*) to repel insects.

In the west, various types of sagebrush (*Artemisia* spp.) were scattered on the ground or burned as insect repellents.

California Indians crushed the leaves of California laurel (*Umbellaria californica*) and spread them on the ground to repel fleas.

Indians of the Southwest rubbed onions (*Allium* spp.) on the skin to repel insects, and the leaves of Rocky Mountain beeweed (*Cleome serrulata*) were crushed as a poultice for insect bites.

Snakebite

Some tribes treated snakebite by sucking the bite and applying a tourniquet: the technique was similar to that used in first-aid nowadays. Poultices were also applied to the bite.

As poultices for snakebite, the Ojibwa used the crushed fresh roots of rattlesnake fern (*Botrychium virginianum*), the crushed roots of sanicle (*Sanicula marilandica*), or the chewed leaves of boneset (*Eupatorium perfoliatum*).

The Rappahannock and other tribes made a poultice from the mashed roots of Virginia snakeroot (*Aristolochia serpentaria*), probably the most famous of the various "snakeroots." The Rappahannock also used the bruised leaves of butterfly weed (*Asclepias tuberosa*). The Seneca chewed the roots of Seneca snakeroot (*Polygala senega*) and applied them as a poultice. The chewed roots of button snakeroot (*Eryngium yuccifolium*) were also used as a poultice in the eastern United States. The Potawatomi used rattlesnake plantain (*Goodyera repens*); they chewed the leaves, swallowing the juice, and then applied the leaves as a poultice.

The Plains Indians drank a decoction of their panacea, calamus (*Acorus calamus*), as a cure for snakebite.

The Hopi used bladderpod (*Lesquerellia fendleri*) for snakebite; they chewed the root, swallowed some of the juice, and then used the root as a poultice.

Menstruation

Menstrual pads were made from pieces of tanned hide, cattail fluff, sagebrush leaves, or the shredded inner bark of willow. Massage was used across North America as a remedy for menstrual cramps.

Women of several eastern tribes drank a strong decoction of the roots of blue cohosh (*Caulophyllum thalictroides*) to control excessive menstrual flow and to relieve menstrual cramps.

The Ojibwa drank an infusion of the roots of black cohosh (*Cicimifuga racemosa*) to cure excessive menstrual flow. For stopped menstrual flow, they drank an infusion of the powdered root of Canada snakeroot (*Sanicula canadensis*). To treat irregular menstruation, they used a decoction of the roots of wild sarsparilla (*Aralia nudicaulis*).

The Algonquin and Cree drank a tea made from the leaves of spotted Joe-Pye weed (*Eupatorium maculatum*) to cure irregular menstruation. Menominee women drank an infusion of the grated roots of the large-flowered trillium (*Trillium grandiflorum*) to cure irregular menstruation and cramps. The Menominee, as well as the Algonquin, also drank a tea of the inner bark of white cedar (*Thuja occidentalis*) for menstrual problems. The Rappahannock used a tea of dried pennyroyal leaves (*Hedeoma pulegioides*) for menstrual cramps, and they used a tea of the split twigs of spicebush (*Lindera benzoin*) for cramps and delayed menstruation. The Cree drank a tea of skullcap leaves (*Scutellaria laterifolia*) to treat delayed menstruation. The Catawba used an infusion of tansy leaves (*Tanacetum vulgare*) to promote menstruation.

Several Plains tribes used a tea of the roots or leaves of various types of sagebrush (*Artemisia* spp.) to treat menstrual problems, though the same infusions were also used as abortifacients.

Childbirth

Massage and pressure on the abdomen were widely used to help childbirth.

The Cree drank an infusion of the mashed above-ground parts of painted trillium (*Trillium undulatum*) to speed delivery.

The Ojibwa used both the leaves and the roots of pitcher plant (*Sarracenia purpurea*) to make a tea that was drunk for several weeks to make childbirth easier, but it was considered strong and dangerous to use.

The Potawatomi drank an infusion of the roots of blue cohosh (*Caulophyllum thalictroides*) to ease childbirth.

The Cherokee drank an infusion of the inner bark of black cherry (*Prunus serotina*) to ease the pain of childbirth, and the Arikara drank the juice of black western chokecherry (*P. melanocarpa*) to stop bleeding after delivery.

The Zuñi mixed a very small amount of corn smut (*Ustilago zeae*) in water and drank it from time to time to speed delivery. Corn smut is a small black fungus that grows on ears of maize; its active ingredient, ustilagine, has been shown to promote uterine contractions.

Transportation

Before the introduction of horses by the Spanish, overland travel was generally on foot. Sleds and toboggans were used to a slight extent for carrying people, but they were principally used for carrying goods. The aboriginal sled, pulled by hand or by dogs over the hard Arctic snow, was a very simple affair, merely a few boards joined by rawhide thongs and perhaps mortised to another two boards used as runners; the built-up sled with side rails was introduced from Siberia only in the eighteenth century. The toboggan, a flat-bottomed device, was used on the softer snow of the Subarctic forest. Snowshoes were also typical of the Subarctic forest. On the Plains, the principal carrying device was the travois, a pair of crossed poles with a ladder- or web-like platform, pulled by a dog. On the Plains, as in many other areas, goods were also packed directly on the backs of dogs.

Travel by water was generally easier than overland travel. Arctic hunters used kayaks on the rivers and oceans, and the larger open-hulled umiaks were used for transporting goods or large numbers of people, as well as for hunting walruses and whales. Throughout the Subarctic and in parts of the Eastern Woodlands, the principal means of transportation in the summer was the birch-bark canoe, and further south canoes were sometimes made with other types of bark. Along the Northwest Coast and along many other parts of the North American coastline, boats were carved out of solid logs. The bull boat, made of buffalo hide on a hemispherical framework, was occasionally used by the Plains Indians. Boats made of bound rushes were used in parts of the southwestern United States and further south.

Toboggans

Toboggans were used primarily by the Indians of the eastern Subarctic. One or two fairly knot-free logs of birch

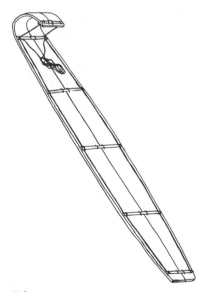

Toboggan

or spruce were split to yield two boards, each of which was not much more than six inches wide and an inch thick, but which might be twelve or more feet long. The boards were trimmed down so that they were only about half an inch thick, and one edge of each board was trimmed as straight as possible, so that the two boards could be placed together. The two outer edges were curved, so that the toboggan was widest about halfway along.

Some toboggans were made with a single board, but two boards gave greater flexibility.

The boards were joined together with four or five widely spaced crossbars made of split sticks. Rawhide thongs passed over each crossbar and through pairs of holes drilled in the boards. A slight groove was cut into the underside of each pair of holes to countersink the thong and thus prevent it from rubbing against the snow. Each crossbar was fastened to four pairs of holes: one at the outer edge of each board, and one at each inner edge. Sometimes two crossbars were used at the very front of the toboggan, one on each side of the boards, and these two crossbars were bound to each other through the paired holes. The boards might also be sewn directly to each other in several places, particularly at the front of the toboggan.

The front of the toboggan was steamed and bent upwards, and the curve was maintained by a strong rawhide thong or a twisted sinew cord fastened from each end of the first crossbar to each end of the second crossbar.

A thong also ran along each side of the toboggan. The crossbars had a notch cut into the underside of each end, allowing the thong to pass the entire length of the toboggan from the second crossbar to the last. When the toboggan was loaded, the lashing could be fastened to these side thongs.

A final thong, used for pulling the toboggan, was also fastened to both ends of the second crossbar. Toboggans were sometimes pulled by dogs, but in prehistoric times an Indian rarely owned more than three or four dogs.

Snowshoes

Snowshoes seem to have developed in northern Asia several thousand years ago and to have spread both west and east. The earliest snowshoes were crude oval or circular forms. Some were made of slabs of wood and later evolved into skis in the Old World. Others were made of twigs bent into a circle or oval, roughly filled with lacing of rawhide or inner bark. But most of the refinements in laced snowshoes (as opposed to all-wood forms) were made in North America, primarily by northern Athapaskans. Snowshoes were vitally important in making it possible to inhabit the northern forests. In the hard windpacked snow of Eskimo country, however, such devices were unnecessary.

Frames.   The most useful classification of snowshoes is based on the type of frame. There were five major types: the bearpaw, the familiar one-piece with pointed heel, the Naskapi two-piece (spliced at each side), the two-piece frame with pointed toe, and the two-piece frame (up to six feet long) with a spliced rounded toe.

The frames of crude bearpaws were made by bending any sort of twig into shape, but the better types of snowshoe frames were made by splitting a sapling of willow, birch, ash, hickory, or other wood into quarters. Each quarter had the heartwood cut away. The wood was trimmed to a rectangular cross-section, steamed, bent, and tied in shape. Where necessary, holes were drilled for the lacing.

Crossbars.   Except for the simplest bearpaws, snowshoes had between one and seven crossbars for reinforcement. Sometimes the crossbar was tied to the frame. Sometimes the end of the crossbar was split, and each half of the split was bent to fit against the frame, to which it was then fastened. But all of the more advanced types had mortised crossbars; a rectangular hole was cut into the frame, and the end of the crossbar (perhaps slightly narrowed) was fitted into this hole.

Netting material.   The netting on finer snowshoes was usually made from rawhide (sometimes greased), though buckskin, sinew, and intestines were occasionally used. Inner bark and other plant materials were sometimes used on cruder types.

Netting techniques.   Crude bearpaw snowshoes often used no particular netting technique. *Rectangular weave* was sometimes the only type of weave used on cruder snowshoes, while on more advanced types it usually formed the middle portion of the snowshoe. *Hexagonal weave*, created by the intersection of three groups of parallel strands, was mainly used in the toe and heel portions.

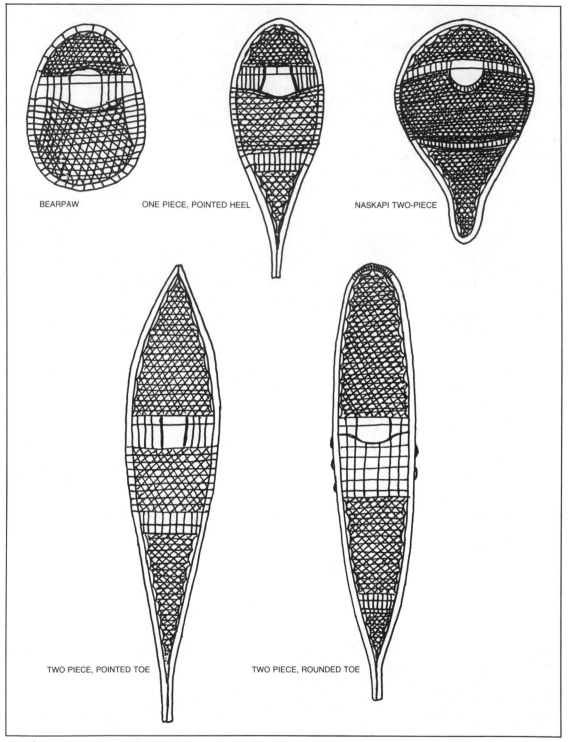

BEARPAW   ONE PIECE, POINTED HEEL   NASKAPI TWO-PIECE

TWO PIECE, POINTED TOE   TWO PIECE, ROUNDED TOE

Snowshoes

Attachment of netting. The netting was attached to the frame by one of three methods. Sometimes the netting was *wrapped* around the frame. On crude bearpaws this was generally the case, while on advanced types this method was mainly used for the rectangular weave around the central portion.

A second method was *reeving*: holes were drilled through the frame, and the netting was "sewn" through these holes. *Selvage thongs* were commonly used for the toe and heel spaces. Holes were drilled as for the reeving method, a thong (often countersunk) was run in and out through these holes, and the main netting was then fastened to the selvage thong.

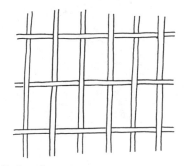

Rectangular weave

Wrapped netting

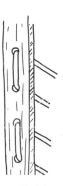

Reeving

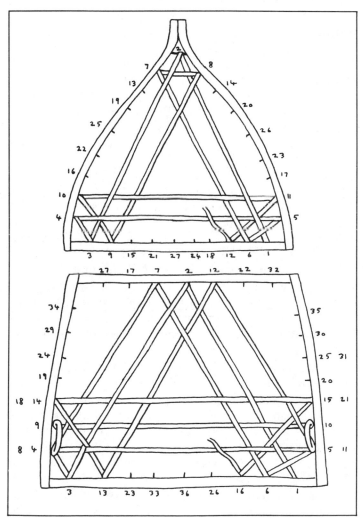

Hexagonal weave

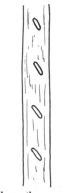

Selvage thongs

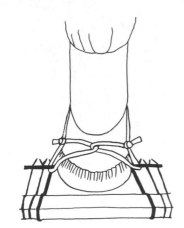

Snowshoe harness

Other traits. Athapaskan snowshoes, in particular, included a number of other advanced traits. All Athapaskan snowshoes, for example, had a toe hole. The ball of the foot was placed on a heavy thong forming the back of the toe hole, and the foot was fastened in such a way that the heel of the snowshoe dragged on the snow, whereas cruder types of snowshoe were fastened more securely to the foot and were lifted completely from the ground like a shoe. Many snowshoes also had an upturned toe to prevent the snowshoe from digging into the snow. Netting was generally used in the toe and heel portions of Athapaskan snowshoes, whereas in cruder forms this was omitted.

All snowshoes required some sort of harness to fasten them to the foot. A common form is shown.

Kayaks

Across most of the Arctic, the hunter's principal means of transportation was the kayak, a slender craft distinguished by a skin covering that enclosed the entire framework except for the cockpit. The framework consisted of gunwales, crossbeams, ribs (frames), stringers (between three and eleven, including a central one that might be regarded as a keelson), a cockpit rim, deck battens, and usually an end-piece—which might take any of several different forms—at bow and stern. The main strength of the kayak lay in its gunwales, the heaviest parts of the vessel.

Most parts were made out of driftwood logs of any sort, preferably found with the bark still on, indicating that they were not decomposed. The logs were carefully split, chipped, sawn, and drilled into shape. The ribs might be made from strips of cedar, or they might be cut from small live willows, preferably slightly crushed to make them more flexible. The cockpit rim was made of a bent strip of wood or whalebone.

Kayaks were made in many styles, depending partly on the environment in which they were to be used. Some kayaks were very narrow, designed for speed at the possible expense of stability. Others were relatively broad, designed for travel on the heavy waves of the open sea. Kayaks ranged up to three feet in width, but most were about one and a half feet wide and about eight inches deep. They were between about ten and thirty feet long, though the average length was somewhere between fifteen and twenty feet. Some kayaks were designed primarily to be light in weight, so that they could be easily hauled over

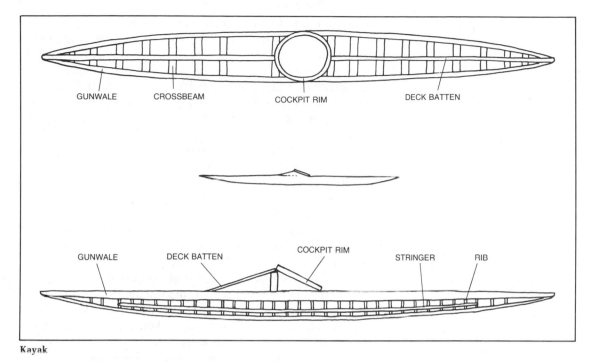

GUNWALE   CROSSBEAM   COCKPIT RIM   DECK BATTEN

GUNWALE   DECK BATTEN   COCKPIT RIM   STRINGER   RIB

Kayak

ice floes. Greenland kayaks often had V-shaped bottoms, many other eastern kayaks had quite flat bottoms, while western kayaks had bottoms that were nearly round in cross-section (actually multi-chined). But compared to other types of boat, all kayaks were slender and streamlined, since they were designed primarily for speed in the hunt.

Assembly.   Several techniques and materials were used to connect the parts of the kayak. Holes were drilled all along the lower edge of the gunwales for the later insertion of the ribs, and mortise slots were cut into the inner sides for the insertion of the crossbeams. Most parts were held together by cord made of baleen, rawhide, or braided sinew, passing through holes drilled near the joints; the pairs of holes were countersunk on the outside to prevent abrasion of the cord. A single length of cord might be knotted around several joints, one after another. Holes were also drilled at an angle through certain joints for the insertion of treenails made of well-dried strips of antler, bone, or wood. A few parts might be joined with a glue of rotten caribou blood, heated with burning splints after the parts were pressed together.

The gunwales were joined together at the ends, together with the end-pieces, if any. The gunwales were then spread apart, and the crossbeams were inserted. In most kayaks, one of the middle crossbeams was angular or rounded rather than straight, and the front of the cockpit rim was fastened to this beam so that the rim slanted downwards from front to back. Sometimes the rim was fastened to the rest of the framework at this stage, but in other types of kayak the rim was fastened to the outside of the cover, as almost a final step in the assembly, rather than to the framework. The two battens were then fastened on, one running from cockpit to bow and the other from cockpit to stern.

The kayak was then turned upside down and placed on supports. The ribs were steamed, bent, and inserted into the holes in the bottom of the gunwales, and either lashed or nailed. The stringers were then sewn and tied in place.

The cover consisted of seal skins (caribou skins were often used in the central Arctic) sewn together to form a single sheet, using a double waterproof stitch known as a "blind stitch." The sheet was soaked and pulled tightly under and over the framework and fastened with a less delicate seam running from cockpit to bow and from cockpit to stern. If the cockpit rim had been previously attached to the framework, the cover was now laced to the top of the rim; otherwise, the cover was now fastened along the bottom edge of the rim, which remained attached to the rest of the framework.

When the cover had dried and shrunk, a caulking mixture of clay and fish oil was applied to the seams, and the entire bottom was smeared with seal or fish oil, to be renewed periodically. The kayak was then ready to be put into the water. The paddler often wore either a waistband or a jacket designed to be waterproof (sewn strips of seal intestine were commonly used), fastened to the cockpit rim with a drawstring. A single-bladed paddle was often used in Alaska. Elsewhere a double-bladed paddle, between seven and twelve feet long, was more common; the two blades were parallel, not feathered like most modern paddles.

The Ojibwa birch-bark canoe

At the risk of a slight exaggeration, it could be said that a kayak was a frame to which a cover was fitted, and a bark canoe was a cover to which a frame was fitted.

The birch-bark canoe was a craft made from materials that were always available in the Subarctic forest: birch bark (*Betula papyrifera*) for the cover, white cedar (*Thuja occidentalis*) or spruce wood (usually black spruce, *Picea mariana*) for the frame (though cedar was preferred), and conifer roots to hold it all together. The canoe was light enough to be portaged around rapids or from one watershed to another, yet durable enough to last for several years with proper care—though, to ensure its longevity, paddlers embarked and disembarked while the canoe was well afloat. Like kayaks, canoes varied in length from about ten feet to over thirty feet, even in pre-voyageur days. But canoes were broader craft, averaging about three feet in width and about a foot in depth. Bow and stern were often identical, but sometimes the bow was distinguished by a slightly greater width and by the way the bark overlapped. Canoes were propelled with single-bladed paddles between four and six feet long.

The making of a canoe involved two stages: (1) cutting and bending and (2) assembly. Usually all the parts were cut and bent to shape before the assembly began, but some people preferred assembling some of the parts before other parts had been finished.

Below is a description of a typical sequence of steps in the making of an Ojibwa canoe. Ojibwa canoes were slightly more elaborate than most other types, but they serve to illustrate the parts and the assembly techniques typical of most bark canoes.

Ojibwa canoes consisted of bark, roots, ribs, sheathing, gunwales, thwarts, end-pieces, and headboards. In addition, a "false frame" was required for molding the bark into shape before the gunwales and other parts had been added.

Most wooden parts were made from cedar logs that were first split *perpendicular* to the growth rings and the bark, beginning at the narrow (top) end of the log, to form quarters. Each quarter was then split in half *parallel* to the growth rings. Each of these halves was in turn split in half *parallel* to the growth rings, and so on. The end-pieces were made in a slightly different manner, as described below.

Particularly in the far north, cedar might be unavailable, and so spruce would be used throughout. In that case, parts were sometimes made with all the splitting done perpendicular to the growth rings.

Bark. The bark was cut, usually in the springtime, from the trunks of large, carefully selected birch trees. The bark had to be thick, it had to have few "eyes," the individual

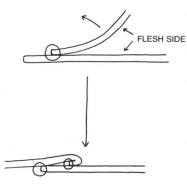

FLESH SIDE

Blind stitch

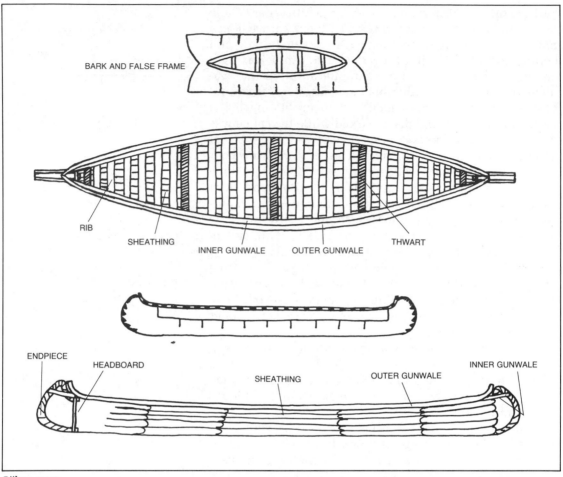

BARK AND FALSE FRAME

RIB

SHEATHING   INNER GUNWALE   OUTER GUNWALE   THWART

ENDPIECE

HEADBOARD

SHEATHING

OUTER GUNWALE

INNER GUNWALE

Ojibwa canoe

layers had to cohere well, and the entire bark had to peel readily from the tree. In the far north, where trees do not grow as large, seven or eight trees might be needed to supply enough bark for a canoe; in that case, most of the pieces would be sewn together before the rest of the assembly was begun. Around the Great Lakes, a single tree might supply enough bark for a canoe, though some people felt that several smaller pieces provided greater versatility in forming the cover.

A ladder or scaffolding was used for removing the bark, though in historical times the tree would be felled. A single vertical cut was made in the bark, and two horizontal cuts were made around the tree, as far apart as necessary to supply the requisite length. A large chisel-ended pole was used to pry the bark free.

Winter bark was said to be stronger, but to remove it

one might have to cut down the tree and pour boiling water on the bark, or carefully light a fire underneath it. A period of thaw might make the task easier.

The bark was rolled up lengthwise and inside out and carried back to the work site. The inside of the bark would become the outside of the canoe.

Roots. Many yards of conifer roots were required to fasten the canoe together. The roots of black spruce, white spruce, tamarack, or jack pine were used, though sometimes the peeled roots of willow (not a conifer) were used instead. They were cut near the trunk and pulled out of the ground, rolled up, and brought back to camp. There they were soaked for a few hours, the bark was pulled off, and they were split into halves or quarters. A bone awl was originally used to punch holes in the bark for the insertion of the roots. No knots were used in sewing; instead, the ends of the root were simply tucked under the first or last few turns.

Ribs. Logs about four or five feet long and up to a foot thick were required for the ribs. The logs were quartered, then split perpendicular to the growth rings into half-inch-thick slabs. They were trimmed until they were about a quarter of an inch thick, two inches wide, and of various lengths. They might be tapered in width and thickness at the ends. They were placed under water for at least three days. After they were removed, they were gathered into bundles of six or more, bent into a semicircle, and tied in that shape until they dried.

Sheathing. The sheathing, which ran longitudinally between the ribs and the bark, was made from cedar logs split into quarters and then split parallel to the growth rings to form thin slabs. Sheathing could be somewhat irregular in form, since the pieces could be arranged in any manner that would present a fairly uniform layer, but usually the majority of pieces were about an eighth of an inch thick, two or three inches wide, and about five to seven feet long.

Gunwales. Logs slightly longer than the finished canoe were quartered and further split for the gunwales. These pieces were trimmed to a little over an inch in width and thickness. Some Ojibwa canoes had only inner and outer gunwales, while others also had a "cap" that covered the two lower gunwales. Inner gunwales were usually bevelled underneath to allow the tops of the ribs to be jammed between them and the bark. Gunwales were also sometimes made of peeled whole saplings rather than split logs. If the gunwales were meant to be sharply upturned at bow and stern, their ends might be split into laminations.

Thwarts.   Ojibwa canoes had from four to seven thwarts, depending on the length of the canoe, though five was the usual number. Often a pair of vertical holes was drilled near each end of a thwart, so that it could be sewn into place. Thwarts were sometimes made of a tougher wood, such as birch.

End-pieces.   The end-pieces of Ojibwa canoes were made from four-foot cedar logs split perpendicular to the growth rings to form quarters, as usual, then split once or twice more in roughly the same direction to form boards, which were trimmed to a rectangular cross-section of about half an inch by three inches. Each board was split down the middle for three feet, parallel to the growth rings, then split into quarters, and so on, until each end-piece consisted of about sixteen parallel splints united at one end. The end-pieces were weighted down underwater and left to soak overnight.

Headboards.   The headboards, which held the end-pieces and gunwales together, were carved from boards about an inch thick, four inches wide, and two feet long. Ojibwa headboards had a lower slot to hold the bottom of the end-piece, a slot in each upper side to hold the gunwales, and a square hole in the upper center to hold the top of the end-piece.

When the end-pieces were removed from the water, they were bent into shape and tied with a spiral binding of bark (e.g. basswood bark), then inserted into the headboards.

False frame.   The false frame was made of two poles or boards held apart by thwart-like spreaders. This frame was about a foot shorter than the assembled gunwales and about six inches narrower. There were three pairs of holes in the false frame to support six stakes, each of which was notched near the top to provide support for the gunwales.

The false frame and its stakes were permanent equipment, used to assemble any number of canoes. Poles of various sizes were also required for assembly.

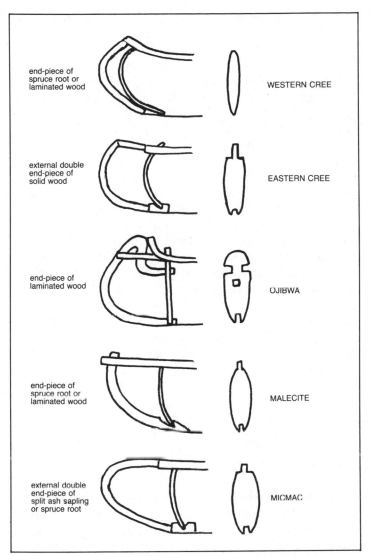

end-piece of spruce root or laminated wood — WESTERN CREE

external double end-piece of solid wood — EASTERN CREE

end-piece of laminated wood — OJIBWA

end-piece of spruce root or laminated wood — MALECITE

external double end-piece of split ash sapling or spruce root — MICMAC

End pieces and headboards

Assembly.   The canoe was usually assembled in the shade or on a cloudy day, so that the bark would not dry out too quickly, and water was sprinkled over the bark from time to time to retard drying.

The building bed was prepared by removing stones and debris from the ground. The false frame was put on the ground, and a dozen or more poles, each three or four feet long, were planted in the ground around the frame, a few inches from its edge. Now that the post holes were established, the posts and the frame were removed, and the bark was put on the ground upside down. The false frame was put on top of the bark and weighted down with rocks. The sides of the bark were turned up, and the posts were replaced in their holes.

Slits (gores) about nine inches long and about a foot apart were cut in the edges of the bark to help form it.

To further aid in the molding of the bark, a few horizontal poles were placed between the bark and the vertical posts. Shorter vertical poles were wedged between the false frame and the inside of the bark and tied to the outer poles.

Beginning at the center of either side of the canoe, the slits were overlapped slightly and sewn up with a spiral stitch. (The edges of the bark were an inch or more from the seam, rather than contained within the stitches.) If necessary, more sheets of bark were sewn to the tops of the sides, or to bow or stern, perhaps with a double running stitch. High pieces always overlapped lower pieces, and pieces nearer the bow overlapped pieces nearer the stern.

The inner gunwales were fastened to the end-pieces and headboards. The six notched stakes were placed in their holes in the false frame, and the inner gunwales were temporarily bound to these stakes. The top edges of the bark were trimmed to shape, with enough bark left so that it could be folded over the inner gunwale toward the inside of the canoe. Bark and inner gunwales were temporarily sewn together. The ends of the bark were trimmed and temporarily sewn to the end-pieces. The outer gunwales and the gunwale caps were temporarily sewn to the inner gunwales and the bark.

All the gunwales were now forced apart in the middle with temporary spreaders. Mortise slots were cut all the way through the inner gunwales, and the permanent thwarts were inserted into these mortises and perhaps also sewn into place.

Final adjustments were made to the shape of the bark. The top edges of the bark were permanently sewn to the gunwales with a spiral stitch, though spaces were left in the binding every few inches so that the ribs could later be inserted between the inner gunwales and the bark. The ends of the bark were permanently sewn to the end-pieces with a long-and-short stitch or a cross stitch.

The false frame could now be lifted out of the canoe, and the boat was suspended a few inches above the ground by ropes tied to six poles planted in the ground. The ribs were temporarily placed in the canoe, marked, removed, and cut to their proper lengths, with room allowed for sheathing.

The insides of the seams were coated with melted pitch, mixed with a little grease to make it less brittle when it dried, and usually also mixed with a little charcoal.

The sheathing was now put in place all over the inside of the canoe except right at the bow and stern. The ends of the pieces overlapped slightly. A few temporary ribs held the sheathing in place while the permanent ribs were hammered in with a punch and mallet, beginning at each end of the canoe. A space of two or three inches was left between each rib.

The canoe was removed from its suspension ropes, the outside of the seams was pitched, and the canoe was left to dry. When it was put into the water, a few leaks would undoubtedly appear, and these would be marked and patched before the canoe was put to use.

Other bark canoes

No prehistoric bark canoes have survived, but vague reports of canoes with bark covers and wooden ribs date back to the early sixteenth century. The overall similarity of construction methods from one side of the continent to the other in historical times suggests that prehistoric canoes were not much different from more recent ones, though construction must have been slower in the days of stone tools.

Gores and panels were sewn together either overlapping or edge-to-edge, but at bow and stern the bark was sewn face-to-face.

If the gores and panels were overlapping, as in Ojibwa canoes, the running stitch and the spiral stitch were commonly used. The running stitch might be made with two thongs, each passing through the same holes but from opposite sides of the bark. Near the middle of the canoe, where the ribs exerted greater pressure, the spiral stitch might again be used, but the stitches would be slanted and closer together.

If, on the other hand, the gores and panels were sewn edge-to-edge, as in many northern canoes, the spiral stitch was again used, but over the bark was placed a batten, consisting of a root or twig split in half. The gores themselves were made by cutting out triangular sections rather than simply slitting the bark.

A spiral stitch was used to fasten the top edge of the

RUNNING STITCH

HARNESS STITCH
(DOUBLE THONG RUNNING STITCH)

SPIRAL STITCH (TWO FORMS)

Stitches for birch bark

SPIRAL STITCH WITH BATTEN

LONG-AND-SHORT STITCH

CROSS STITCH (TWO FORMS)

Stitches for birch bark

bark to the gunwales; sometimes both ends of the thong were used at once, but from opposite sides, resulting in something like an upside-down cross stitch. The stitching might run all along the gunwale, or it might stop where each rib was to be inserted.

At bow and stern, the long-and-short stitch and the cross stitch were commonly used to fasten the bark and end-pieces together. If the end-piece consisted of a single carved board, a series of holes might be drilled through it, so that the bark could be sewn to both sides with a double running stitch.

The different types of canoe were distinguished mainly by the shape of the bow and stern, which in turn was determined by the shape of the end-pieces. Some Ojibwa canoes had great hook-like ends, Micmac canoes had low round ends, while most other types had end-pieces rising in a more modest curve toward the ends of the gunwales. Some end-pieces were formed from a bent piece of solid wood rather than from bent laminations, and bent roots were frequently used. Other end-pieces, as previously mentioned, consisted of a wide board cut to a slight curve and fitted edge-on. Not all canoes had headboards. Eastern Cree canoes were distinguished partly by the fact that instead of having a single internal end-piece at each end, they had double solid-wood end-pieces, sewn onto the outside of the bark; the headboard was independent of the end-pieces, and, as in Micmac canoes, it sat on a frog, a small notched piece of wood. (Also, while most canoe bottoms were fairly straight from bow to stern, Eastern Cree canoes had "rocker" bottoms, suitable for turning quickly in rapids.) Often the space behind the headboard was packed with wood shavings or moss.

Virtually all birch-bark canoes consisted of gunwales, thwarts, ribs, sheathing, and end-pieces, fitted into a bark covering. Gunwales varied considerably, however. Some canoes had only inner gunwales, some had inner gunwales and caps, some had inner and outer gunwales, and some had inner and outer gunwales as well as caps.

Canoes of the Maritimes were distinguished by the fact that no false frame was used. Instead, the gunwales and thwarts were fitted together beforehand and used as a building frame. When the bark had been cut and sewn, the frame was raised, placed on stakes that stood on the bark, and sewn to the edge of the bark. Canoes built without the use of a false frame had rather long and wide bottoms, and the sides of the canoe had to curve in sharply at the top.

Some very unusual types of bark canoe were built on the perimeter of the real "canoe country," i.e. the eastern Subarctic. In the far north, some canoe frames resembled those of kayaks, and some northern canoes even had coverings of skin, perhaps the result of Eskimo influence or the scarcity of large birch trees. South of the Subarctic, canoes were made from the bark of spruce, pine, elm, and probably other kinds of trees, and some of these vessels had rather crude frameworks.

Dugouts

Dugouts were much simpler than canoes or kayaks in their manner of construction. The basic process involved cutting down a tree (driftwood logs were also used) and trimming it to shape by alternately burning and chopping. The red-cedar canoes of the Northwest Coast, however, were first adzed to shape on the outside, and the inside was then cut into blocks that were split out; no fire was used to remove the wood. Holes were drilled from the outside, and pegs were inserted. When the worker cut down to the pegs on the inside, he knew he had hollowed the inside to the right thickness. Northwest Coast canoes were also spread in the center to increase width and stability. To make the wood flexible enough for spreading, water and urine were poured in, and heated rocks were added to the mixture. Water was also sprinkled over the top of the canoe, and a torch was used to heat the bottom. The sides of the canoe were then pulled apart, temporary spreaders were inserted, and the permanent thwarts were sewn into mortise holes with cedar withes. Separately carved prow and stern pieces were pegged and sewn into place. Seats were also pegged into place.

Fire

The North American Indians had two general methods for starting a fire: by using a wooden fire set consisting primarily or solely of a shaft and hearth, and by striking two pieces of flint, quartz, or pyrite together.

Wooden fire-sets

There were three types of wooden fire-sets: the two-piece set, the four-piece set, and the far less common pump-drill set. Fire sets of all types were very similar to drills used for boring holes, though the latter had a stone bit set in the bottom of the shaft, somewhat in the manner of an arrowhead (and, of course, no hearth was used). It is interesting to speculate on whether these devices were first used for making holes or first for used making fires.

The two-piece set. In most of North America, fire was made with a simple two-piece set. It had a wooden shaft approximately as thick as a finger and from one to three feet long. Often the shaft was slightly thicker in the center than towards the ends. The lower end of the shaft was rounded, and it fitted into a cavity in the hearth, which was a wooden board or rod placed flat on the ground.

The cavity might be dug no more than a quarter of an inch deep, since the shaft would soon deepen it, and it was usually made a fraction of an inch from one edge of the hearth. A notch, usually deeper than the cavity, was dug from the edge of the hearth to the cavity, and it often extended right to the center of the cavity. The notch might be a horizontal groove, or it might run almost straight downward.

Tinder was prepared and placed beside the notch, and often a few grains of sand and charcoal were dropped into the cavity. The right foot or knee was placed on the hearth to hold it steady, and the shaft was placed in the cavity.

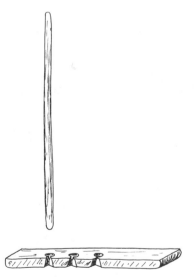

Two-piece fire set

The hands were placed flat and parallel on each side of the top of the shaft, and the shaft was twirled in a rapid alternating motion. The hands gradually slid down to the bottom, so they were brought to the top again as quickly as possible, and the drilling was repeated.

Whenever the hands rose to the top, the shaft was not in motion, and the drill and hearth cooled slightly, delaying progress. To avoid this problem, two or three people often worked the shaft at the same time. As one person's hands reached the bottom, another person put his hands at the top and took over the drilling.

If the cavity and its notch had not been properly cut, a ring of brown "sawdust" would accumulate around the cavity. If, on the other hand, they had been cut to the right shape, a lump of black, almost sticky "soot" would start to accumulate in the notch, or on the ground just below it. That is why the notch, cut deeper than the cavity, was so important: the powdered wood fell through the bottom of the cavity and accumulated in one small spot, thus retaining the heat rather than dispersing it.

As the black dust accumulated—perhaps only seconds after the start of the drilling—a wisp of smoke began to rise. But this thin stream of smoke was not sufficient. If the drilling were stopped at this point, the smoke would cease rising. Instead, the drilling was continued, perhaps harder and faster than before. At some point, the wisp of smoke would suddenly turn into a strong cloud of smoke. A change had taken place: the thick cloud of smoke came not from the friction of the drill and the cavity, but from combustion within the lump of black dust.

When the worker was sure that the dust was ignited, he stopped drilling and fanned the dust and tinder gently, or blew on them, to supply more air. The dust and tinder burst into flame, and the tinder was quickly but carefully placed under a waiting "tipi" of small twigs.

So far three combustible materials had been used: wood dust, tinder, and twigs. When the twigs were well aflame, slightly larger twigs were laid on, and larger pieces were gradually added on top of these. If the fuel were added too quickly, though, the heat would be dispersed through the cold wood and the fire would go out, so more fuel was added only when the previous fuel was burning steadily.

The four-piece set.   In the Arctic, in central Canada, and to a lesser extent in more southern areas, the fire kit consisted of four parts: a shaft, a hearth, a bow, and a socket.

The hearth was similar to that used in the two-piece set. The shaft, however, was somewhat shorter and thicker, the top was cut to a point, and sometimes the cross-section was slightly angular in order to provide a better grip for the thong. The bow consisted of a slightly curved piece of wood, ivory, or antler, with a rather loosely fitting thong of plant or animal fiber tied to both ends. The bow was sometimes flexible, but it did not need to be, since tension on the thong was maintained principally by the right hand. The socket was usually a small square piece of wood, bone, or stone with a slight cavity in the bottom, though the Eskimos sometimes used a slightly longer piece of wood with the actual stone socket neatly inset into the center.

The thong was coiled once or twice around the shaft, in such a way that the coil was to the left of the rest of the thong, and the top of the coil pointed toward the hand holding the bow. The bottom of the shaft was set into the cavity on the hearth, and the top of the shaft fitted into the cavity under the socket, which was held in the left hand.

The left hand pressed lightly on the socket, forcing the shaft downwards, and the right hand pulled the bow back and forth. The shaft rotated with an alternating motion, as did the shaft in the two-piece set, but the bow made the work much faster with less effort, and even a lone worker was able to finish the work without pausing.

Eskimo four-piece sets included some peculiar variations. In many cases the socket was designed to be held in the mouth; the socket might be crescent-shaped, but with a flat projection, meant to be gripped by the teeth, on the concave side. Sockets of this type left one hand free to hold the hearth (or, if the drill was intended to bore holes, one hand was left free to hold the material being pierced). What was more peculiar about Eskimo four-piece sets was the shape of the cavity in the hearth. In some cases the cavity and the notch resembled those in sets from other regions, but a shelf was cut along the side of the hearth, and the burning dust fell from the notch onto this shelf rather than onto the snow. Many hearths, however, had cavities in the center of the hearth rather than toward one edge. The usual notch was omitted, and instead there might be a groove running partway down the length of the hearth. Other hearths had two or more cavities dug and drilled against each other, so that the dust which was drilled from one hole collected in the next. Other hearths, strangely enough, had no means at all for

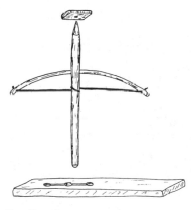

Bow fire set

collecting the dust, and the worker presumably had to continue drilling until a ring of dust around the drill began to ignite.

Other Eskimos used fire sets that resembled the above types, including a socket held either in the hand or in the mouth, but a plain thong was used instead of a bow. Sometimes a bone or ivory handle was attached to each end of the thong. In either case, the thong had to be held with two hands, so if the socket was designed to be held in the hand, a second worker was required to operate the thong.

Both the bow drill and the thong drill were also used by the Eskimos and the Subarctic Indians for boring holes, in which case a stone point needed to be lashed to the bottom of the drill. The bow drill was used for boring small holes in wood, bone, antler, or ivory. The thong drill was used for boring larger holes in wood when making boats and sleds.

The pump-drill set. The pump-drill set had a shaft and hearth similar to those in other types of fire set, but the shaft fitted loosely into a hole in the center of a crossbar. A thong ran from one end of the crossbar to the top of the shaft, where it was tied, and from there down to the other end of the crossbar. A flywheel was wedged onto the shaft near the bottom. No socket was needed. The shaft was turned several times, so that the thong was wound up on the shaft, causing the crossbar to rise. The worker then pressed down on the crossbar, causing the thong to unwind and thereby causing the shaft to spin. As the shaft spun, it wound the thong up in the other direction.

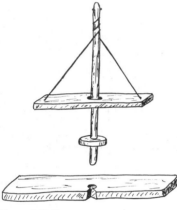

Pump-drill fire set

The pump drill was quite widely used for drilling holes, especially when delicate work needed to be done. Its chief advantage was that it could be operated with one hand. But as a fire drill it was not very practical. The only people known to have used the pump drill as a fire drill are the Iroquois, who built a very large version with a four-foot shaft. It is possible they adopted the device in historical times, since the earliest explorers only mention less complex devices.

Materials for wooden fire-sets. The materials for a fire set varied considerably. Common materials for both the drill and hearth included willow, poplar, cedar, pine, and mesquite. Ash, oak, basswood, slippery elm, and sassafras were used in some parts of eastern North America. Yucca and agave stalks were often used in the Southwest for both the drill and the hearth. In some areas, a harder wood was used for the drill. In the Great Basin, drills were often compound. The Shoshone, for example, lashed a section of sagebrush to the inside of a split in a longer shaft of willow or serviceberry. In many areas, the hearth was made of rotten or charred wood, and often the lower end of the drill was also charred in a previous fire before being used to start a new one.

A very common tinder was the dried inner bark of various cedars, rubbed into fine shreds and sometimes charred. Various species of dried bracket fungus (hard fungus growing on trees) were also widely used, and the blackfeet also used puffball spores. Other materials included dry rotten wood, well-rubbed dry grass or moss, the frayed outer bark of a birch tree or the inner bark of a dead birch, the frayed bark of big sagebrush, the dried fibers of Indian hemp, the fibers from bracken fern rhizomes, willow catkins, and dried buffalo dung.

Stone fire-sets

The Eskimos and the Indians of central Canada also obtained fire by striking together two hard stones. These stones might be flint, white quartz, or pyrite (fool's gold, iron sulphide), used in any combination. One stone was held in the fingertips of the left hand, and the tinder was held in the palm of the same hand. The other stone was held in the right hand and struck against the surface of the first stone until sparks fell onto the tinder and began to ignite it.

The bow drill was used until quite recently in northern Europe, but it has left no trace in most European languages. The percussion technique, on the other hand, can still be seen in the English word "pyrite," derived from the Greek *pyr*, "fire," and in the German word for flint, *Feuerstein* ("firestone").

Slow matches and torches

To save the trouble of trying to obtain a spark for a new fire, a "slow match" was often used, particularly when people were travelling. The slow match generally consisted of the same materials used for tinder: rotten wood, bracket fungus, cedar bark, sagebrush bark, and so on. The material, however, was less finely shredded, and it was kept in a more compact mass. The bark of cedar or sagebrush was shredded, gathered into an elongated bundle, and tied at several points to hold it together; sagebrush bark was also braided. Sometimes less inflammable materials were added to slow the burning.

The slow match was lit, but it was only allowed to smolder. It might then be carried in a buffalo horn or between two clamshells. It was blown on occasionally if it seemed likely to go out. If the slow match was a wad of material rather than a "rope," more material might be added from time to time. When a new fire was needed, the slow match was applied to a small pile of tinder and blown or fanned.

In the Subarctic, torches were often made of birch bark. A square of birch bark was rolled up diagonally from one corner and tied, or a strip of bark was folded several times and inserted in the end of a cleft stick. The Indians of British Columbia used bundles of cedar twigs as torches. The Navaho used strips of yucca leaf to tie shredded cedar bark into a bundle for use as a torch.

The fireplace

With stone axes as the only tools, most Indians cut as little firewood as possible. Limbs were broken from dead standing trees and often burned in half by being laid across the fire. The fireplace itself usually consisted of a ring or platform of heavy stones, which both regulated and retained the heat.

One of the principal uses of fire, of course, was for cooking.

The Eskimo fireplace was rather modest. A bowl-shaped lamp of soapstone was filled with the oil from crushed seal blubber. A wick of twisted moss or cotton-grass fluff (*Eriophorum* spp.), rubbed with oil, was placed in the lamp and lit. The lamp was used mainly for light and heat, though food was sometimes cooked by suspending a four-sided soapstone bowl above it.

In other parts of North America, food was often roasted in the flames, or wrapped and baked in the ashes. Food was also boiled in water, and a vessel of some sort was then required. A clay pot might be set on the ground, with a ring of fuel around it, or the pot might be suspended by a rope around its neck. But other types of vessel were also used for boiling. Twined and coiled baskets were commonly used in western North America. Even birch-bark vessels were used; if the flames rose no higher than the water level, the water would draw the heat away from the bark and prevent it from burning.

Stone-boiling was another widespread technique.

Stones were heated in a fire, picked up with wooden tongs, and dropped into a basket or box containing soup or mush. The stones might need to be rolled around to prevent burning the bottom of the container, and they might be replaced by new ones if the food failed to boil sufficiently. On the Plains, food was often stone-boiled in shallow pits lined with rawhide.

Pit-cooking was done primarily in western North America. A pit was dug and lined with stones, and a fire was built over the stones and left to burn until they were red-hot. The burnt wood and ashes were removed, or pushed between the stones, and the food was added, sometimes after it was wrapped in maize husks or skunk-cabbage leaves. The pit was covered with a layer of vegetation and a layer of earth, and left for several hours—or days—until the food was cooked.

Food could also be steam-cooked in a pit; wet vegetation, such as seaweed, was added, or a stick was planted in the center while the pit was being covered, then lifted out afterwards to allow water to be poured in. The same techniques were used to steam wood that needed to be bent.

Preparation of hides

The hides of animals supplied clothing for most North American Indians, but hides were also used for the covers of lodges and boats, for containers, and, when cut into strips, for cordage. Hides were used either tanned or untanned, and in either case the hair might be left on or it might be scraped off.

Skinning and butchering

Animals were usually bled, gutted, and skinned as soon as possible after they had been killed. The hide became progressively more difficult to remove after that time. The skin of deer and most other large animals was slit from neck to anus, and a further cut was made along the underside of each limb. The skin was peeled or, if necessary, cut away from most of the flesh and fat. The tendons were removed from the legs to be used as cordage, and the flesh was slit on both sides of the backbone to remove the longer tendons from that area. Some of the bones might be saved to be made into tools. The internal organs would be eaten right away, though the brain and perhaps the liver would be saved for tanning the hide. The blood might be used for soup. The flesh could be eaten right away, though it might be dried and stored as jerky or pemmican.

Rawhide

To convert a hide into rawhide, two tools were required: a flesher and a depilator.

The flesher was usually a leg bone from any large animal. One end of the bone was ground to a chisel edge, and often the edge was serrated. A thong loop was attached to the top of the flesher. The worker's hand passed through the thong loop and held the tool so that the little finger was closest to the cutting edge.

The depilator was usually made from either a leg bone

Flesher

Depilator

or a rib. If made from a leg bone, most of one side was cut away, and one edge of the cut-away portion was sharpened. A rib bone might be sharpened along one edge, or it might be used just as it came from the animal. The tool was used with both hands.

The hide was soaked in water for two or three days until the hair began to loosen. It was then placed on a peeled log, and the remaining flesh was chopped off with the fleshing tool. When the flesh side was finished, the hide was reversed, and the hair was scraped off with the depilator. The top layer of skin (the epidermis or grain) was also scraped off, giving a suede-like texture to the hide. The hide was re-moistened during the work if it began to dry out very much.

The hide might then be allowed to dry, but if so it would become stiff, unless it had come from a small animal, such as a rabbit. If the hide was to be cut later, e.g. for cordage, it would need to be soaked until it was soft.

Sometimes the hide was softened after fleshing and depilating. The softening process consisted of twisting, rubbing, and kneading the hide for a considerable length of time, perhaps after tying it around a tree or pole.

Tanning

A hide to be tanned was submitted to the same processes of soaking, fleshing, and depilating as rawhide. The hide was then washed and wrung out until nearly dry. The actual tanning process involved using an animal's brain, usually taken from the same animal that had supplied the hide. The brain was simmered for a few minutes with just enough water to cover it, then mashed with the water to form a paste. When the mixture had cooled, it was rubbed into the hide, sometimes with a round stone, and the hide was rolled up and left for about a day. The hide was then thoroughly rubbed and kneaded until it was soft.

The final step was smoking. Often the hide was sewn into a roughly conical form, with a small hole at the apex, and suspended over a small pit in which a smoky fire had been made. Twigs might be placed inside the hide to hold it open. Rotten wood, green wood, or bark might be used to produce the smoke. The hide was smoked for any length of time from ten minutes to several hours. Afterwards the hide was reversed and smoked on the other side.

The smoking kept the hide supple even if it got wet. It probably also helped to preserve it against rotting or being eaten by vermin. Excessive heat during the smoking process could damage the hide, and so a fringe (cotton cloth was used in historical times) was sometimes sewn onto the bottom of the cone to direct the smoke without having the hide too close.

The above description of Indian tanning is only a generalized one. Every culture had its own method of tanning, but the main processes were basically the same almost everywhere: soaking, removing the flesh and hair, braining, stretching (softening), and smoking.

Sometimes wood ashes were added to the water for the initial soaking, or the hide might be rolled up in wet ashes.

To depilate a hide, the Ojibwa placed it over the end of a peeled log planted obliquely in the ground. The worker pressed his body against the end of the log to hold the hide in place and pushed the depilator away from himself.

Tanning mixtures nearly always included brains, either freshly boiled or reconstituted from a paste that had been previously cooked and dried. To the brains might be added liver, fat, marrow, or meat broth. Moss, sagebrush leaves, or yucca fiber were sometimes added to the mixture if it was to be dried for later use.

Most tribes softened hides by pulling and kneading them, but sometimes a sharp-edged flat stone was scraped across the hide. Some of the Ojibwa laced deer hides into a rectangular frame just prior to the smoking process. A long-handled stone-tipped tool was then rubbed back and forth across the hide to soften and stretch it.

The last three steps—braining, stretching, and smoking—might be repeated three or four times, particularly for elk or moose. The amount of time for each step varied from one tribe to another; the brain mixture, for example, might be left in the hide for a few hours or for several weeks. Sometimes each step in the tanning process was preceded or followed by soaking and/or drying.

Hides might also be treated with the hair left on. The pelts of small animals, such as rabbits, needed no other treatment than drying. The pelts of larger animals were treated either as rawhide or as tanned hides, except that the initial soaking was omitted.

Buffalo hide

The treatment of buffalo hide on the Plains differed in several respects from the treatment of other types of hide. Buffalo hides were often cut in half to make them less cumbersome. The hide was usually staked out on the ground, though horizontal rectangular wooden frames were occasionally used, especially in winter. The flesh was scraped off with the usual chisel-shaped fleshing tool, but the hair was chopped off with an adze-like tool that also removed a fair amount of the hide. In many cases, no pre-soaking was done to loosen the hair; the Crow, however, first soaked the hide for several days in a mixture of water and wood ashes. A brain mixture was then rubbed in, sometimes with the aid of a smooth stone.

The next steps varied considerably, though often the hide was dried, soaked, and partially dried again. Several techniques were used to soften the hide: pulling the hide by hand, scraping it with either sharp-edged stones or coarse-grained stones, or pounding it with stones. Quite often the hide was pulled over a short but thick section of sinew rope, both ends of which were tied to a slanted fixed pole. The process of soaking, drying, and softening might be performed two or three times. The hides were not always smoked afterwards; tipi hides were smoked by building a fire in the finished tipi.

Eskimo treatment of hides

The Eskimos used several unique kinds of tools and techniques for preparing hides. The principal tool was a scraper, which varied considerably in form. Some scrapers had a straight or bent handle of wood or antler, to which a head of ground flint or nephrite was bound with rawhide thongs. Other scrapers had much shorter handles of wood or ivory, elaborately carved to fit the fingers; the forward end was mortised for the insertion of the stone blade, and no rawhide lashing was required.

The central Eskimos used two scrapers. One scraper consisted of a sharpened caribou scapula and was used as a flesher. The other scraper was one of the types previously described: a stone head lashed to a long bone or wooden handle. This second tool was used to soften the hide after it had been fleshed.

An additional instrument, the fat scraper, was required for seal skins. This tool also varied considerably in form. Some consisted of a ring-shaped section of walrus ivory, some consisted of a strip of ivory bent and tied in a U-shape, while others were round or slightly elongated bowl-shaped pieces of bone.

Eskimo tanning of seal hides was often characterized by the use of urine, which probably served to dissolve the fat and to prevent decay. Some Eskimos, however, allowed hides to rot before the hair was removed.

The Greenland Eskimos prepared seal pelts for clothing by scraping the flesh side to remove the meat and a certain amount of the skin, then soaking the hide in urine for one day. The hide was pegged out to dry, sprinkled with more urine, rubbed with a pumice stone, and then rubbed between the hands until soft.

Seal skins used by the Greenland Eskimos for sole leather were soaked in urine for two or three days. The hair was pulled out, the hide was soaked in fresh water for three days, and it was then stretched out and dried.

The Greenlanders did not use urine if the seal skin was to be used for kayaks. Instead, some of the fat was left on, the hide was rolled up and left to rot for several weeks, the hair was pulled out, and the hide was soaked in salt water for several days.

The western Eskimos also used urine, but the central Eskimos treated seal skins essentially as rawhide, softening them by scraping, rubbing, or chewing. Most Eskimos also used caribou hides, with or without the hair, as softened rawhide rather than as tanned hides, though the Alaskan Eskimos tanned caribou hide, with the hair on, using boiled fish eggs in the same way that brains were used further south.

Cordage

String and rope of plant or animal fiber were required for almost everything the Indians made—moccasins, snowshoes, fishing lines, nets, traps, bows, arrows, spears, boats, lodges, and so on. Fortunately there were many materials that could supply cordage. The most important materials are discussed below, though many others are known to have been used, and it is likely that almost any strong and pliable fiber was used at one time or another.

The materials and methods used for making cordage were often the same as those used for making baskets, mats, and blankets, though cordage fibers were sometimes stronger and more flexible.

Sometimes the material for cordage was taken from the plant or animal and used after virtually no processing. Other materials were twisted into two or more plies, like most of the rope, string, and thread we use today. Still other materials were processed by *braiding*; the process might be regarded as a form of angular plaiting, similar to the technique often used in basketry. Certain kinds of material, such as sinew, were treated in several different ways.

Each method of treatment had its advantages and disadvantages. When little or no processing was used, the material had to be very pliable and strong. Multiple-ply (usually two-ply) twisting produced a stronger and more flexible cordage, but it required fibers that were well-separated, non-elastic, and preferably rough-textured. Braiding was a rather slow method, but it usually guaranteed that the material would not unravel.

Multiple-ply twisting

Multiple-ply twisting first required that the individual fibers be separated. The techniques for the most commonly used plants will be described later.

One might take any bundle of parallel fibers and give it a twist throughout its length. The result would be a "single-ply" cord or yarn. Unfortunately, such a cord would be likely to unravel. Single-ply twisting was used to make a very crude type of cordage out of withes (flexible branches). It was also used for making yarn of various sorts woven on a loom; each thread in a woven fabric was prevented from unravelling by the other threads that crossed it.

The essential point about multiple-ply cordage, however, is that the plies work against each other and therefore hold each other in place. In a two-ply cord, for example, each of the two bundles is twisted *clockwise*, and these two strands are twisted *counter-clockwise* around each other (or vice versa).

There were three principal methods of making multiple-ply twisted cordage. I call them the "thigh method," the "fingertip method," and the "spindle method." All these methods were somewhat alike and resulted in more or less the same sort of finished product.

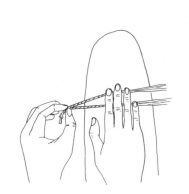

Thigh method

Thigh method. The "thigh method" was by far the most common form of multiple-ply twisting. The ends of two bundles of parallel fibers were knotted together, and the bundles were laid across the right thigh, a fraction of an inch apart, with the knot pointing to the left. (Alternately, a single bundle of fiber was bent in half, with the loop or bight taking the place of the knot.) The knot projected a few inches to the left of the thigh.

The knot was held firmly with the left hand. The right palm was brushed forward over the two bundles, rolling each of them into a spiral. The palm was pressed down on the two bundles, the bundles were pushed together, and the palm was pulled backward, allowing the two spirals to spring together in the opposite direction.

The cord was then pinched with the left hand at the point where the finished cord came to an end (i.e. on the right side of the right hand). The bundles were pulled a few inches to the left, and the process was repeated. As the fibers ran out, new fibers were laid in place. The fibers were usually kept well-moistened throughout the work.

Fingertip method. The "fingertip method" was used particularly for making bowstrings. Two bundles of fiber were knotted together at their ends and held between the tips of the left thumb and index finger, with the bundles falling across the raised palm. The nearest bundle was twisted two or three times with the right hand, then held under the third finger of the left hand. The second bundle was likewise twisted, then brought across the first bundle and held in place by the second finger of the left hand. The process was continued until three or four inches of cord had been completed. The left thumb and index finger then pinched the cord further down, where the spiral came to an end, and the steps were repeated. This technique was fairly slow, but it required less practice than the thigh method, and it produced a well-twisted cord.

The "fingertip method" was used for fine cordage that had to be free from irregularities, but two somewhat similar techniques, to be described later, were used on the Northwest Coast for heavier ropes made from the inner bark and the branches of western red cedar.

Fingertip method

Spindle method. On the Northwest Coast, the Kwakiutl and other tribes used spindles both for making multiple-ply cordage and for producing single-ply yarn to be woven on a simple loom-like device. (The spinning of yarn for use on a loom or loom-like device has been described in chapter 8, "Clothing.") The Kwakiutl spindle was fairly typical of those used on the Northwest Coast. It was quite large, with a three-foot maple rod tapering almost to a point at both ends. The rod was inserted into a six-inch disk or whorl of whalebone, wood, or stone, which sat on the rod approximately halfway along.

Before the fiber was put onto the spindle, it was converted into a loose single-ply cord or "roving." The Kwakiutl planted a three-foot pole in the ground at an angle. The fiber was tied to the top of the pole, twisted, and rolled around the pole. New fibers were laid into the previous ones and similarly twisted and wound onto the pole, until about six feet of roving had been produced. The ball of roving was removed, and more lengths were similarly prepared. The fiber was not moistened before being spun.

The Kwakiutl then spun the roving on the spindle. One end of the roving was twisted several times around the rod just above the whorl. The lower tip of the spindle was placed on the ground, the fiber was held out at a slight angle by the left hand, and the lower half of the spindle rod was rolled down the right thigh. The fiber was thus given a tighter twist, and at the same time it was wound onto the spindle.

But the result was still a single-ply cord, like that used

for loom-weaving, and so a second ball of cord was likewise spun on the spindle. The ends of both balls of cord were then attached to the rod, and both cords were held in the left hand; one cord ran between the left thumb and forefinger, and the second cord ran between the third and fourth fingers. The spindle, however, was rolled up the thigh instead of downwards.

Braiding

Sinew, rawhide, and buffalo hair were sometimes braided. Plant fiber was less often braided, though tumplines (carrying straps held across the forehead or chest) consisted of wide braided bands of plant fiber. Braiding is essentially a process of laying left and right strands alternately over each other. Illustrated are the steps for three-strand and four-strand braiding. Braiding can be (and was) done with far more than four strands, though braiding with a large number of strands is a rather clumsy process. More often, several lengths of three- or four-strand cord were braided, and then these lengths were braided together to produce a thicker cord. On the Northwest Coast, heavy harpoon lines for whaling were made by enclosing several lengths of four-strand braided cord in a wide spiral of the same sort of cord.

Sinew

The most widely used source of cordage in North America was sinew (tendons), the long white fibers that join muscle to bone. The sinew of birds and small mammals was occasionally used, but sinew was most often taken from the legs and back of deer and other larger animals. The leg tendons were cut off just after skinning, but the longer back tendons required cutting into the muscles just to the left and right of the backbone.

Sinew was treated in several different ways. Usually the tendons were first split into thinner fibers; the fibers could be pulled or cut apart when fresh or after soaking, or the dry sinew could be lightly beaten and pulled apart. The split fibers might be moistened, perhaps in the mouth, and used directly for binding. They could also be twisted to become two-ply cord, or they could be braided.

Sinew is very strong, it shrinks as it dries, and it also contains a natural "glue," so it was considered an excellent binding material. Often it was fastened without tying a knot; the beginning of the sinew was simply tucked under

Three-strand braiding

the first few turns and pulled tight, and the other end was treated in a similar manner.

Rawhide

Rawhide thongs were made by cutting a disk-shaped piece of fresh or well-soaked rawhide into a spiral. In historical times, the disk of hide was sometimes placed on a board, a steel knife was stuck into the board, and the hide was pulled against the knife blade. Whether or not a similar technique was used in the days of stone tools is unknown.

Thongs cut from the sheet and allowed to dry were pliable enough to be used for tying, especially if they were flexed somewhat before use. Wet thongs were more useful, however, since they shrank as they dried and thus provided a firmer bond.

Unfortunately the opposite was also true: rawhide stretched in the presence of moisture. Snowshoe frames were usually filled with rawhide lacing, which needed to be kept tight. To obviate the problem, rawhide was often stretched tightly between two poles and left to dry after it had been cut. Caribou hide, however, was said to be less prone to shrinking and stretching than other types of rawhide.

The Kwakiutl used a rather unusual technique for sealskin thongs. A single thong was tied at one end to a stake, pulled tight, and twisted. It was then bent double, and the two halves were allowed to spring together to form a two-ply cord. Perhaps the same technique was used elsewhere.

More often, rawhide was braided. Snares for big game, for example, were frequently made of braided rawhide. Sometimes the strands were twisted individually before being braided together.

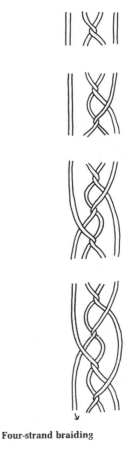

Four-strand braiding

Conifer roots

Throughout the Subarctic, one of the most commonly used cordage materials was the roots of various conifers: black spruce (*Picea mariana*), white spruce (*Picea glauca*), jack pine (*Pinus banksiana*), and tamarack (*Larix laricina*). The roots were soaked or boiled, and the bark was scraped off. They were then split into halves or quarters. The order of the steps varied somewhat.

On the Northwest Coast, the roots of western red cedar (*Thuja plicata*), Sitka spruce (*Picea sitchensis*), Engelmann spruce (*Picea engelmanni*), and sometimes lodgepole pine (*Pinus contorta*) were treated in a similar fashion, though they were frequently scorched in order to loosen the bark.

Western red cedar (*Thuja plicata*)

The roots, bark, and branches of western red cedar were all used for cordage on the Northwest Coast.

The bark was removed from the roots by heating them over a fire and pulling them through a set of tongs, a stick split halfway and bound around the center. The roots were then split or quartered and ready for use.

Bark for cordage was taken from the trunks of trees about a foot thick. The bark was pulled away in large strips, and the outer bark was cracked off and discarded. To prevent killing the trees, only one strip was removed from each. Methods of treating the bark generally included splitting it into layers, pounding it to loosen the fibers, and drying it. Sometimes the fiber was boiled for a day or two, or soaked for from ten to thirty days, at some point in the preparation. It was then made into two-ply cordage by moistening it and twisting it on the thigh, or left dry and spun on a spindle. (Western yellow cedar, *Chamae-cyparis nootkatensis*, was treated in the same manner to produce a softer fiber used for clothing.)

Another type of rope was made from thin strips of unbeaten inner bark. The strips were gathered in three to five bundles, and each bundle was given a preliminary twisting (single-ply). The ends of all the bundles were then tied together, held between the big toe and the second toe, and twisted around each other in a manner similar to the "fingertip method" described earlier.

Strips of unbeaten bark were also braided together, usually as three-strand cordage.

The branches were also used for cordage. These had to be quite long and thin, and were carefully selected. They were gathered in the spring, peeled (usually after being heated over a fire), either left whole or split into halves or quarters, and then twisted until pliable. If a whole branch was too thick to twist halfway down, it was bitten in the middle and bent double; the twisted half of the twig caused the other half to twist around it.

Very heavy multiple-strand rope was made from the peeled but unsplit branches. They were beaten with the back end of a wedge and then steamed; red-hot stones were covered with dulse, the branches were placed on top, another layer of dulse was added, and water was poured on. Mats were put on the pile, and the branches were left to steam for about ten minutes. When the branches were removed, a rope was tied around their ends and to a stake driven into the ground. Each branch was twisted individually and at the same time twisted around the other two, somewhat in the manner described above for strips of bark. A less crude type of rope was made by first twisting two pairs of branches together, and then twisting a third pair onto the previously twisted pairs.

Willow (*Salix* spp.)

Willow was a major source of cordage fiber in the western Arctic and most of the Subarctic, but it was also used in other areas. Individual shoots with the bark still attached were roughly twisted into a single-ply "cord" used for building lodges and wiers. Strips of the entire bark were sometimes pulled from the branches and used with no further treatment. The inner bark was collected in the spring, separated from the outer bark, and twisted on the thigh into two-ply cordage. The roots were peeled and soaked as a fourth type of cordage.

Basswood (*Tilia americana*)

The inner bark of the basswood tree was the most important cordage material of the western Great Lakes region. The bark was removed from the tree in the springtime.

The entire bark was fastened in the water at the edge of a lake for about ten days. The outer bark was then peeled off and discarded, and the inner bark was cut into narrow strips and hung up to dry. If finer cord was needed, the bark was separated into thinner layers before being cut. To produce a stronger cordage, the bark was sometimes boiled for an hour or so, often with wood ashes added to the water.

The bark could be used in this form, or it could be further processed to become twisted cordage. The fiber was softened by rubbing it between the hands or pulling it through a hole in a deer scapula or pelvic bone. The material was then spun on the thigh as two-ply cordage.

Indian hemp and dogbane (*Apocynum cannabinum* and *A. androsaemifolium*)

Indian hemp was a major source of cordage in most of the United States. The related dogbane was treated in the same way but regarded as inferior. Methods of preparing the fiber varied somewhat, but the basic steps were more or less as follows. The stalks were gathered in the autumn, when the first frost had killed the leaves; plants no more than a year old were preferred. The leaves and smaller branches were removed and discarded. The stalks were crushed between the fingers or pulled over a horizontal pole, and then split in half. The outer skin and the inner pith were scraped away, and the fibers were rubbed between the fingers. When the fibers were completely separated, they were spun on the thigh to become two-ply cordage.

Milkweed (*Asclepias* spp.)

Various species of milkweed were often used for cordage on both sides of the continent, but especially in California. Milkweed was treated in the same manner as Indian hemp, to which it is somewhat related, but it was regarded as slightly weaker.

Stinging nettle and false nettle (*Urtica dioica* and *Boehmeria cylindrica*)

Stinging nettle is said to be an alien species, and yet it was often used in many parts of North America in historical times. The related but native false nettle was also used in eastern North America. Nettles were also important sources of cordage fiber in much of the Old World; the English word "nettle," related to the word "net," comes from a root meaning "to twist."

The Ojibwa cut the stalks in the autumn and stripped off the leaves. The stalks were tied in bundles and hung to dry. They were then soaked just long enough to loosen the fibers, beaten, and spun on the thigh.

On the Northwest Coast, nettle stalks were likewise cut in the autumn. The Kwakiutl split the stems, coiled them, and hung them to dry in the sun. They were then further dried near a fire. The outer skin and pith were cracked off and discarded. The fibers were beaten, thoroughly rubbed, and pulled over a rib bone until completely separated from each other, then spun on a spindle. Other tribes on the Northwest Coast used similar techniques, and the fibers were often spun on the thigh rather than on a spindle, though in either case the finished product had a double ply.

Yucca and agave (*Yucca* spp. and *Agave* spp.)

Yucca was the principal source of cordage in the South-west.

The Zuñi used various species of yucca for cord. They took the young leaves from the center of the plant, folded and tied them in bundles, then boiled them with wood ashes until they were soft. The leaves were then chewed and scraped between the front teeth to separate the fibers, and dried for later use. Before being spun, the fibers were soaked again. The fibers were usually spun on the thigh to make cordage, but occasionally they were spun on a spindle to make single-ply yarn for clothing.

The Havasupai selected the inner leaves from dead specimens of various broad-leaved species. The leaves were pounded with a stone, flexed and soaked until the fibers were separated, and then braided, usually into three-strand cord.

Agave (maguey) was treated in a similar fashion, and in Mexico it was spun and woven into clothing.

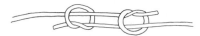

Fisherman's knot

Other important materials

Other types of animal fiber were sometimes used for cordage. Thin strips of baleen, the long flexible teeth of plankton-eating whales, were used by the Eskimos for seal nets and small snares. The split and twisted intestines of mammals were used to a limited extent in several areas. The Plains Indians sometimes used the longer hair of buf-falo for rope: several lengths of two-ply twisted cord were prepared, and these were braided together.

Many tribes of the Northwest Coast used the stipes ("stems") of bull kelp (*Nereocystis luetkeana*) for trolling lines. The stipes were soaked in fresh water and dried; these steps might be performed several times. The stipes were usually joined end to end with what is nowadays known as a "fisherman's knot". Occasionally the dried stipes were braided together. Another commonly used ma-terial on the Northwest Coast was the entire bark of bitter cherry (*Prunus emarginata*), cut from the tree in a spiral and used for binding projectile points and fishhooks; it was sometimes also pounded and twisted into two-ply cord. The inner bark of various species of maple (*Acer* spp.), twisted into two-ply cord, was used from British Columbia to California. The inner bark of silverberry (*Eleagnus commutata*) was twisted into two-ply cord on the Plateau; in the same region, the lower edges of cattail leaves (*Typha latifolia*) were sometimes twisted into two-ply cord for sewing cattail or rush mats. The entire bark of big sagebrush (*Artemisia tridentata*) was a common source of two-ply cordage on the Plateau and the Great Basin. Indians of the Eastern Woodlands also made twisted or braided cordage from the inner bark of mulberry (*Morus* spp.), leatherwood (*Dirca palustris*), eastern white cedar (*Thuja occidentalis*), and slippery elm (*Ulmus fulva*).

Basketry and pottery

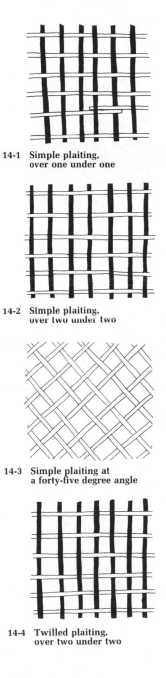

ood needed to be harvested, stored, and cooked, so containers of some sort were required. These containers could be made of clay, stone, wood, gourds, sheets of bark, folded rawhide, or woven plant material.

Basketry

The three basic types of stitch in basketry are *plaiting*, *twining*, and *coiling*. Each type of stitch is usually associated with certain types of *start* and certain types of *border*—the beginning and end of the basket.

Plaiting. The fibers or rods which form the vertical members of the side of a basket are known as *warps*. The horizontal members are known as *wefts*. In plaiting, the wefts simply go alternately over and under the warps (figs. 14-1 to 14-4). The weave may be "over one under one" (i.e. the weft goes over one warp and then under one warp), "over two under two," or any of several other combinations.

In "twilled" plaiting (fig. 14-4), the weft shifts over by one stitch with each succeeding row, creating a diagonal pattern. Twilled plaiting is therefore also known as "diagonal" plaiting, not to be confused with "angular" plaiting, (fig. 14-3), in which the warps and wefts (indistinguishable from each other) actually run at an angle of forty-five degrees to the sides of the basket.

Simple work baskets were often made in an "openwork" stitch. (For the sake of clarity, most of the illustrations depict openwork.)

The warps at the start of a plaited basket could be either "radial" or "non-radial." Four-sided plaited baskets were non-radial: a square or rectangular "mat" was woven, and the protruding elements were turned up to become the warps of the four sides of the basket. These baskets, in other words, had no "start" as such. Round baskets, on

14-1 Simple plaiting, over one under one

14-2 Simple plaiting, over two under two

14-3 Simple plaiting at a forty-five degree angle

14-4 Twilled plaiting, over two under two

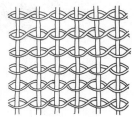

14-5 Simple twining, over one under one

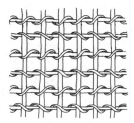

14-6 Twilled twining, over two under two

14-7 Three-strand twining

14-8 Wrapped twining

the other hand, had warps radiating out from a center, which meant that a distinct starting technique was required, and the wefts ran in a spiral around this center.

Two starts for radial plaiting are shown in figs. 14-9 and 14-10.

The start shown in fig. 14-10 was slightly complicated, but it was often used in the Southwest for both plaiting and twining. It began with two flat bundles of warps. Each bundle was bound at the center by interweaving (plaiting) a weft fiber from one side to another, until a square had been created. An "over one under one" stitch is shown, but other plaiting stitches were also used. The two bundles were then laid crosswise and pressed together. (The Hopi and Zuñi also bound the corners together.) A weft fiber was inserted in one corner, and the usual plaiting or twining was begun.

One peculiarity of plaiting is that if there is an even number of warps, which would normally be the case (since they form a cross at the center), then as the wefts go around the basket, some of them will always be under the warps, and the others will always be over the warps—an unacceptable situation. One remedy for this problem was to have, in each row, a single stitch that passed over one or more warps than usual, thereby creating an odd number of stitches. Another solution was to poke the end of an extra warp into the basket at the beginning, as shown in fig. 14-9.

Several types of border used for plaited baskets are shown in figs. 14-16 to 14-22. Those shown in figs. 14-16 and 14-17 were highly variable. The rod shown on top of the warps in fig. 14-18 was sometimes omitted.

Twining. The difference between plaiting and twining is that in the latter type of weave, the wefts are used in pairs. One weft goes over the warp, while the other weft goes under the same warp, and the pair of wefts is twisted a hundred and eighty degrees before enclosing the next warp (fig. 14-5). The stitch has a slanted appearance. The twist is normally in the same direction for every stitch and every row (though not in wrapped twining). Terms such as "twilling" (fig. 14-6) and "openwork" are equally applicable to twining. Finely twined baskets were often watertight.

The warps of twined baskets usually radiated from a distinct start. Several types of start used for twined baskets are shown in figs. 14-10 to 14-15. In most cases, the first "pair" of wefts was actually a single weft bent in half,

14-9 Start for plaiting

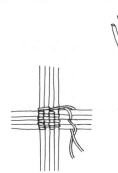

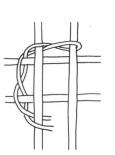

14-10 Start for plaiting or twining

14-11 Start for twining

14-12 Start for twining

14-13 Start for twining

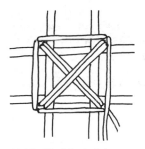
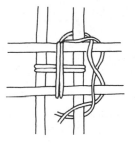

14-14 Start for twining

14-15 Start for twining

14-16 Border for plaiting or twining

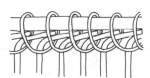

14-17 Border for plaiting or twining

14-18 Border for plaiting or twining

14-19 Border for plaiting

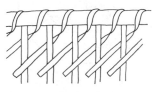
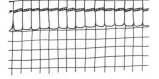
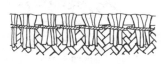

14-20 Border for plaiting

14-21 Border for plaiting

14-22 Border for plaiting

though unbent pairs of wefts were used for the rest of the basket.

Coiling. Plaiting and twining are fairly similar, but coiling is a totally different type of weave. In coiling, a coil or spiral of *foundation* material—either fibers or rods—is sewn together with a finer material, the *thread*, which encircles the foundation material with an overhand stitch (fig. 14-23 to 14-25).

While plaiting and twining could be done with no other tool than a knife, coiling also required an awl to punch holes for the thread.

Some common types of start are shown in figs 14-26 to 14-28.

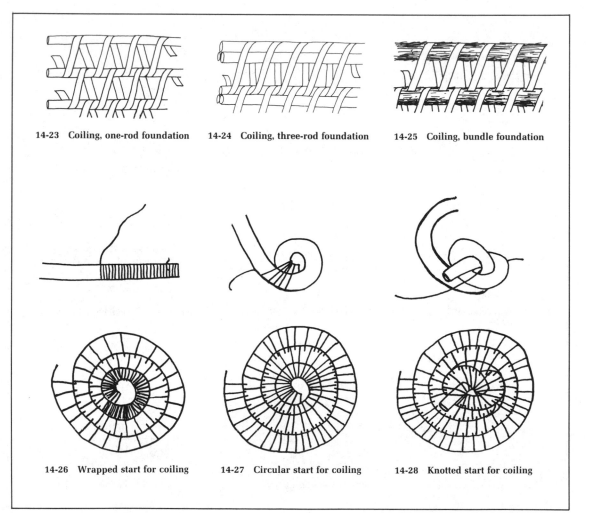

14-23 Coiling, one-rod foundation   14-24 Coiling, three-rod foundation   14-25 Coiling, bundle foundation

14-26 Wrapped start for coiling   14-27 Circular start for coiling   14-28 Knotted start for coiling

The start shown in fig. 14-26 was the most common. The ends of the fibers or rods were wrapped with thread. The beginning of the thread was held in place simply by being enclosed by several more turns of the thread. Once an inch or so had been wrapped, the foundation was bent into a circle and the actual sewing began.

Fig. 14-27 shows a Navaho start. The foundation was bent into a tight circle and completely wrapped with thread before the sewing began.

Fig. 14-28 illustrates a Salish technique for strips of conifer root. The ends of the foundation fibers were tied in an overhand knot. The sewing began by inserting the thread into the center of the knot.

Most coiled baskets had no distinct technique for the border, though in most cases the last row of foundation material was gradually reduced in thickness, so that the termination of the work was less visible.

Coiled baskets, like twined baskets, were often water-tight.

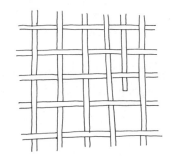

14-29 Addition of warps

Replacement and addition of warps and wefts. New warps were needed for two reasons: to *replace* warps that had run out, and to increase the actual *number* of warps. As the warp ran out, a new warp was added, usually by simply laying the beginning of the new warp parallel to the end of the old warp. But on the bottom of the basket, as the circumference increased, the actual number of warps needed to be increased, or the weft stitches would become too wide. Several ways of adding new warps are shown in figs. 14-24 to 14-31, which illustrate plaiting, though the techniques were equally applicable to twining.

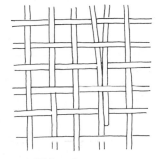

14-30 Addition of warps

Wefts also needed to be added, usually to replace ones that had run out. In most cases the beginning of the new weft was simply laid against the end of the old weft, though it might be knotted to the previous weft or to the warp.

No specific formulas can be given for the addition of warps and wefts, since each basket was unique. Sometimes new warps were added four at a time (one at each "corner"), perhaps after every two or three rows of weaving, while in other baskets the warps were added in a rather freeform manner.

Preparation of materials. Twigs, roots, and bark were usually gathered in the spring, but leaves were gathered whenever they were large enough. Virtually all materials

14-31 Addition of warps

were gathered and allowed to dry completely, then soaked before use and kept moist during the work. Extremely moist material, however, might swell during the work and shrink later, producing gaps in the work. Peeling and splitting, if necessary, were done either before or after the drying. Further treatment of specific materials is described below.

Northwest Coast. The Kwakiutl and several other tribes made four-sided plaited baskets from the inner bark of western red cedar (*Thuja plicata*). The bark was stripped from the tree, the outer bark was cracked off, and the inner bark was split into three layers: the middle layer was saved for rope, and the coarse outer layer and fine inner layer were used for baskets and mats. Each layer of bark was split into strips, usually about half an inch wide. The baskets were made with a variety of plaiting stitches, plain or twilled, straight or angular. Sometimes the bottom was plaited with wide strips, and these were split into three as they became the warps of the sides of the basket. Often a narrow double strip of bark was twined around the bottom edge. A common method of finishing the border was to bend the warps straight down and twine a double strip of bark under the last weft (fig. 14-21).

Both the inner bark and the split twigs of red cedar were also used to make twined baskets on the Northwest Coast.

The Tlingit, Haida, and other tribes made twined baskets from the split roots of Sitka spruce (*Picea sitchensis*). The Aleuts and some of the western Eskimos made finely twined baskets of various grasses.

Plateau. The Salish of the Plateau region made coiled baskets from the finely split roots of western red cedar, and occasionally from spruce or juniper.

In much of the Plateau region, twined bags and flexible baskets were more common than rigid baskets. The materials included the split stems of rush (*Scirpus* spp.) and the split leaves of cattail (*Typha latifolia*). Other materials included the inner bark of willow and the entire bark of big sagebrush (*Artemisia tridentata*), silverberry (*Eleagnus commutata*), greasewood (*Purshia tridentata*), white clematis (*Clematis ligustifolia*), and orange honeysuckle (*Lonicera ciliosa*)—the same materials that were used to make clothing. Twisted cordage of Indian hemp (*Apocynum cannabinum*) was often used as a weft.

Plains. In the upper Missouri region, the Arikara, Hidatsa, and Mandan made plaited burden baskets with four U-shaped ribs for reinforcement (fig. 14-32). The basic material was the inner bark of black willow (*Salix nigra*) or Manitoba maple (*Acer negundo*), cut into strips about a quarter of an inch wide.

14-32 **Plains burden basket**

The rim of the basket was made from a peeled willow, oak, or hickory sapling. A sharp diagonal cut was made to each end, and the sapling was bent into a circle and bound with wet sinew.

Four more saplings were required for the ribs; two were slightly longer than the others. Each rib was bent into a U-shape. The two longest ribs were tied with sinew to the outside of the rim, parallel to each other but about a foot apart, with the ends projecting slightly above the rim. The two shorter ribs were tied on in the same manner, but at right angles to the longer ribs. The bottoms of these shorter ribs might be either outside or inside the longer ribs. The ribs were tied together where they intersected at the bottom.

The strips of bark were then plaited together to form the bottom and sides of the basket. A twilled "over three under three" stitch was common. At the corners, the bark strips were looped in a circle around each rib from the outside to the inside, so that the ribs were concealed.

The border is shown in fig. 14-20.

Eastern Woodlands. Around the Great Lakes, bags were plaited from the inner bark of eastern white cedar (*Thuja occidentalis*). A foot-long horizontal bar was suspended by a string at each end, and the bark strips were laid over the bar and plaited downward, usually at an angle. The rim was finished by twisting the strips around each other (fig. 14-17). The bar was removed, and a few stitches were sewn into each bottom corner for reinforcement.

Birch-bark containers, however, were far more common around the Great Lakes than woven bags.

The principal food-container of the Iroquois was a barrel made of sewn sheets of elm bark, though twined baskets were also made, using Indian hemp, maize husks, and cattail leaves.

Throughout most of the southeastern United States, four-sided plaited baskets were made from the stems of cane (*Arundinaria* spp.), peeled and split into thin strips.

The Houma of Louisiana made coiled baskets from palmetto leaves (*Sabal palmetto*).

In much of the eastern United States for the last three centuries, baskets have been made from splints—strips pounded or cut from logs of ash, oak, hickory, and other woods. The technique was adopted from white settlers.

California. In California, crude twined baskets (often conical) were made from the split roots of pines and other conifers, the twigs of willow and hazel, and the stems of rush (*Scirpus* spp.).

The finely twined baskets of the Pomo had warps made from the peeled but unsplit shoots of various species of willow, though hazel was occasionally used. The wefts were made from the roots of either sedge (*Carex barbarae*) or rush (*Scirpus pacificus*); the outer layer of the root was discarded, and the core was split into fine threads. Coiled baskets were made with the same materials.

Southwest. Crudely plaited or twined burden baskets, either four-sided or rounded, were made throughout the Southwest. The most commonly used material was willow twigs, whole or split, peeled or unpeeled. Sometimes two heavy U-shaped ribs, either crossing at the bottom or parallel, were incorporated into the basket for reinforcement.

The finer baskets of the Hopi and Zuñi were made with radial plaiting and were usually quite shallow. Peeled but unsplit willow or sumac twigs were used for the warps, and the peeled unsplit twigs of various kinds of "rabbit-bush" (*Bigelovia graveolens, Chrysothamnus graveolens,* and *Verbesnia encelioides*) were used for the wefts. The start was that shown in fig. 14-10. At the border, the ends of the warps were cut off, and the weft was bound with a spiral stitch of split yucca leaves.

The Pueblo Indians also made shallow containers known as "ring baskets." Strips of yucca leaf were plaited to make a mat with an "over two under two" weave. The mat was soaked until flexible and forced into a rim made of a sumac twig. The projecting strips of yucca were cut to form a circle larger than the rim. The strips were then bent over the rim, usually outwards, gathered in groups of four or more, and held in place by a doubled yucca cord (or strip) twined around beneath the rim (fig. 14-22).

The Apache made excellent twined baskets from the peeled twigs of willow, cottonwood, or mulberry. The twigs were about a quarter of an inch thick at the base and about a yard long. Twigs for the warps were left whole. Twigs for the warps were split lengthwise into three parts, starting at the butt end, by holding one part in the teeth and the other parts in the hands, and the pith was scraped away. A common type of start was that shown in fig. 14–10, using two to six twigs in each bundle.

Apache burden baskets (fig. 14–33) were nearly cylindrical, though the bottom was slightly narrower than the top. These baskets had ribs at the sides and a hoop at the border. The ribs were two U-shaped rods which crossed at the bottom, and the tops of the ribs were fastened to the hoop. The start of the basket was the same as that described above. After the bottom of the basket had been started, it was put into the hoop-and-rib framework. The twining continued, and the ribs were incorporated directly into the twining by enclosing them in the stitches. At the top of the basket, the projecting warps were either cut off short or bent sidewards, and a weft fiber was coil-stitched around the hoop and the last two or three rows of twining (fig. 14–18). Often a second hoop was fastened on top of the first.

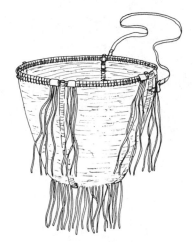

14-33   Apache burden basket

The Apache also made globular or ovoid water jars with funnel-shaped mouths, using the shoots of squawberry (*Vaccineum stamineum*) or sumac (*Rhus trilobata*). Again, the weft shoots were split into three parts. The twining was always twilled, and the hoop around the border was composed either of rods or of bundles of bark or grass. Two leather lugs (vertical straps) were sewn to the jar to support a carrying strap. Pine pitch (*Pinus edulis*) was melted (probably in boiling water) and rubbed into the jar with a yucca-fiber brush.

For coiled baskets, the Apache used a foundation of whole willow, cottonwood, or mulberry twigs, with split twigs of the same material for thread. The start was that of fig. 14-26.

The Havasupai made excellent twined baskets of acacia twigs (*Acacia greggii*). Peeled unsplit twigs were used for the warps, and twigs split into three parts were used for the wefts. The start was that shown in fig. 14-12.

In the lower Southwest, the Papago made square-bottomed angular-plaited baskets of split reed stems (*Phragmites communis*) and split sotol leaves (*Dasylirion wheeleri*).

Mats

Mats were often made with the same techniques and materials used in basketry, though some kinds of mats were sewn rather than woven.

Around the Great Lakes, large mats were used for the

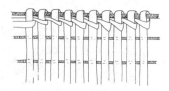

14-34   Eastern Woodlands cattail mat

walls, roofs, or floors of wigwams. Cattail leaves (*Typha latifolia*) were gathered and dried in late summer. A simple frame was built, consisting of a horizontal pole tied between two vertical poles. The ends of the leaves were bent over a long piece of cord and twisted to one side, so that each leaf hid the end of the previous one (fig. 14-34). The long cord was then temporarily fastened to the horizontal pole with another cord, which was wrapped in an elongated spiral around the first cord and the pole. A slightly curved bone needle, about nine inches long, with a hole at one end or in the center, was used to sew the leaves together. The thread consisted of two-ply twisted basswood bark. The lines of sewing were about eight or nine inches apart. The bottom of the mat might be finished in the same manner as the top, though often the bottom was left without a finished border, so that the mat would stand up more easily against the frame of the wigwam.

Mats were also made of rushes (*Scirpus validus*) in the Great Lakes region. The rushes were suspended from a cord and a pole in the same manner as cattail leaves, but instead of being sewn, they were twined together with basswood-bark cord at half-inch intervals.

Other mats of this region were made by plaiting strips of the inner bark of white cedar (*Thuja occidentalis*) or eastern red cedar (*Juniperus virginiana*), suspended in the same manner. All four edges were finished with a spiral stitch of bark.

Mats similar to the above types were made on the Northwest Coast and the Plateau, particularly by the Salish. Cattail leaves (*Typha latifolia*) and rush stems (*Scirpus acutus*) were sewn with a hardwood needle two or more feet long and triangular in cross-section, using a two-ply twisted thread of stinging nettle, Indian hemp, or the white lower edges of cattail leaves. A "mat creaser," a small board with a groove along one edge, was pressed down along the line of sewing to soften the rushes and prevent the thread holes from splitting. The two edges of the mat parallel to the leaves or stems were usually finished with a braided length of cattail or rush. The other two edges were finished by folding the leaves over and enclosing them in one or two rows of twining; the technique was identical to the basketry border of fig. 14-21. Other mats were made by twining rush stems together, using the above-mentioned thread materials for the weft.

On the Northwest Coast, mats were also made by plaiting strips of western red cedar (*Thuja plicata*). The strips on the left and right edges of the mat were simply folded and woven back into the fabric; the strips at the top and bottom edges were finished with the technique of fig. 14-21, using a narrow strip of bark as the twining material. Superior mats were made with angular plaiting.

In the Southwest, mats were plaited from yucca leaves (*Yucca* spp.), sotol leaves (*Dasylirion wheeleri*), reed stems (*Phragmites communis*), and the inner bark of cedar (*Thuja* sp.) and juniper (*Juniperus* sp.).

Birch-bark containers

Birch bark (*Betula papyrifera*) was usually peeled from the trees in late spring, while the sap was flowing. Winter bark was said to be stronger, but boiling water had to be poured over the log, or a fire built under it, in order to get the bark to peel. Birch trees vary a lot in the structure of their bark: some have thinner bark than others, some have too many "eyes," and some, for unknown reasons, peel better than others.

14-35　Birch-bark containers

After peeling off the entire thickness of bark, one or two outer layers were usually discarded. The inside of the bark formed the outside of the container. Bark could be used right away. If it had been stored for a while (flat, weighted down with stones), it needed to be soaked for about two or three days until it was supple; soaking for too long tended to make the bark curl, however. Roasting over a fire could also make the bark more supple.

The bark was then laid out and cut to shape. Several forms are shown in fig. 14-35. The seams were punched with an awl and sewn together with the split roots of spruce or other conifers. Twisted basswood bark was used as the sewing material in the northeastern United States (basswood is rare in Canada).

The rim of a birch-bark container was usually bound, either inside or outside, with a split shoot, such as willow, sewn in place with a spiral stitch.

Containers were made with the grain of the bark either horizontal or vertical; in either case, some of the seams would be weaker than others. If the grain was horizontal, the spiral stitch around the rim needed to be staggered to prevent putting all the stress on one horizontal line.

If the container was intended to hold liquids, the outside of the seams needed to be coated with pitch. A square or notch was cut out of the bark of a coniferous tree in the spring. After a few days, pitch was put in boiling water. (Sometimes it was put into a loosely woven bag before being immersed, to hold back twigs and other debris.) The melted resin rose to the surface and was scooped off. Usually a little charcoal was added to the pitch, probably to make it spread more easily. The pitch was then spread thickly over the seams.

Resin was also obtained from boiled jack pine cones or boiled poplar buds.

Birch-bark containers were only made to any great extent, of course, where white birch was common, namely in the Subarctic. In other parts of the continent, similar but more primitive containers were made from sheets of pine, spruce, cedar, poplar, and elm bark, sometimes with the outer layer partly chipped off.

Pottery

Pottery was made to a varying extent nearly throughout the United States and in most of southern Canada.

Clay is easily recognized. It has a soapy texture and a putty-like consistency, fine enough to retain fingerprints. It is usually found in the beds or banks of streams, or in the ravines of dried riverbeds.

Pure clay will check or crack when drying, so when it was to be used for pottery it was spread out to dry thoroughly, crushed to powder, and mixed with some form of tempering: fine sand, crushed pottery shards, crushed soapstone or mica, powdered shells, or occasionally hair or vegetable fiber. The tempering might constitute anywhere between five and eighty percent of the entire material. If the clay was found already mixed with other material, it might be possible to use it without added tempering.

On the other hand, sometimes the clay contained too many impurities. It would be dried and crushed, and the largest stones would be picked out by hand. The remaining clay would be "winnowed": it was allowed to fall through the fingers, or it was tossed in a basket, and the stones fell to the ground while the wind blew the pure clay onto a blanket.

Clay found dry might need to be soaked for a week or longer before it acquired the right plasticity.

The tempered clay was mixed with enough water to form a dough, then kneaded for at least fifteen minutes to get rid of air bubbles. If work had to be stopped at any time, the lump of clay could be kept immersed in water.

Indian potters used only two methods for making pottery, sometimes in combination. Small pots were simply pressed into shape with the thumbs and fingers. Larger pots were built up in coils. Usually the base was formed by pressing clay into some sort of mold, such as an old clay dish, a shallow basket, or a hollowed piece of wood. The inside of the mold was given a coat of temper or grease. The bases of aboriginal pots were round or pointed, not flat, so that they could be placed in sand or among rocks.

When the base was formed, more clay was rolled into a long "sausage" shape, bent into a coil, and pressed into place to begin the sides. More coils were added until the pot was completed. In the Southwest, the coils were pressed into place so that they overlapped, while in the Eastern Woodlands the coils were added in a more vertical fashion (fig. 14-36). The walls had to be of a uniform thickness if the pot was to dry without cracking.

Certain tools were sometimes used to press the coils into shape. A round pebble or a mushroom-shaped clay anvil could be held against the inside wall, while a paddle-shaped stick was used to slap the adjacent part of the outside wall.

If the pot was to have a narrow neck, the lower half of the pot was made first and allowed to dry and harden for a few hours before the shoulders and neck were added.

The finished pot was dried completely in the sun. If the sun was too hot, however, or if there was no sun, it was dried inside. When completely dry, it was lifted out of the mold in which the base had been formed. The outside was moistened, then scraped with pieces of gourd shell, clam shells, bones, stones, or broken pieces of pottery.

Some pots were given one or more coats of "slip," fine clay mixed with a lot of water. The slip was put on when the pot was dry, and each coat was allowed to dry before the next was applied. The pot could also be given a fine polish with a smooth stone when the slip itself had dried to leather hardness.

The completely dried pot was then fired, preferably on a windless day so that the heat would be uniformly distributed. The fuel, consisting of wood, bark, or dry dung, was stacked over, under, and around the pot. The fire was allowed to burn for half an hour or an hour, and more fuel was added when necessary. The pot was then removed and left to cool.

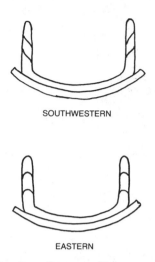

SOUTHWESTERN

EASTERN

14-36 Start of pottery coiling

Appendix: food plants

The data is restricted to Canada and the United States. A few minor or doubtful species have been omitted. Algae, fungi, lichens, and ferns are listed first. Other plants are listed alphabetically by species or genera within families. Note the warning messages ("CAUTION") under family and other headings.

ALGAE CAUTION: nearly all saltwater algae are edible, but members of the genus *Lyngbya* are toxic; these are dark bluish-green algae composed of mats of fine filaments. Certain sour-tasting brown algae, *Desmarestia* spp., are slightly toxic.

Alaria esculenta. Kelp. Cooked by Indians in Alaska.

Macrocystis integrifolia. Giant Kelp. When coated with herring spawn, eaten raw or cooked by Northwest Coast Indians.

Porphyra spp. Laver. Eaten raw or cooked on Northwest Coast.

FUNGI CAUTION: there are many poisonous species of fungi.

Agaricus spp. Meadow Mushroom, etc. Eaten in Alaska, British Columbia, and California, and by the Iroquois.

Armillaria mellea. Honey Agaric. Apparently eaten in British Columbia and Montana.

Boletus sp. Boletus. A yellow and green species was eaten in California.

Bovista plumbea. No common name. Young plants eaten by the Omaha.

Calvatia spp. Puffball. Eaten by the Omaha and Iroquois.

Cantharellus spp. Chantarelle. Eaten in British Columbia.

Coprinus comatus. Shaggy Mane. Eaten in British Columbia.

Lycoperdon spp. Pear Puffball. Eaten by the Omaha and Zuñi.

Morchella esculenta. Morel. Boiled in Nebraska, North Dakota, and South Dakota. A species of morel was eaten by the Iroquois.

Pachyma cocos. Tuckahoe. The large underground growth of this fungus was eaten in the southeastern United States.

Phaeolepiota aurea. Golden Phaeolepiota. Eaten in British Columbia.

Pleurotus ulmarius. No common name. Young plants eaten by the Omaha.

Polyporus spp. Bracket Fungus. *P. farlowii* eaten in New Mexico, *P. versicolor* probably eaten by the Dakota, *P. sulphureus* probably eaten in British Columbia, other species eaten by the Iroquois and in California.

LICHENS CAUTION: most lichens are bitter and mildly toxic; boiling in large amounts of water is recommended.

Bryoria fremontii and *B. tortusa.* Black Tree Lichen. Cooked in the northwestern United States and in British Columbia, usually by boiling or baking for a long time.

Cetraria islandica. Iceland Moss. Eaten in several parts of North America.

Cladonia rangiferina. Reindeer Moss. Taken from the stomach of caribou and eaten by the central Eskimos; also boiled as an emergency food in the Subarctic.

Parmelia physodes. No common name. Cooked for soup in Wisconsin. CAUTION: Kingsbury lists *P. molliuscula* as toxic.

Sticta amplissima. No common name. Cooked by the Menominee and Ojibwa.

Umbilicaria dilenii. Rock Tripe. Boiled by the Huron.

FERNS AND FERN ALLIES

Dryopteris dilatata. Mountain Woodfern. Rootstocks harvested in spring and pit-baked by Alaskan Indians.

Equisetum spp. Horsetail. Tubers eaten in Minnesota, fertile (unbranched) shoots eaten in British Columbia, plant dried and ground in New Mexico. CAUTION: horsetail is poisonous in large quantities; the toxin is similar to the thiaminase in bracken.

Lycopodium lucidulum and *L. selago.* Clubmoss. Plants eaten by the Ojibwa.

Onoclea sensibilis. Sensitive Fern. Rootstocks eaten by the Iroquois.

Osmunda cinnamomea. Cinnamon Fern. "Fiddleheads" (sprouts) boiled by the Menominee.

Polystichum munitum. Giant Hollyfern. Rootstocks roasted in British Columbia.

Pteridium aquilinum. Bracken. Rootstocks debarked and roasted, young sprouts boiled. Eaten in many areas, from Alaska to California to Wisconsin. CAUTION: large amounts of mature bracken have caused thiaminase poisoning in livestock.

ACERACEAE

Acer spp. Maple. Sap and cambium of several species eaten in many areas.

AESCULACEAE

Aesculus californica. California Buckeye. Nuts boiled in several changes of water in California as an emergency food. CAUTION: highly toxic when raw.

AGAVACEAE

Agave spp. Agave, Mescal, Century Plant. Crown pit-roasted in the Southwest. Stalks, flowers, and seeds sometimes cooked. CAUTION: the raw plant causes a serious irritation, especially in the mouth.

Nolina microcarpa. Bear Grass. Seeds and shoots eaten in New Mexico. CAUTION: the flowers are quite toxic.

Yucca spp. Yucca. Fruit, stems, and flowers eaten raw or cooked in the Southwest.

ALISMACEAE

Sagittaria spp. Arrowhead. Tubers boiled or roasted in many parts of the United States and southern Canada.

AMARANTHACEAE

Acanthochiton wrightii. No common name. Entire above-ground plant cooked by the Hopi.

Amaranthus spp. Amaranth, Pigweed. Leaves and seeds eaten in many parts of the United States, and several species cultivated.

AMARYLLIDACEAE

Allium spp. Onion, Garlic, Leek. Bulbs and leaves eaten raw or cooked in most of North America.

Androstephium caeruleum. No common name. Bulbs eaten in Texas.

Bloomeria aurea. Golden Stars. Bulbs eaten in California.

Brodiaea spp. Brodiaea. Bulbs of several species eaten raw or roasted in western North America.

Dichelostemma capitatum and *D. pulchellum.* Blue Dicks, Ookow. Bulbs eaten in California and Arizona.

Triteleia laxa and *T. peduncularis.* Triteleia. Bulbs eaten in California.

Zephyrantes atamasco. Atamasco Lily. Bulbs used by the Creek Indians as an emergency food. CAUTION: listed by Kingsbury as highly toxic.

ANACARDIACEAE

Rhus spp. Sumac. Fruit eaten whole, or used to make a hot or cold beverage, in many parts of the United States and southern Canada. Peeled roots of R. *Glabra* (smooth sumac) eaten raw. CAUTION: poison ivy and poison oak (*Toxicodendron* spp.) are similar but have yellow or white fruit.

ANNONACEAE

Asimina triloba. Pawpaw. Fruit eaten in the central and eastern United States.

AQUIFOLIACEAE

Nemopanthus mucronata. Mountain-Holly. Berries eaten by the Potawatomi.

ARACEAE CAUTION: most members of the Arum Family contain calcium oxalate, which can cause an intense burning sensation in the mouth. The corms ("roots") become quite edible, however, after thorough baking or boiling, sometimes preceded by slicing and drying.

Arisaema triphyllum Jack-in-the-Pulpit, Indian Turnip Corms cooked in the Eastern Woodlands.

Calla pallustris. Wild Calla. Rootstocks cooked in the Eastern Woodlands.

Colocasia esculenta. Elephant's Ear, Taro, Dasheen. Corms cooked in southeastern United States.

Lysichitum americanum. Western Skunk Cabbage. Rootstocks steamed in autumn on Northwest Coast, flower-stalks and young leaves also steamed.

Orontium aquaticum. Golden Club. Corms and seeds cooked in Eastern Woodlands.

Peltandra spp. Arrow-Arum. Corms cooked in southeastern United States.

Symplocarpus foetidus. Eastern Skunk Cabbage. Rootstocks, young leaves, and shoots cooked by the Iroquois.

ARALIACEAE

Aralia nudicaulis and *A. racemosa.* Wild Sarsparilla and American Spikenard. Fruit of A. *nudicaulis* eaten in British Columbia. Roots and young tips of A. *racemosa* eaten in Eastern Woodlands.

Oplopanax horridum. Devil's Club. Roots and young stems eaten in Alaska.

ARISTOLOCHIACEAE

Asarum canadense. Wild Ginger. Rootstocks used as a flavoring in eastern North America.

ASCLEPIADACEAE

Asclepias spp. Milkweed, Butterflyweed. Shoots, young pods, and flower buds of most milkweeds eaten raw or cooked in several parts of the United States. CAUTION: the raw plants are unpalatable and often toxic; it is probably best to cook all milkweeds. *A. labriformis* should definitely be avoided. *A. tuberosa*, *A. syriaca*, and *A. speciosa*, all common species, are probably less dangerous than most others.

BERBERIDACEAE

Berberis spp. Barberry, Holly Grape, Oregon Grape, Agarita. Berries eaten in many parts of North America.

Podophyllum peltatum. May Apple, Mandrake. Fruit eaten raw or cooked in the central and eastern United States. CAUTION: the rest of the plant is quite toxic.

BETULACEAE

Alnus rubra. Red Alder. Cambium eaten in British Columbia.

Betula lutea. Yellow Birch. Sap added to maple sap by the Ojibwa.

Corylus spp. Hazel. Nuts eaten in most of the United States and southern Canada.

BORAGINACEAE

Amsinckia lycopsoides and *A. tesselata.* Fiddleneck. Shoots of *A. lycopsoides* eaten in California, seeds of *A. tesselata* in Utah. CAUTION: fiddleneck is listed as toxic to certain animals.

Cynoglossum grande. Hound's Tongue. Cooked roots eaten in California.

Lithospermum spp. Gromwell, Puccoon, Stoneseed. Roots and leaves eaten in western North America. CAUTION: the roots of *L. ruderale* were used as a contraceptive.

Plagiobotrys fulvus. No common name. Shoots and seeds eaten in California.

BUXACEAE

Simmondsia chinensis. Jojoba. Nuts eaten raw or parched in California.

CACTACEAE

Cereus giganteus. Saguaro. Fruit, including rind and seeds, eaten in Arizona and California.

Echinocactus spp. Mound Cactus. Seeds from the fruit of *E. polycephalus* (cottontop cactus) eaten in California. The stems of *Echinocactus* spp. contain thirst-relieving juice.

Echinocereus spp. Hedgehog Cactus. Fruit and stems eaten in many parts of the southwestern United States.

Ferocactus spp. Barrel Cactus. Fruit eaten in many parts of the southwestern United States. Pulp of stem crushed to give a thirst-relieving liquid. Seeds and boiled stems of *F. wislizeni* eaten by the Pima. CAUTION: the juice contains oxalic acid, which in quantity can cause nausea.

Lemaireocereus thurberi. Organpipe Cactus. Fruit and crushed seeds eaten in California, Arizona, and Mexico.

Mamillaria spp. Ball Cactus. Fruit eaten in the southwestern United States, and the Crow Indians ate the fruit of *M. missouriensis.*

Opuntia spp. Prickly Pear, Cholla, etc. Fruit eaten raw or cooked in western United States and southern Canada. Stems, seeds, and flowers also cooked.

Peniocereus greggii. Deerhorn Cactus. Fruit eaten in Texas.

CAPPARIDACEAE

Cleome serrulata. Rocky Mountain Beeweed. Leaves and flowers boiled in New Mexico. Leaves also dried for winter use.

Isomeris arborea. Bladderpod. Pods cooked in California.

Polanisia trachysperma. Clammy-Weed. Young plants cooked in California.

Wislizenia refracta. Jackass Clover. Young plants cooked by the Hopi. CAUTION: according to Kingsbury, the plant is highly toxic to livestock.

CAPRIFOLIACEAE

Lonicera ciliosa and ***L. involucrata.*** Honeysuckle. Berries eaten in northwestern North America.

Sambucus spp. Elderberry. Fruit eaten raw or cooked in many parts of North America. CAUTION: large amounts of the raw berries can cause nausea in some people. The rest of the plant is also fairly toxic.

Symphoricarpos albus and ***S. occidentalis.*** Snowberry, Waxberry. Berries eaten in central and western North America.

Viburnum spp. Highbush Cranberry, Nannyberry, etc. Berries of several species, but especially *V. trilobum* (highbush cranberry), eaten in many parts of North America. Most are bitter.

CELASTRACEAE

Celastrus scandens. American Bittersweet. Inner bark and twigs boiled in Minnesota and Wisconsin. CAUTION: possibly toxic.

CHENOPODIACEAE

Allenrolfea occidentalis. Iodine Bush, Pickle Bush, Chico. Seeds ground for bread or gruel in Utah.

Atriplex spp. Saltbush. Boiled young leaves and ground seeds of many species eaten in western United States.

Chenopodium spp. Lamb's Quarters, etc. Some species alien. Seeds and leaves eaten in many parts of the United States and further south. CAUTION: *C. ambrosioides* can be toxic in large quantities.

Cycloloma atriplicifolium. Cycloloma. Seeds added to pinole by the Zuñi.

Monolepsis nuttaliana. Patata, Patota. The Pima boiled the roots; the seeds were boiled, partially dried, parched, and then ground for pinole.

Salicornia spp. Glasswort, Samphire, Pickleweed. Seeds ground and cooked in Utah, Nevada, and California. Stems also edible raw or boiled.

Sarcobatus vermiculatus. Greasewood. Young twigs boiled in the western United States, seeds also eaten. CAUTION: the leaves can have toxic levels of oxalates.

Suaeda spp. Sea Blite, Seep Weed. Leaves and seeds cooked in Arizona, Utah, Nevada, and California.

COCHLOSPERMACEAE

Amoreuxia palmatifida. No common name. Roots eaten in Arizona.

COMMELINACEAE

Tradescantia spp. Spiderwort. Shoots eaten raw, leaves cooked, in Arizona and other areas.

COMPOSITAE

Achyrachaena mollis. Blow-Wives. Achenes ("seeds") roasted in California.

Agoseris aurantiaca. No common name. Leaves eaten in Utah and Nevada.

Ambrosia trifida. Giant Ragweed. Cultivated for its seeds in several areas.

Arctium lappa. Burdock. Alien. The Iroquois cooked the young leaves and the peeled young stalks, and the peeled roots were boiled or dried for winter.

Artemisia spp. Sagebrush. Seeds of many species cooked in Utah and Nevada. Young leaves of *A. dracunculoides* baked in Arizona and California. CAUTION: large amounts of the seeds can be toxic.

Aster macrophyllus. Large-Leaf Aster. Roots and young leaves cooked by the Ojibwa.

Balsamorhiza spp. Balsam Root. Seeds (unshelled) and peeled roots (the latter dug in spring) of several species cooked in western North America. Young leaves, stalks, and flower buds sometimes eaten raw or cooked.

Blennosperma nanum. Common Blennosperma. Seeds roasted and ground in California.

Chrysothamnus confinis. Douglas Rabbitbush. Buds eaten in New Mexico.

Cirsium spp. Thistle. Many species alien. Roots and peeled stems eaten raw or cooked in many parts of the United States and southern Canada.

Crepis glauca. Hawksbeard. Leaves eaten in Utah and Nevada.

Dicoria brandegei. Single-Fruited Dicoria. Flowers and ground seeds eaten in Arizona.

Happlopappus parishii. No common name. Seeds eaten in California.

Helianthus spp. Sunflower. Seeds of several species, especially *H. annuus*, eaten in many parts of the United States. Tubers of *H. doronicoides*, *H. maximiliani*, and especially *H. tuberosus* (Jerusalem artichoke) eaten raw or boiled. *H. annuus* and *H. tuberosus* were sometimes cultivated.

Hemizonia fasciculata and **H. luzulaefolia.** Tarweed, Spikeweed. leaves of *H. fasciculata* boiled as an emergency food in California. Seeds of *H. luzulaefolia* roasted for pinole in California.

Iva ciliata. Marsh Elder. Cultivated for its seeds in several parts of the United States.

Lactuca spp. Wild Lettuce, Some species alien. Young leaves cooked in Utah, Nevada, and New Mexico.

Lasthenia glabrata. Smooth Lasthenia. Seeds ground and eaten dry in California.

Layia glandulosa and **L. platyglossa.** Layia. Seeds eaten in California.

Liatris punctata. Blazing-Star. Roots cooked by the Tewa of New Mexico.

Lygodesmia grandiflora. Rush-Pink. Leaves boiled by the Hopi.

Madia spp. Madia, Tarweed. *M. sativa* is alien. Seeds ground and cooked in California. Oil extracted from the seeds of *M. sativa*.

Malacothrix californica. Desert Dandelion. Seeds eaten in California.

Microseris nuttans and **M. procera.** No common name. Roots eaten in western United States.

Pectis angustifolia. Chinch Weed. Leaves and shoots eaten in Arizona and New Mexico.

Petasites palmatus. Western Coltsfoot. Plant burned for use as salt in western United States.

Rudbeckia laciniata. Cutleaf Coneflower. Young stems eaten in new Mexico. CAUTION: somewhat toxic.

Solidago spp. Goldenrod. Seeds and leaves of several species eaten in Utah, Nevada, and Arizona. CAUTION: toxic to livestock.

Sonchus asper. Prickly Sowthistle. Alien. Young leaves cooked in California.

Taraxacum officinale. Dandelion. Alien. Young leaves cooked, roots eaten raw, in many parts of the United States.

Thelesperma spp. Cota. Stems and leaves boiled as a beverage in the Southwest.

Viguiera multiflora. No common name. Seeds eaten in Utah and Nevada. CAUTION: toxic in quantity.

Wyethia spp. Mule Ears. Seeds, roots, and young leaves and stems eaten in western United States.

Xanthium sp. Cocklebur. Seeds of *X. strumarium* or *X. spinosum* eaten in New Mexico. CAUTION: Kingsbury, however, lists the seeds as highly toxic.

CONVOLULACEAE

Cuscuta curta and ***C. umbellata.*** Dodder. Seeds parched and ground in New Mexico.

Ipomoea leptophylla and ***I. pandurata.*** Man Root, Wild Sweet Potato. The very large roots were roasted as an emergency food in Montana and Wyoming, but more frequently eaten in the southeastern United States. CAUTION: possibly toxic in large amounts.

CORNACEAE

Cornus spp. Dogwood and Bunchberry. Fruit eaten raw in many parts of North America. The widespread *C. canadensis* (bunchberry) is less bitter than most.

CRASSULACEAE

Dudleya spp. Dudleya, Live-forever. Young leaves eaten raw in California.

Sedum spp. Stonecrop. Leaves and roots eaten raw by Eskimos and in British Columbia. CAUTION: some species are cathartic and emetic in large amounts.

CRUCIFERAE

Barbarea verna and ***B. vulgaris.*** Winter Cress. Alien. Leaves eaten raw in eastern United States.

Brassica campestris and *B. nigra.* Mustard. Alien. Young leaves cooked in California.

Cakile edulenta. Sea Rocket. Powdered root added to flour in Canada.

Capsella bursa-pastoris Shepherd's Purse. Alien. Above-ground plant eaten in several areas.

Cardamine rotundifolia. Mountain Watercress. Leaves cooked in eastern United States.

Caulanthus inflatus. Desert Candle, Squaw Cabbage. Young plant boiled, seeds pounded into flour in Utah, Nevada, and California.

Dentaria spp. Crinkleroot, Toothwort. Roots eaten raw or boiled in central and eastern United States. The Ojibwa covered the roots of *D. maxima* with a blanket for four or five days, so that they fermented and became less acrid.

Descurainia spp. Tansy Mustard. Seeds and young plants eaten in western United States.

Lepidium spp. Peppergrass. Some species alien. Seeds and leaves eaten in California, Louisiana, and other areas.

Nasturtium officinale. Watercress. Alien. Eaten by the Iroquois and in California.

Rorippa spp. Cress. Some species alien. One or more species eaten in western North America, though changes in nomenclature make identification difficult.

Sisymbrium officinale. Hedge Mustard. Alien. Seeds parched, ground, and boiled in New Mexico.

Stanleya spp. Indian Cabbage, Princes Plume. Boiled leaves and ground seeds eaten in southwestern United States. CAUTION: sometimes contains toxic levels of selenium.

CUCURBITACEAE

Cucurbita spp. Squash, Pumpkin, Buffalo Gourd, etc. Cultivated in many areas and also harvested wild. Fruit cooked in various ways. Seeds cooked and eaten, or boiled to extract oil.

Lagenaria vulgaris. Gourd. The Ojibwa ate the young fruit.

CYCADACEAE

Zamia floridana and *Z. pumila.* Coontie. Starch was extracted from roots of these and perhaps other species by the Seminoles; the roots were mashed, soaked, sieved, fermented, drained, and finally spread out to dry. CAUTION: the leaves are toxic to livestock.

CYPERACEAE

Carex spp. Sedge. Stems and base of stems eaten in Utah, Nevada, and Oregon.

Cyperus spp. Chufa, Nutgrass. Tubers eaten in southern United States.

Scirpus spp. Rush, Tule, Bulrush. Rootstocks eaten raw, or pounded to make bread, in most parts of the United States. Young shoots, seeds, and pollen also eaten.

EBENACEAE

Diospyros virginiana. Persimmon. Fruit eaten in southeastern United States.

ELEAGNACEAE

Eleagnus commutata. Silverberry. The Blackfeet ate the fruit raw or in soup.

Shepherdia argentea and **S. canadensis.** Buffaloberry, Soapberry. Extremely bitter fruit eaten in western North America. In British Columbia, the berries of S. canadensis were mixed with other berries and water and beaten into a foam.

EMPETRACEAE

Empetrum nigrum. Crowberry. Berries eaten in northwestern North America.

ERICACEAE

Arbutus menziessi and **A. xalapensis.** Madrone, Arbutus. Fruit eaten in California.

Arctostaphylos spp. Bearberry and Manzanita. Fruit eaten in many parts of North America.

Gaultheria spp. Wintergreen and Salal. Fruit eaten in most of North America.

Gaylussacia spp. Huckleberry. Fruit eaten in eastern United States.

Oxydendron arboreum. Sourwood. Young leaves eaten in southeastern United States.

Vaccinium spp. Blueberry, Cranberry, and Deerberry. Fruit eaten in most of North America.

EUPHORBIACEAE

Euphorbia serpyllifolia. Thyme-Leaf Spurge. Roots and leaves eaten by the Zuñi. CAUTION: the plant contains an acrid toxin.

Reverchonia arenaria. No common name. Berries eaten in Arizona. The Hopi used the oil of the seeds on their stone griddles. CAUTION: Kingsbury lists the raw plant as quite poisonous.

FAGACEAE

Castanea spp. Chestnut. Nuts eaten in eastern United States.

Chrysolepsis spp.   Chinquapin.   Nuts eaten in California and Oregon.

Fagus grandifolia.   Beech.   Nuts and buds eaten in eastern North America.

Lithocarpus densiflora.   Tanbark-Oak.   Acorns eaten in California.

Quercus spp.   Acorns eaten in many parts of the United States, particularly in California. Most species require leaching.

FOUQUIERACEAE

Fouquiera splendens.   Ocotillo.   Seeds and flowers eaten in California.

GENTIANACEAE

Frasera speciosa.   No common name.   Roots eaten by the Apache. CAUTION: the roots can be eaten either raw or cooked, but are toxic in quantity. *F. carolinensis* is cathartic and emetic.

GERANIACEAE

Erodium cicutarium and *E. moschatum.*   Storksbill.   Alien. Young plants eaten raw or cooked in northwestern United States.

GNETACEAE

Ephedra spp.   Jointfir.   Seeds roasted and ground for bread in California and New Mexico. Entire plant used to make a hot beverage.

GRAMINEAE   CAUTION: the cooked grains of uninfected grasses have never been shown to be seriously toxic, but a few problems occur with several grasses. Usually the problems result when feeding large amounts of the raw foliage to livestock. Many cases of poisoning are due to fungus infections, particularly by ergot (*Claviceps* spp.), which produces vertical pink or purple growths that replace the grain; on small-seeded grasses, the ergot growth may be nearly invisible.

Agropyron spp.   Quack Grass, Wheat Grass.   Grains of one or more species eaten in Utah and Nevada.

Agrostis spp.   Bent Grass.   Grains of one or more species eaten in Oregon.

Arundinaria gigantea.   Cane.   Grains eaten in southeastern United States.

Avena fatua.   Wild Oat.   Alien.   Grains eaten in California.

Beckmannia syzigachne.   Slough Grass.   Grains eaten in western United States.

Bromus spp.   Brome.   Grains eaten in Utah, Nevada, and California.

Cinna latifolia. Drooping Woodreed. Grains eaten in Utah and Nevada.

Deschampsia caespitosa. Tufted Hairgrass. Grains eaten in Utah and Nevada.

Echinocloa crusgalli. Barnyard Grass. Grains eaten in Great Basin and Southwest. Sometimes cultivated.

Elymus spp. Wild Rye. Grains eaten in western United States.

Eragrostis spp. Lovegrass. Grains of one or more species (probably E. *pectinacea*) eaten in Utah.

Festuca octoflora and **F. ovina.** Fescue. Grains eaten in Utah and Nevada. CAUTION: large amounts of fescue are toxic to livestock.

Glyceria spp. Manna Grass. Grains eaten in Utah, Nevada, and Oregon.

Hordeum spp. Barley. Grains eaten in western United States.

Koeleria cristata. Junegrass. Grains eaten in New Mexico.

Lolium temulentum. Darnel. Alien. Grains eaten in California. CAUTION: sometimes reported to be toxic.

Oryzopsis hymenoides. Indian Ricegrass. Grains eaten in western United States.

Panicum spp. Witch Grass, Panic Grass. Grains of several species eaten in Arizona, California, and Mexico.

Phragmites communis. Reed. Gum from injured stems eaten in Utah, Nevada, and Oregon. Shoots, roots, and ground stalks eaten in California. The grains are also edible; the hull is difficult to remove, but the grain can be cooked without removing the hull.

Poa fendleriana and **P. scabrella.** Muttongrass, Blue-grass. Grains eaten in Utah and Nevada.

Puccinellia airoides. Nuttal Alkali-Grass. Grains eaten in Utah and Nevada.

Sorghum vulgare. Sorghum. Alien. Grains eaten by the Pima of Arizona. CAUTION: cyanide compounds have sometimes reached toxic levels in the fresh plant fed to livestock.

Sporobolus spp. Dropseed. Grains eaten in Utah, Arizona, and New Mexico. No threshing required; as the name suggests, the seed drops from the hull.

Trisetum spicatum. Spike Trisetum. Alien. Grains eaten in Utah and Nevada.

Zea mays. Maize, Indian Corn. Cultivated in many areas.

Zizania aquatica. Wild Rice. Grains eaten in central and eastern United States and southern Canada.

HYDRANGEACEAE

Philadelphus microphyllus. Littleleaf Mock-Orange. Fruit eaten in New Mexico.

HYDROPHYLLACEAE

Hydrophyllum spp. Waterleaf. Roots and sprouts eaten in several parts of North America.

Phacelia ramosissima. Branching Phacelia. Leaves and stems cooked in California.

JUGLANDACEAE

Carya spp. Hickory and Pecan. Nuts eaten in central and eastern United States.

Juglans spp. Walnut, Nogal, Butternut. Nuts eaten in most of United States.

JUNCAGINACEAE

Triglochin maritima. Arrowgrass. Seeds parched and ground in Great Basin and California. CAUTION: The plant contains hydrocyanic acid and is poisonous when raw.

LABIATAE

Agastache spp. Horsemint. Seeds and leaves eaten in northern and western United States.

Lycopus asper and **L. uniflorus.** Bugleweed. Rootstocks eaten in Minnesota, Wisconsin, and British Columbia.

Mentha canadensis. Wild Mint. Leaves eaten or used as a beverage in many areas.

Monarda spp. Wild Bergamot, Oswego Tea, Beebalm. Leaves used as flavoring or beverage in eastern United States.

Pogogyne parviflora. Pogoyne. Seeds added to pinole in California, leaves used as a beverage.

Poliomintha incana. Rosemary Mint. Leaves and flowers eaten in Arizona.

Salvia spp. Sage, Chia. Seeds and flowering tops used as food or beverage in southwestern United States.

Stachys scopulorum. Hedge Nettle. Seeds eaten in Utah and Nevada. CAUTION: S. *arvensis* is toxic to livestock.

LAURACEAE

Sassafras albidum. Sassafras. Leaves used in soup in eastern and southern United States.

Umbellularia californica. California Laurel, Bay Laurel. Fruit and roasted kernel eaten in California.

LEGUMINOSAE CAUTION: legumes often contain toxic alkaloids, though many species were cooked to drive off the poison. All unfamiliar species should be eaten in moderation.

Acacia greggii. Acacia, Catclaw. Mature beans or entire pods ground for food in Arizona and California. CAUTION: A. *greggii* sometimes contains lethal amounts of cyanide in the limestone areas of Arizona. *A. berlandieri* contains an amine which is toxic if large amounts of the plant are eaten.

Amphicarpa bracteata and ***A. pitcheri.*** Hog Peanut. Roots and beans eaten in central and eastern United States.

Apios americana. Groundnut, Potato Bean. Tubers eaten raw, boiled, or roasted in central and eastern United States.

Astragalus spp. Milk-Vetch. Roots, pods, and seeds eaten raw or boiled in central and western United States. CAUTION: *Astragalus* can contain toxic amounts of selenium. Also, both *Astragalus* and the closely related *Oxytropis* have often produced a mysterious illness called "loco."

Baptisia tinctoria. Yellow Wild-Indigo. Shoots cooked in northeastern United States.

Canavalia ensiformis. Jack Bean. Cultivated for its beans in the Southwest

Cercidium torreyanum. Paloverde. Beans ground into meal in Arizona and California.

Cercis occidentalis. California Redbud. The Navaho roasted the pods and ate the seeds.

Gleditsia triacanthos. Honeylocust. Pods ground and used as a sweetener in the southeastern United States and the Mississippi region.

Glycyrrhiza lepidota. Licorice. Roots eaten raw or cooked from Alaska to New Mexico.

Gymnocladus dioica. Kentucky Coffeetree. Roasted nuts eaten in the eastern United States. CAUTION: listed by Kingsbury as toxic.

Hoffmannseggia densiflora. No common name. Tubers cooked in the Southwest.

Lathyrus spp. Wild Pea. Pods and peas roasted, stalks and sprouts eaten raw or cooked, in many parts of the United States. CAUTION: toxic in large quantities.

Lotus strigosus. Lotus, Bird's Foot Trefoil. Entire aboveground plant cooked in California.

Lupinus spp. Lupine. Roots and leaves cooked in British Columbia, Washington, Oregon, and California. CAUTION: lupines contain toxic alkaloids, especially in the seeds.

Medicago lupulina and ***M. sativa.*** Alfalfa and Black Medick. Alien. Seeds and branches of *M. sativa* cooked in Utah, seeds of *M. lupulina* eaten in California.

Olneya tesota. Tesota, Ironwood Tree. Seeds eaten raw or roasted in Arizona.

Oxytropis lamberti. False Locoweed. Roots eaten in Arizona. CAUTION: see *Astragalus*, above.

Parkinsonia aculeata. Jerusalem Thorn, Horse Bean. Beans eaten fresh or ground in southwestern United States.

Petalostemmum spp. Prairie Clover. Roots eaten raw by Plains Indians.

Peteria scoparia. Camote-de-Monte. Rootstocks roasted or boiled in New Mexico.

Phaseolus spp. Bean. Wild and cultivated beans eaten in many parts of Mexico, the United States, and southern Canada.

Prosopis spp. Mesquite and Screwbean. Ripe beans (sometimes parched first) or whole pods ground into meal in Southwest; the Pima also ate the catkins. CAUTION: a steady diet of mesquite beans is toxic to livestock.

Psoralea spp. Indian Breadroot. Roots of several species, especially *P. esculenta*, eaten fresh, roasted, or ground into flour throughout the United States. The leaves of *P. orbicularis* were cooked in California.

Trifolium spp. Clover. Some species alien. Entire plant eaten raw or cooked in British Columbia, Arizona, and California; seeds used for pinole in California.

Vicia americana and ***V. gigantea.*** Vetch. Young stems and whole pods of *V. americana* cooked in California and New Mexico, seeds of *V. gigantea* eaten in northwestern United States and British Columbia. The Kwakiutl roasted the green pods until they began to split, then ate the seeds. CAUTION: raw vetch may be toxic.

LENNOACEAE

Ammobroma sonorae. Sand Root. Roots and stems eaten raw or cooked in Arizona and California. The succulent plant is a source of liquid in the desert.

Pholisma arenarium. Desert Christmas Tree. Stems eaten in California.

LILIACEAE
CAUTION: most members of the lily family are quite edible, but there are a few highly poisonous species, particularly *Zigadenus* spp. (death camas) and *Veratrum viride* (false hellebore). It is often easy to mistake poisonous species for edible ones.

Aletris farinosa. Stargrass. Bulbs eaten in Louisiana.

Asparagus officinalis. Asparagus. Alien. Shoots cooked by the Iroquois and in New Mexico.

Calochortus spp. Mariposa Lily. Bulbs of many species eaten in western North America, raw, boiled, roasted, pounded into flour for gruel, or dried for winter use.

Camassia quamash and ***C. leichtlinii.*** Camas. Bulbs cooked by the Plains Indians, or dried and ground into flour.

Chlorogalum spp. Soap Plant, Amole. Bulbs and shoots roasted in California. CAUTION: the plant was also used as a fish poison.

Dasylirion wheeleri and **D. texanum.** Sotol. Heart of the plant cooked in the Southwest.

Disporum trachycarpum. Fairy Bells. Berries eaten raw by the Blackfeet.

Erythronium spp. Trout Lily, Dogtooth Violet, Glacier Lily. Bulbs eaten in many parts of North America.

Fritillaria spp. Fritillary, Rice Root. Bulbs eaten raw, boiled, or dried in many parts of North America.

Hesperocallis undulata. Desert Lily. The large deeply buried bulbs were eaten in Arizona.

Leucocrinum montanum. Sand Lily, Star Lily. Bulbs eaten by the Crow Indians.

Lilium spp. Bulbs of several species eaten in many parts of the United States and southern Canada.

Maianthemum canadense. Wild Lily-of-the-Valley, Canada Mayflower. Berries eaten by the Potawatomi.

Medeola virginiana. Cucumber Root. Tubers eaten in north-eastern United States.

Polygonatum biflorum and **P. caniculatum.** Solomon's Seal. Rootstocks eaten by the Iroquois.

Smilacena racemosa and **S. stellata.** False Solomon's Seal. Roots and berries eaten in several areas.

Smilax spp. Carrionflower, Greenbrier. Rootstocks, shoots, and berries eaten mainly in the southeastern United States.

Streptopus amplexifolius. Clasping Twisted-Stalk. Berries eaten by the Thompson of British Columbia.

Uvularia perfoliata and **U. sessifolia.** Bellwort. Rootstocks and shoots eaten in the eastern United States.

LINACEAE

Linum lewisii. Prairie Flax. Seeds eaten on the Plains.

LOASACEAE

Mentzelia albicaulis. White-stemmed Stickleaf. Seeds parched and ground in Montana, Oregon, and Arizona.

LORANTHACEAE

Phoradendron californicum. Mistletoe. Pima Indians boiled the berries without removing them from the stem. CAUTION: the fruits of P. villosum and P. flavescens are suspected of being toxic.

MALVACEAE

Callirhoe spp. Poppy Mallow. Roots eaten in several areas of the United States.

Gossypium hirsutum. Cotton. Seeds eaten in Arizona.

Sidalcea malvaeflora. Checker-Bloom. Leaves cooked in Utah, Nevada, and California.

MARTYNACEAE

Martynia spp. Martynia, Unicorn Plant, Devil's Claw. Young pods cooked by the Apache. The Pima and Papago ate the dried seeds raw or cooked.

MYRTACEAE

Sizygium spp. Eugenia. Fruit eaten in Florida and elsewhere.

NYCTAGINACEAE

Abronia latifolia and *A. tragans.* Sand Verbena. Roots eaten in western United States.

NYMPHAEACEAE

Nelumbo lutea. American Lotus. Tubers at the end of the rootstocks, collected in spring and fall, roasted and then boiled in western and eastern United States, or sliced and strung up to dry. Seeds and leaves also eaten.

Nuphar advena and *N. polysepalum.* Spatterdock and Wokas. Tubers collected in the fall (or in the spring before flowering) and eaten raw, boiled, or roasted in northern and eastern United States. Seeds ground into meal for soup or bread.

Nymphea odorata. Fragrant Waterlily. Buds eaten by the Ojibwa.

NYSSACEAE

Nyssa sylvatica. Sour Gum, Black Gum. Fruit eaten in southeastern United States.

OLEACEAE

Fraxinus pennsylvanica. Red Ash. Cambium eaten by the Ojibwa.

ONAGRACEAE

Boisduvalia densiflora. No common name. Seeds used for pinole in California.

Epilobium angustifolium and *E. latifolium.* Fireweed, Willow Herb, River Beauty. Pith of stalk eaten raw in northwestern United States and in Canada. A species of *Epilobium* was used to make bread in Arizona, Utah, and Nevada.

Clarkia spp. No common name. Seeds of one species used for pinole in California.

Oenothera spp. Evening Primrose. Pods and seeds eaten in southwestern United States.

ORCHIDACEAE

Calypso bulbosa. Calypso. Bulbs eaten raw or cooked on Northwest Coast.

OROBANCHACEAE

Orobanche spp. Broom-Rape, Cancer-Root. The entire plant, but especially the succulent rootstock, was eaten raw or cooked in Utah, Nevada, and California.

OXALIDACEAE

Oxalis spp. Wood Sorrel. Some species alien. Whole plant eaten raw or cooked in several parts of the United States. CAUTION: sometimes contains dangerous amounts of oxalates.

PALMACEAE

Erythea armata. Blue Palm. Fruit and base of young leaves eaten in California.

Sabal palmetto. Palmetto. Core of tree boiled in southeastern United States.

Serenoa repens. Saw Palmetto. Fruit eaten in southeastern United States.

Washingtonia filifera. Fan Palm, Desert Palm, Petticoat Palm, Western Washington Palm. Fruit, base of young leaves, and ground seeds eaten in California.

PAPAVERACEAE

Dicentra canadensis. Squirrel Corn. Tubers eaten in New York State. CAUTION: some species of *Dicentra* are toxic to cattle.

Escholzia californica. California Poppy. Leaves boiled or roasted in California.

Platystemon californicus. Creamcups. Leaves cooked in California.

PASSIFLORACEAE

Passiflora incarnata. Maypop. Fruit eaten in southeastern United States.

PHYTOLACCACEAE

Phytolacca americana. Poke Berry, Poke Salad. Young shoots boiled by the Iroquois. CAUTION: the roots, seeds, and other parts are poisonous.

PINACEAE

Abies spp. Fir. Sap, cambium, and seeds eaten in eastern and western North America.

Juniperus spp.   Juniper.   Berries eaten fresh, cooked, or dried and ground into bread in western North America.

Larix occidentalis.   Western Larch.   Sap and cambium eaten in British Columbia.

Picea spp.   Spruce.   Seeds and cambium eaten in northwestern North America.

Pinus spp.   Pine.   Seeds, cambium, sap, and catkins eaten in many parts of North America, mainly in the west.

Pseudotsuga spp.   Douglas-Fir.   Cambium and seeds eaten in British Columbia and California.

Thuja plicata.   Western Red Cedar.   Cambium eaten in Alaska, Oregon, and Montana.

Tsuga spp.   Hemlock.   Cambium eaten in western North America.

PLANTAGINACEAE

Plantago major.   Plantain.   Alien.   Young leaves eaten in New Mexico.

POLEMONIACEAE

Gilia staminea.   Gilia.   Seeds eaten in California.

POLYGONACEAE   CAUTION: members of this family contain oxalic acid, toxic in large doses.

Eriogonum spp.   Desert Trumpet, Wild Buckwheat.   Boiled leaves and raw young stems eaten in Arizona, Utah, and California.

Oxyria digyna.   Mountain Sorrel.   Leaves and stems eaten raw or boiled in most of western North America.

Polygonum spp.   Knotweed, Bistort, Lady's Thumb. Rhizomes (dug in the spring), young shoots, and seeds eaten from Alaska to California.

Rumex spp.   Garden Sorrel, Sheep Sorrel, Dock, Canaigre.   Some species alien.   Leaves, seeds, and roots eaten from Alaska to California. Most important native species is R. *hymenosepalas* (canaigre); young leaves and stems boiled or roasted in the Southwest.

PORTULACACEAE

Calandrinia ciliata.   Red Maids.   Alien.   Seeds and young leaves eaten in California.

Claytonia spp.   Spring Beauty.   Entire plant, especially tubers, eaten in many areas.

Lewisia spp.   Bitter Root.   Roots steamed, boiled, or roasted in western North America.

Montia spp.   Miner's Lettuce.   Entire plant, including roots, eaten raw or cooked in western North America.

Portulacca spp. Purslane. *P. oleracea* (common purslane) is alien. Seeds and leaves eaten in western United States, *P. oleracea* also eaten by the Iroquois.

Talinum auranticum. No common name. Roots cooked in Arizona, New Mexico, and Texas.

PRIMULACEAE

Dodecantheon hendersonii. Henderson's Shootingstar. Roots and leaves roasted in California.

Glaux maritima. Sea Milkwort. Rhizomes eaten in the spring in British Columbia.

PYROLACEAE

Moneses uniflora. Wood Nymph. Berries eaten in Montana and Alaska.

RANUNCULACEAE
CAUTION: many members of the buttercup family are toxic, some extremely so. The toxic alkaloids of those listed below were destroyed by cooking.

Aquilegia sp. Columbine. Roots of one species eaten in the northwestern United States.

Caltha palustris. Marsh Marigold. Leaves and stems boiled in eastern United States.

Paeonia brownii. Western Peony. Cooked roots eaten in California.

Ranunculus spp. Buttercup. Seeds, roots, and sometimes entire plant boiled or roasted in southwestern United States.

RHAMNACEAE

Ceanothus fendleri and ***C. integerrimus.*** Wild Lilac. Seeds eaten in California and Texas.

Condalia spp. Crucillo, Jujube. Fruit eaten in southwestern United States.

ROSACEAE

Amelanchier spp. Juneberry, Serviceberry, Saskatoon, Shadblow. Fruit eaten in most of North America.

Crataegus spp. Hawthorn. Fruit eaten in most of United States and southern Canada.

Fragaria spp. Strawberry. Fruit eaten in most of North America.

Heteromeles arbutifolia. Toyon Berry, Christmas Berry. Fruit eaten in California.

Holodiscus discolor and ***H. dumosa.*** Ocean Spray. Seeds eaten in California and New Mexico.

Osmaronia cerasiformis. Osoberry, Indian Plum. Fruit occasionally eaten in British Columbia and Washington.

Potentilla anserina and ***P. pacifica.*** Silverweed. The bitter roots were steamed in pits on the West Coast. *P. anserina* also eaten in Montana.

Prunus spp. Cherry and Plum. Fruit eaten in most of North America. CAUTION: cherry trees contain cyanogenic glycoside, particularly in the leaves and bark; the seeds of *P. serotina* (black cherry) seem to be especially dangerous.

Pyrus spp. Crabapple and Chokeberry. Fruit eaten in northern United States and in Canada.

Rosa spp. Rose. Fruit eaten in northern United States and in Canada. Shoots occasionally eaten.

Rubus spp. Raspberry, Blackberry, Dewberry, Salmonberry, etc. Fruit eaten in most of North America. Sprouts (new plants) of several species picked in the spring, peeled, and eaten raw. The fresh or dried leaves were used as a hot beverage, though in the merely wilted stage—between fresh and dried—they are slightly toxic.

Sorbus spp. Mountain Ash. Fruit eaten in British Columbia and by the Ojibwa.

RUBIACEAE

Galium kamtschaticum. Licorice Plant. Root eaten in Alaska.

Mitchella repens. Partridgeberry. Fruit eaten in Texas and eastern United States.

SALICACEAE

Populus spp. Poplar, Aspen, Cottonwood. Cambium, sap, sprouts, buds, catkins, and seeds eaten in many areas.

Salix spp. Willow. Cambium and shoots eaten in Alaska.

SANTALACEAE

Comandra pallida. Bastard Toadflax. Fruit eaten in Utah and Nevada.

SAPOTACEAE

Bumelia lanuginosa and ***B. reclinata.*** Bumelia. Fruit eaten in southern United States.

SAXIFRAGACEAE

Ribes spp. Gooseberry and Currant. Fruit eaten in almost every part of North America.

SCROPHULARIACEAE

Mimulus spp. Monkeyflower. Shoots and leaves eaten raw or cooked in southwestern United States.

Moldavica parviflora. Dragonhead. Seeds eaten in Utah and Nevada.

Pedicularis spp. Wood Betony, Lousewort. The above-ground plant was cooked by the Iroquois, and the Alaskan Eskimos ate the entire plant.

SOLANACEAE CAUTION: many plants in this family are quite toxic.

Capsicum spp. Chili. Fruit eaten in Southwest. Cultivated in Mexico, but not in Southwest until historical times.

Chamaesaracha coronopus. No common name. Berries eaten by the Hopi and Navaho.

Lycium spp. Wolfberry, Tomatillo. Berries eaten raw or cooked in Arizona, New Mexico. and California.

Physalis spp. Ground Cherry. Fruit eaten raw or cooked in many parts of the United States. CAUTION: the raw fruit may be slightly toxic.

Solanum spp. Nightshade, Wild Potato. Tubers of S. *fendleri* and S. *jamesii* eaten raw or boiled with clay (to reduce sourness) in Arizona and New Mexico. Ripe berries of S. *nigrum* and S. *triflorum* eaten in New Mexico and California. Leaves of S. *douglasii* cooked in California. CAUTION: plants of this genus (including the cultivated potato) contain solanine, a puzzling substance that is sometimes highly toxic.

SPARGANIACEAE

Sparganium eurycarpum. Burr Reed. Tubers and base of stem eaten in Oregon.

STAPHYLEACEAE

Staphylea trifolia. Bladdernut. Seeds eaten in eastern United States.

TAXACEAE

Taxus brevifolia. Pacific Yew. Fruit eaten in California. CAUTION: the rest of the tree, including the seed of the fruit, is poisonous.

Torreya californica. California Nutmeg. Nuts eaten in California.

TILIACEAE

Tilia americana. Basswood. Sap used to make syrup by the Ojibwa.

TYPHACEAE

Typha spp. Cattail. Rootstock, base of stem, flower head, pollen, and seeds eaten in western North America.

ULMACEAE

Ulmus fulva. Slippery Elm. Cambium eaten in eastern North America.

UMBELLIFERAE CAUTION: many edible members of this family can be confused with *Conium maculatum* (poison hemlock) and *Cicuta* spp. (water hemlock), all of which are extremely poisonous.

Apium graveolens. Celery. Alien. Plant cooked in California.

Coriandum sativum. Coriander. Alien. Leaves and powdered root eaten, mainly as a condiment, in Arizona and New Mexico.

Cymopterus spp. Gamote, Corkwing. Roots, leaves, and seeds eaten in western United States.

Daucus pusillus. Rattlesnake Weed. Roots eaten raw or boiled by the Nez Perce and Navaho.

Heracleum lanatum. Cow Parsnip. Flower-stalks and leaf-stems peeled and eaten raw or cooked in the spring before the flowers opened. Roots sometimes cooked and eaten. Used in central and western North America. CAUTION: contact with the plant sometimes causes a skin irritation.

Ligusticum sp. Lovage. Cooked stems and raw or cooked roots of one species eaten in northwestern United States and in British Columbia.

Lomatium spp. Biscuit Root, Cous. Roots of many species dug up in the spring and eaten raw or cooked, or dried and ground into flour, in western United States. Young leaves and flowers sometimes cooked. Flowers of *L. triternata* mixed with pemmican. CAUTION: *L. dissectum* possibly toxic.

Musineon spp. No common name. Roots eaten raw or cooked by the Blackfeet and Crow.

Oenanthe sarmentosa. No common name. Tubers boiled in Oregon.

Osmorhiza chilensis and ***O. claytoni.*** Sweet Cicely. Roots dug in spring and cooked in Wisconsin and British Columbia. Stems of *O. claytoni* also eaten.

Pastinaca sativa. Wild Parsnip. Alien. Roots eaten in Alaska and eastern United States.

Perideridia spp. Yampa. Roots dug in spring and eaten raw, boiled, or steam-cooked in western North America.

Pseudocymopterus aletifolius. No common name. Leaves eaten raw or cooked in New Mexico.

Sanicula tuberosa. Sanicle. Roots eaten raw in California.

Sium suave. Water Parsnip. Leaves and stems eaten in Montana and Oregon, rootstocks eaten in British Columbia. CAU-

TION: resembles, and often grows near, *Cicuta* (water hemlock); the flowers of *Sium suave* may be poisonous.

URTICACEAE

Celtis spp. Hackberry, Palo Blanco. Fruit, sometimes pounded with the seed, eaten in most of the United States.

Morus spp. Mulberry. Fruit eaten in many areas of the United States.

Salsola kali. Russian Tumbleweed. Alien. Seeds and shoots eaten in the Southwest.

Urtica dioica. Stinging Nettle. Alien? Tops of plants boiled by the Iroquois and others.

VALERIANACEAE

Valeriana edulis. Tobacco Root, Edible Valerian. Roots and seeds cooked in northwestern North America. CAUTION: possibly toxic when raw.

VERBENACEAE

Verbena hastata. Blue Vervain. Seeds eaten in California.

VIOLACEAE

Viola pedunculata. California Golden Violet. Leaves eaten in California.

VITACEAE

Parthenocissus quinquefolia. Virginia Creeper. Fruit eaten raw, stalks peeled and boiled, root also eaten, in Wisconsin, Minnesota, and Montana. CAUTION: Kingsbury lists the fruit as probably toxic.

Vitis spp. Grape. Fruit eaten in most of United States. Sap and twigs used for beverages.

ZOSTERACEAE

Zostera marina. Eelgrass. Rootstocks and leaf bases eaten raw or cooked in British Columbia.

Selected bibliography

Adney, Edwin T., and Chappelle, Howard I. The Bark Canoes and Skin Boats of North America. Bulletin 230. Washington: United States National Museum, 1964.

Adovasio, James M. Basketry Technology: A Guide to Identification and Analysis. Chicago: Aldine Publishing Company, 1977.

Arima, Eugene Y. A Contextual Study of the Caribou Eskimo Kayak. Mercury Series. No. 25. Ottawa: National Museums of Canada, 1975

The Athapaskans: Strangers of the North. Ottawa: National Museums of Canada, 1974.

Barnett, Homer G. The Coast Salish of British Columbia. Eugene: University of Oregon Press, 1955.

Barrett, S.A., and Gifford, E.W. Miwok Material Culture. Bulletin of the Public Museum of the City of Milwaukee. No. 2 (1933), pp. 117-376.

Birket-Smith, Kaj. The Caribou Eskimos, Material and Social Life and Their Cultural Position. Report of the Fifth Yule Expedition 1921-24. Vol. 5, part 3. Copenhagen: Gyldendal, 1929.

Bixby, Lawrence B. Flint Chipping. American Antiquity, Vol. 10, no. 4, pp. 353-61 (1945).

Black, Meredith Jean. Algonquin Ethnobotany: An Interpretation of Aboriginal Adaptation in Southwestern Quebec. Mercury Series. No. 65. Ottawa: National Museums of Canada, 1980.

Boas, Franz. The Central Eskimo. 6th Annual Report of the Bureau of American Ethnology (1888), pp. 399-675.

_____. Ethnology of the Kwakiutl. 35th Annual Report of the Bureau of American Ethnology, parts 1 and 2.

_____. The Kwakiutl of Vancouver Island. 1909. Reprint. New York: AMS Press, 1975.

_____. The Social Organizations and Secret Societies of the Kwakiutl Indians, Based on Personal Observations and Notes Made by George Hunt. Report of the United States National Museum for 1985 (1897).

Bodenheimer, F.S. Insects as Human Food. The Hague: Dr. W. Junk, Publishers, 1951.

Campbell, Walter Stanley. The Cheyenne Tipi. American Anthropologist (New Series) Vol. 17, no. 4 (Oct.-Dec. 1915), pp. 685-94.

_____. The Tipis of the Crow Indians. American Anthropologist (New Series) vol. 29, no. 1 (Jan.-March 1927), pp. 87-104.

Clark, Annette McFadyen. Koyukuk River Culture. Mercury Series. No. 18. Ottawa: National Museums of Canada, 1974.

Cooper, John M. Snares, Deadfalls, and Other Traps of the Northern Algonquians and Northern Athapaskans. 1938. Reprint. New York: AMS Press, 1978.

Davidson, Daniel Sutherland. Snowshoes. Memoirs of the American Philosophical Society. Vol. 6 (1937).

Densmore, Frances. Chippewa Customs. Bureau of American Ethnology. Bulletin 86 (1929).

_____. Uses of Plants by the Chippewa Indians. 44th Annual Report of the Bureau of American Ethnology (1928), pp. 275-397.

Driver, Harold E. Indians of North America. 2nd ed., rev. Chicago: University of Chicago Press, 1961.

Drucker, Philip. The Northern and Central Nootkan Tribes. Bureau of American Ethnology. Bulletin 144 (1951).

Easby, Dudley T., Jr. Early Metallurgy in the New World. Scientific American, April 1966.

Erichsen-Brown, Charlotte. Use of Plants for the Past 500 Years. Aurora, Ont: Breezy Creeks Press, 1979.

Ewers, John C. Indian Life on the Upper Missouri. Norman: University of Oklahoma Press, 1968.

Grinnell, George Bird. Blackfoot Lodge Tales: the Story of a Prairie People. Lincoln: University of Nebraska Press, 1962.

_____. The Lodges of the Blackfeet. American Anthropologist (New Series) vol. 3, no. 4 (1901), pp. 650-668.

Guthe, Carl E. Pueblo Pottery Making: A Study of the Village of San Ildefonso. Papers of the Southwestern Expedition, no. 2. New Haven: Yale University Press, 1925.

Hamilton, T.M. Native American Bows. York, Pennsylvania: G. Shumway, 1972.

Hara, Hiroko Sue. The Hare Indians and Their World. Mercury Series. No. 63. Ottawa: National Museums of Canada, 1980.

Hatt, Gudmund. Moccasins and Their Relation to Arctic Footwear. Memoirs of the American Anthropological Association. No. 3, pp. 149-250 (1916).

Hearne, Samuel. A Journey from Prince of Wales' Fort to the Northern Ocean, 1769, 1770, 1771, 1772. Ed. Richard Glover. Toronto: Macmillan, 1958.

Hellson, John C. Ethnobotany of the Blackfoot Indians. Mercury Series. No. 19. Ottawa: National Museums of Canada, 1974.

Hill, W.W. The Agricultural and Hunting Methods of the Navaho Indians. Yale University Publications in Anthropology. No. 18, pp. 1-194 (1938).

Hoffman, Walter J. The Menomini Indians. 14th Annual Report of the Bureau of American Ethnology, 1892-3.

Holmes, William H. Aboriginal Pottery of the Eastern United States. 20th Annual Report of the Bureau of American Ethnology, pp. 1-237 (1903).

_____. The Lithic Industries. Part 1, Handbook on Aboriginal American Antiquities. Bureau of American Ethnology. Bulletin 60 (1919).

Hough, Walter. Fire-making Apparatus in the United States National Museum. United States National Museum. Annual Report for 1888, pp. 531-87 (1890).

_____. The Hopi Indian Collections in the United States National Museum. United States National Museum. Proceedings. Vol. 54, pp. 235-297 (1919).

Kinietz, W. Vernon. The Indians of the Western Great Lakes 1615-1760. Ann Arbor: University of Michigan Press, 1940.

Kingsbury, John Merriam. Poisonous Plants of the United States and Canada. Englewood Cliffs, New Jersey: Prentice-Hall, 1964.

Kluckhohn, Clyde, et al. Navaho Material Culture. Cambridge, Mass.: Belknap Press, 1971.

Knowles, Sir Francis H.S. The Manufacture of a Flint Arrowhead by Quartzite Hammer-stone. Occasional Papers on Technology. No. 1. Pitt Rivers Museum, University of Oxford, 1944.

_____. Stone-Worker's Progress. Occasional Papers on Technology. No. 6. Pitt Rivers Museum, University of Oxford, 1953.

Kroeber, Alfred L., and Barrett, S.A. Fishing Among the Indians of Northwestern California. Berkeley: University of California Press, 1960.

Lips, Julius E. Trap Systems among the Montagnais-Naskapi Indians of Labrador Peninsula. Stockholm: Statens Etnografiska Museum, 1936.

Lowie, R.H. The Assiniboine. American Museum of Natural History. Anthropological Papers. No. 4, pp. 1-270 (1910).

_____. The Material Culture of the Crow Indians. American Museum of Natural History. Anthropological Papers. No. 21. part 3, pp. 201-270 (1922).

_____. The Northern Shoshone. American Museum of Natural History. Anthropological Papers. No. 2, part 2 (1909).

_____. Notes on Shoshonean Ethnography. American Museum of Natural History. Anthropological Papers. No. 20, part 3, pp. 185-314 (1924).

Lyford, Carrie. The Crafts of the Ojibwa (Chippewa). Washington: United States Bureau of Indian Affairs, 1943.

_____. Iroquois Crafts. Washington: United States Bureau of Indian Affairs, 1945.

Mandelbaum, D.G. The Plains Cree. American Museum of Natural History. Anthropological Papers. No. 37, pp. 155-316 (1940).

Mason, Otis T. Aboriginal American Basketry. United States National Museum. Annual Report for 1901-2 (1904). Washington, 1902.

_____. Aboriginal American Harpoons. United States National Museum. Annual Report for 1900, pp. 189-304 (1902).

_____. Aboriginal Skin-Dressing. United States National Museum. Annual Report for 1889, pp. 553-89 (1891).

_____. North American Bows, Arrows, and Quivers. United States National Museum. Annual Report for 1893, pp. 631-681 (1894).

_____. Primitive Travel and Transportation. United States National Museum. Annual Report for 1894, pp. 237-593 (1896).

Material Culture Notes. Denver: Denver Art Museum, 1969.

Miles, Charles. Indian and Eskimo Artifacts of North America. New York: Bonanza Books, 1963.

Mindeleff, Cosmos. Navaho Houses. 17th Annual Report of the Bureau of American Ethnology, part 2, pp. 475-517 (1898).

Murdoch, J. Ethnological Results of the Point Barrow Expedition. 9th Annual Report of the Bureau of American Ethnology (1892).

Nelson, Ernest W. The Eskimo about Bering Strait. 18th Annual Report of the Bureau of American Ethnology, part 1 (1899).

Nelson, Richard K. Hunters of the Northern Forest. Chicago: University of Chicago Press, 1973.

Newman, Sandra Corrie. Indian Basket Weaving: How to Weave Pomo, Yurok, Pima, and Navaho Baskets. Flagstaff: Northland Press, 1974.

Niethammer, Carolyn. American Indian Food and Lore. New York: MacMillan Publishing Co., 1974.

Oswalt, Wendell. Alaskan Eskimos. Scranton, Pennsylvania: Chandler Publishing Co., 1967.

Parker, Arthur Carswell. Parker of the Iroquois. Ed. W.N. Fenton. Syracuse: Syracuse University Press, 1969.

Pope, Saxton. Yahi Archery. University of California Publications in American Archaeology and Ethnology. Vol. 13, part 3 (1918).

Powers, Stephen. Tribes of California. 1877. Reprint. Berkeley: University of California Press, 1976.

Rau, Charles. Prehistoric Fishing in Europe and North America. Smithsonian Contributions to Knowledge. Vol. 25. Washington, 1884.

Ritzenthaler, Robert E. The Building of a Chippewa Indian Birch-Bark Canoe. Bulletins of the Public Museum of the City of Milwaukee. Vol. 19, no. 2. Nov. 1950.

Rostlund, E. Freshwater Fish and Fishing in Native North America. University of California Publications in Geography. Vol. 9 (1952).

Russell, Frank. The Pima Indians. 26th Annual Report of the Bureau of American Ethnology, pp. 17-390 (1908).

Skinner, Alanson. Notes on the Eastern Cree and Northern Salteaux. American Museum of Natural History. Anthropological Papers. No. 9, pp. 1-116 (1911).

Smith, Huron. Ethnobotany of the Forest Potawatomi Indians. Bulletins of the Public Museum of the City of Milwaukee. Vol. 7, no. 1, pp. 1-230 (1933).

_____. Ethnobotany of the Menomini Indians. Bulletins of the Public Museum of the City of Milwaukee. Vol. 4, no. 1, pp. 1-174 (1923).

_____. Ethnobotany of the Meskwaki Indians. Bulletins of the Public Museum of the City of Milwaukee. Vol. 4, no. 2, pp. 175-326 (1928).

_____. Ethnobotany of the Ojibwe Indians. Bulletins of the Public Museum of the City of Milwaukee. Vol. 4, no. 3, pp. 327-525 (1932).

Spier, Leslie. Havasupai Ethnography. American Museum of Natural History. Anthropological Papers. Vol. 29, part 3, pp. 83-392 (1928).

_____. Zuñi Weaving Technique. American Anthropologist (New Series), vol. 26, no. 1 (1924).

Stewart, Hilary. Indian Fishing: Early Methods on the Northwest Coast. Vancouver: Douglas and McIntyre, 1977.

Swanton, John R. The Indians of the Southeastern United States. Bureau of American Ethnology. Bulletin 137 (1946).

Tanner, Clara L. Southwest Indian Craft Arts. Tucson: University of Arizona Press, 1968.

Taylor, J. Garth. Canoe Construction in a Cree Cultural Tradition. Mercury Series. No. 64. Ottawa: National Museums of Canada, 1980.

Teit, James A. The Thompson Indians of British Columbia. Ed. Franz Boas. American Museum of Natural History. Memoirs. Vol. 2, (1900).

Turner, Lucien. Ethnology of the Ungava District. 11th Annual Report of the Bureau of American Ethnology (1894), pp. 167-350.

Turner, Nancy J. Food Plants of the British Columbia Indians. Part 1. Coastal Peoples. Handbook no. 34. Victoria: British Columbia Provincial Museum, 1975.

_____. Food Plants of British Columbia Indians. Part 2. Interior Peoples. Handbook no. 36. Victoria: British Columbia Provincial Museum, 1978.

_____. Plants in British Columbia Indian Technology. Handbook 38. Victoria: British Columbia Provincial Museum, 1979.

Underhill, Ruth. Pueblo Crafts. Washington: United States Bureau of Indian Affairs, 1944.

_____. Workaday Life of the Pueblos. Washington: United States Bureau of Indian Affairs, 1946.

Vogel, Virgil J. American Indian Medicine. Norman: University of Oklahoma Press, 1970.

Waterman, T.T. North American Indian Dwellings. Geographical Review, vol. 14, no. 1 (Jan. 1924), pp. 1-25.

Waugh, F.W. Canadian Aboriginal Canoes. The Canadian Field-Naturalist, vol. 33, no. 2 (May 1919), pp. 23-33.

Weiner, Michael A. Earth Medicine—Earth Food: Plant Remedies, Drugs, and Natural Foods of the North American Indians. 1st rev. and expanded ed. New York: Macmillan, 1980.

Weltfish, Gene. Prehistoric North American Basketry Techniques and Modern Distributions. American Anthropologist (New Series), vol. 32, pp. 454-495 (1930).

Wheat, Margaret M. Survival Arts of the Primitive Paiutes. Reno: University of Nevada Press, 1967.

Whiting, A.F. Ethnobotany of the Hopi. Bulletin 15. Flagstaff: Museum of North Arizona, 1939.

Wissler, Clark. Costumes of the Plains Indians. American Museum of Natural History. Anthropological Papers. Vol. 17, part 2, pp. 39-91 (1915).

_____. Indian Costumes in the United States: a Guide to the Study of the Collections in the Museum. Guide Leaflet no. 63. New York: American Museum of Natural History, 1926.

_____. Material Culture of the Blackfoot Indians. American Museum of Natural History. Anthropological Papers. Vol. 5, part 1 (1910).

Yanovsky, Elias. Food Plants of the North American Indians. Miscellaneous Publication no. 237. Washington: United States Department of Agriculture, 1936.

Zimmerly, David W., ed. Contextual Studies of Material Culture. Mercury Series. No. 43. Ottawa: National Museums of Canada, 1978.

_____. Hooper Bay Kayak Construction. Mercury Series. No. 53. Ottawa: National Museums of Canada, 1979.